WOLFGANG CAPITO
FROM HUMANIST TO REFORMER

STUDIES
IN MEDIEVAL AND
REFORMATION THOUGHT

EDITED BY

HEIKO A. OBERMAN, Tübingen

IN COOPERATION WITH

E. JANE DEMPSEY DOUGLASS, Claremont, California
LEIF GRANE, Copenhagen
GUILLAUME H. M. POSTHUMUS MEYJES, Leiden
ANTON G. WEILER, Nijmegen

VOLUME XVII

JAMES M. KITTELSON

WOLFGANG CAPITO
FROM HUMANIST TO REFORMER

LEIDEN
E. J. BRILL
1975

WOLFGANG CAPITO

FROM HUMANIST TO REFORMER

BY

JAMES M. KITTELSON

LEIDEN
E. J. BRILL
1975

ISBN 90 04 04312 8

TABLE OF CONTENTS

ACKNOWLEDGMENTS

Thanks for support go to the Woodrow Wilson National Fellowship Foundation, which ten years ago provided funds to begin graduate work and then a year's stipend for research abroad; to the Center for Reformation Research, which granted a fellowship in 1966 that allowed extended work in paleography and bibliography, as well as the pleasure of the company of genial spirits who gathered in St. Louis that summer; to the European libraries and their staffs, in particular the Bibliothèque nationale et universitaire and the Archives municipales of Strasbourg, which provided productive working conditions and then copies of all the materials that were overlooked in 1966-67; to the research foundation of The University of Iowa, which allocated funds to pay for typing an early draft of the manuscript; to Dean Arthur E. Adams and the College of Humanities at The Ohio State University for a quarter's assigned research duty; to the secretarial staff of the Department of History, who typed the final draft.

Appreciation must also go to Dr. Lewis W. Spitz of Stanford University, whose own research first led me to the world of humanists and reformers, and in whose voluminous files of work to be done, the name of Wolfgang Capito once resided. Dr. Beate Stierle of Göttingen, who discovered Capito's manuscript lectures on Romans, graciously shared her treasure. M. Jean Rott of Strasbourg, paleographer, editor, and researcher *par excellence*, has kindly sent copies of archival materials and even of his own transcripts of such sources. So too have Dr. Frank Baron of Munich, Dr. Abraham Friesen of the University of California at Santa Barbara, and Dr. Thomas A. Brady, Jr., of the University of Oregon, a fellow researcher of Alsatica with whom conversation is always a productive delight. Others have read parts or all of the various versions of this work: Dr. Donald W. Sutherland of The University of Iowa; Dr. James D. Tracy of the University of Minnesota; and Dr. Ulrich Gäbler of the Institut für Schweizerische Reformationsgeschichte, Zurich, who also provided a copy of a manuscript letter at a critical point, and who arranged for the copying of the Romans lectures. Dr. Clarence Forbes, Professor Emeritus of Classics at The Ohio State University, checked Latin translations.

Finally, this work might never have seen publication were it not for the interest of Prof. Dr. Heiko A. Oberman, the editor of this series, who also provided very useful criticism from an anonymous but perceptive and careful reader.

One person epitomizes all these contributions: presider over the most important institution in my world, quick critic, closest companion—Margaret Ann, to whom this work, as all else, with its faults, is dedicated.

ABBREVIATIONS

BAO   Ernst Staehelin, ed. *Briefe und Akten zum Leben Oekolampads.*

BB   Traugott Schiess, ed. *Briefwechsel der Brüder Ambrosius und Thomas Blaurer, 1509-1548.*

BDS   Robert Stupperich, *et al.*, eds. *Martin Bucers Deutsche Schriften.*

EE   P. S. Allen, ed. *Opus Epistolarum Des. Erasmi Roterodami.*

QGT   Manfred Krebs and Hans Georg Rott, eds. *Quellen zur Geschichte der Täufer.* VII, VIII.

Th. B.   Johann Wilhelm Baum, ed. and copier. Thesaurus Epistolicus Reformatorum Alsaticorum.

WA   *D. Martin Luthers Werke. Kritische Gesamtausgabe.*

WABr   *Briefwechsel.*

WADB   *Deutsche Bibel.*

ZW   Emil Egli, ed. *Corpus Reformatorum. Huldreich Zwinglis Sämtliche Werke.*

FOREWORD

The powerful Reformation movement of the sixteenth century touched the lives of nearly all Europeans. It profoundly altered the careers of one group of men in particular. They were the northern humanists with their program of cultural and religious renewal according to the models of classical and Christian antiquity. Before Luther's appearance they had long criticized the immorality of the clergy, the superstitiousness of the laity, and what they regarded as the sterility of scholastic theology. When the Indulgence Controversy erupted, they adopted Luther as their own. They publicized his cause, and they intervened for him at the courts of bishops and the chanceries of princes in Germany and throughout Europe. But when the full import of Luther's program became evident in the early 1520's, their solidarity was shattered. While those of Erasmus, generation realized that Luther's affair was not their affair, the younger men became reformers. The Reformation as it really happened would be unrecognizable without the humanists.

There are a few safe generalizations about the relationship between northern humanism and the Reformation. First, many of the younger humanists did desert Erasmus and they did become the shock-troops of the Reformation. From the outset they constituted the most articulate and influential group within the reform movement, and many of them ended their lives as reformed pastors with a local reformation their most prized accomplishment. Secondly, their conversion was critical to the success of reform, less, perhaps, because they added sheer numbers to the reform party, than because they were the Reformation's most constructive and accomplished recruits. Finally, the humanists carried with them into the Reformation attitudes and values that they held before their conversions. Their lives and careers thus marked the link between, as well the transition from, the Renaissance to the Reformation.

Grave conceptual and material problems lurk behind such truisms. In the first place, there is no satisfactory explanation for the conversion of so many young humanists into reformers. After all, their common mentor and cultural hero, Erasmus, and with him most of his peers, publicly broke with Luther in the famous controversy over free will. And it is clear that Erasmus did so as much from a

fundamentally different religious point of view as he did from timidity
or the putative conservativeness of old age. By itself the suggestion of
a generational conflict between younger and older humanists [1]
amounts to little more than avoiding an explanation for the irony
that Erasmus' most avid disciples in the 1510's established the Reformation in the 1520's and 1530's. Nor is it satisfying, without careful
definition, simply to assert that Luther's theology was superior to
that of Erasmus, More, Reuchlin, and Colet,[2] should a mere historian
feel competent to make that judgment. All that can be said at present
is that Luther's message was assuredly different from Erasmus', and
that the young humanists who became Luther's followers began
quickly to concern themselves with true doctrine and with right
practice in a way they never had before. Their new deeds fit their
new words in a manner that divided them cleanly from Erasmus.
However difficult it is to explain such profound spiritual changes,
an explanation must be attempted, at least in specific cases.

But how deep was the change from humanist to reformer? Was it
sufficiently profound to be called a conversion in the individual
and a revolution in large? At least during the early years, the young
humanists seem to have misunderstood Luther and to have taken him
for another follower of Erasmus. Zwingli, for example, certainly
retained an Erasmian spiritualism throughout his career, and in
other respects evidenced such a continuing allegiance to humanistic
values that the nature of his conversion remains a live issue. One
historian has maintained that, at least in the realm of ethics, Martin
Bucer never became fully evangelical.[3] There is at least the possibility that some of those who made the Reformation did not fully
understand or appropriate Luther's evangelical message.

Put in a different perspective, the last paragraph addresses the

---

[1] Bernd Moeller, "Die deutschen Humanisten und die Anfänge der Reformation," *Zeitschrift für Kirchengeschichte*, LXX (1959), 47-61, esp. 51-52, for a survey
of the problem.

[2] Gerhard Ritter, "Die geschichtliche Bedeutung des deutschen Humanismus,"
Historische Zeitschrift, CXXVII (1923), 450-451. In fairness it should be added that
Ritter was not attempting here to explain the humanists' conversion to the
Reformation, but his view that humanism was a "weak half-way house" on
the way to Reformation has become common. For a delimited affirmation of this
view, see the afterword below.

[3] For the debate on Zwingli's indebtedness to humanism, see Gottfried
Locher, "The Change in the Understanding of Zwingli in Recent Research,"
Church History, XXIV (1965), 3-24, and the literature cited there. On Bucer, see
Karl Koch, *Studium Pietatis. Martin Bucer als Ethiker*, (Neukirchen, 1962), pp.
43-70.

problem of what affect the Renaissance values of the humanists-turned-reformers had upon the Reformation. To be sure (and with Luther's agreement, it must be added), they saved the Reformation from obscurantism. They expressed their humanistic values in building one of the Reformation's most enduring institutions—the public school. The dividing line between humanism and the Reformation cannot be equated with the difference between rationality and irrationality. But there are other equally subtle questions. Many of the converted humanists exhibited a concern for wider social issues, such as welfare legislation, that were lower on Luther's scale of values. And their success in establishing reform through generally non-violent means may have rested upon shared attitudes toward politics that can be explained only by reference to their careers as humanists. They may also have brought with them into the Reformation on the one hand a more ecumenical spirit or on the other a greater tendency to systematize than did Luther. In these and other ways the converted humanists not only established but also profoundly shaped the Reformation.

Any attempt to characterize the complex relationship between humanism and the Reformation must begin with individuals. To be sure, even the most individualistic characters find themselves part of a group whose basic point of view they share. And however much the solitary intellectual may be free to innovate, the historically-significant figure either creates a group that depends upon himself or is part of such a group. Nevertheless, thoughts and values are always held by individuals, particularly at the higher ranges of intellectual endeavor. And ideas and values first find expression in the careers of individuals, and only through them in institutions. Accordingly, there is perhaps no branch of historical studies for which biography is so crucial to the understanding as it is in the investigation of a revolutionary era such as the Reformation.

Wolfgang Capito was one of the humanists. His life personified the epoch-making transition from humanism to the Reformation. He was educated in the nominalist tradition at Freiburg, but, like so many young German intellectuals, he quickly became a disciple of Erasmus. To the humanistic study of languages and ancient texts he coupled a fervent desire for religious reform while he was a professor and cathedral preacher at Basel. He enthusiastically supported Luther and then forsook the contemplative life to become the personal chaplain and adviser of the Archbishop of Mainz. He quickly acquired influence out of proportion to his position, and from 1520 to 1523 he tried vainly to moderate Luther while frustrating the prosecution of Luther and the young reform movement. Finally, in the course of over a year, he converted to the evangelical faith and became a reformer. He moved to Strasbourg and led the fight to purify the church there. Until his death in 1541 he was co-architect with Bucer of the moderating and mediating policy for which Strasbourg was famous during the Reformation era. At the same time Capito gradually discarded the cultural values he espoused as a humanist and replaced them with values he considered more appropriate to his Reformation faith.

In spite of Capito's importance in his own right, and as an example of the humanist who became a reformer, knowledge of his life is fragmentary. Johannes Sturm, Strasbourg's famous educator, wrote a brief life of his friend in 1542 that he published in a volume of student exercises he dedicated to Melanchthon's biographer, Joachim Camerarius.[4] Seventeenth and eighteenth-century ecclesiastical historians included thumbnail sketches of Capito in their confessional accounts of the Reformation.[5] They, like Sturm, used materials that have subsequently been lost. Nevertheless, the only full biography of Capito came in 1860 from Johann Wilhelm Baum, the indefatigable student of reformed church origins. He contented himself with long citations from Capito's works and a chronology from an 1850 Bachelor of Divinity thesis.[6] Moreover, Capito was forced to share this biography with his colleague Bucer, on whom Baum also wrote in the same volume. Accordingly, neither Capito the humanist nor Capito the reformer emerges clearly from Baum's pages. It is safe to report that there is no well-founded picture of Capito's life available to the modern student of northern humanism and the Reformation.

---

[4] *Ioan. Sturmii et Gymnasii Argentoratensis Luctus ad Ioachimum Camerarium.* (Argentorati, 1542).

[5] Abraham Scultetus, *Annalium Evangelii passim per Europam decimo quinto salutis portae seculo renovati* (Heidelbergae, 1618), I, 9. Melchior Adamus, *Vitae Germanorum Theologorum, qui seculo ecclesiam Christi voci scriptisque propagarunt et propugnarunt* (Heidelbergae, 1620), pp. 88-92. Daniel Gerdesius, *Introductio in Historiam Evangelii seculo XVI. Passim per Europam Renovati Doctrinaeque Reformatae. Accedunt Varia Quibus ipsa Historia Illustratur Monumenta Pietatis atque Rei Litterariae* (Groningae et Bremae, 1744), I, 115-119.

[6] Johann Wilhelm Baum, *Capito und Butzer, Strassburgs Reformatoren.* III, *Leben und Ausgewählte Schriften der Väter und Begründer der Reformierten Kirche* (Elberfeld, 1860). Jean-Charles Hoffet, *Esquisse Biographique sur Capiton* (Strasbourg, 1850), followed the older accounts for Capito's earlier life. He dedicated his thesis to Baum.

Two aspects of Capito's career are well known. In 1907 two learned monographs shed light on his service at the court of Albert of Mainz. The conservative Lutheran historian Paul Kalkoff [7] argued that Capito was Luther's conscious follower between 1520 and 1523, and Fritz Herrmann, [8] a younger man, agreed, while giving Capito's exploits a prominent place in his study of the evangelical movement at Mainz. Neither scholar considered Capito's religious thought during this period, but their agreement that he aided Luther's cause from his influential position has become standard doctrine.

Capito's relations with the Anabaptists have interested historians since the mid-nineteenth century, long before the modern renaissance of studies in the so-called Radical Reformation. In general, scholars have agreed that Capito promoted a remarkably tolerant policy toward religious dissidents, and have disagreed only on his motives. Timotheus-Wilhelm Röhrich, the father of Alsatian Reformation studies, considered Capito's mildness a function of his personal relations with some radicals. [9] Others have suggested that he was fundamentally sympathetic to Anabaptist theology. [10] But in 1889 Camill Gerbert, in his basic study of the radical movement in Strasbourg, maintained that Capito's differences with Bucer concerned policy only and grew from his powerful pastoral concerns. [11] Present understanding of Capito's attitude toward the radicals and of his theology comes, nevertheless, from Otto Erich Strasser of the University of Bern, who returned to the older view. In two studies he argued that before 1532 Capito leaned theologically toward the Anabaptists, but later rejected their spiritualism. [12]

---

[7] Paul Kalkoff, *W. Capito im Dienste Erzbischof Albrechts von Mainz. Quellen und Forschungen zu den entscheidenden Jahren der Reformation*. I, *Neue Studien zur Geschichte der Theologie und Kirche* (Berlin, 1907).

[8] Fritz Herrmann, *Die Evangelische Bewegung zu Mainz im Reformationszeitalter* (Mainz, 1907), p. 77 n. 173, termed Kalkoff's study "outstanding."

[9] Timotheus-Wilhelm Röhrich, *Geschichte der Reformation im Elsass und besonders in Strassburg* (Strassburg, 1830-1832), 3 vols., esp. II, 77-79.

[10] [   ] Heberle, "W. Capito's Verhältnis zum Anabaptismus." *Zeitschrift für die Historische Theologie*, XXVII (1857), 285-310. Johann Martin Usteri, "Die Stellung der Strassburger Reformatoren Bucer und Capito zur Tauffrage," *Theologische Studien und Kritiken*, LVII (1884), 456-525.

[11] Camill Gerbert, *Geschichte der Strassburger Sectenbewegung zur Zeit der Reformation, 1524-1534* (Strassburg, 1889).

[12] O. E. Strasser, *Capitos Beziehungen zu Bern. IV, Quellen und Abhandlungen zur Schweizerischen Reformationsgeschichte* (Leipzig, 1928), and *La pensée theologique de Wolfgang Capiton dans les dernières années de sa vie. XI, Mémoires de l'Université de Neuchâtel* (Neuchâtel, 1938). See also his "Un chrétien humaniste: Wolfgang

The lack of a modern, analytical biography of Capito turns partly on the state of the primary sources. There is no critical edition of his thirty-nine published works, copies of which are scattered in the Bibliothèque Nationale et Universitaire, the Archives Municipales, and the Seminaire Protestant in Strasbourg, as well as Basel's Universitätsbibliothek, Zurich's Centralbibliothek, and Munich's Bayerische Staatsbibliothek. His early years to 1507 are virtually a blank, providing material for little more than speculation. His extant correspondence is more plentiful for the years after 1515, but again the originals are widely dispersed.[13] Fortunately, in the nineteenth century Baum and his students made handwritten copies, which they desposited at the Bibliothèque Nationale et Universitaire in Strasbourg,[14] and his correspondence with more important figures has been published in modern editions of their works. Insofar as they are presently known, all the extant materials bearing on Capito's life have been investigated in preparation for this study.

A biography of Capito falls naturally into three parts. The first two chapters trace his development as a reforming northern humanist, and the third and fourth his attitude toward and conversion to the evangelical movement. The next three chapters describe the career of the reformer, as he worked to purify the church of Strasbourg, to maintain unity among the chief reformers, and to establish the new churches of the Reformation. A final chapter that discusses the changes in his religious and cultural values forms a natural conclusion. Throughout, the effort is to penetrate, as deeply as possible, Capito's own thought and motives, and thereby to write true biography while presenting a case study in the relationship between humanism and the Reformation.

The biographer faces the temptation of according so-called secondary figures a full life and works in the hope that he may rescue their

---

Capiton," *Revue d'Histoire et de Philosophie Religieuses*, XX (1940), 1-14, where he sees Capito's humanism in his understanding of human reason.

[13] The most important collection is the St. Thomas Archives of the Archives municipales in Strasbourg. See Jean Adam, *Inventaire des Archives de Chapitre de St. Thomas de Strasbourg* (Strasbourg, 1937). For the curious history of the Capito manuscripts, see Baum, *Capito und Butzer*, pp. 584-585.

[14] Johannis Guil. Baum, compiler and copier, Thesaurus Epistolicus Reformatorum Alsaticorum. 26 vols. (Hereafter cited as Th. B.) Where complete, it has been used in this study. For a description and index, see Johannes Ficker, ed., *Thesaurus Baumianus. Verzeichniss der Briefe und Aktenstücke* (Strassburg, 1905). There is now a microfilm copy of Th. B. at the Foundation for Reformation Research in St. Louis, Missouri.

careers from undesevered oblivion. This temptation has been eschewed here. Capito was sufficiently important in the intellectual and religious currents of the early sixteenth century to merit study for his own sake. But as a humanist he was no Reuchlin, Erasmus, or More. And as a reformer he was overshadowed not only in Germany by Luther, Melanchthon, and Zwingli, but also in Strasbourg itself by the enigmatic figure of Bucer. Capito was too mild, too ambivalent for genuine greatness in the harsh age of the Reformation. The details of his domestic and personal life, and of his religious thought, accordingly have little value in and of themselves. To be sure, his thought and deeds bore the stamp of his own personality and circumstances, and his peculiarity must be identified. But he was primarily an intellectual and religious reformer who was powerfully influenced by the greater intellects and personalities of his time, by Erasmus and Luther in particular. His was an imitative genius, whose abiding importance lies in the fact that he was a humanist who became a reformer.

Although not of the traditional life and works sort, this study is a biography, for the life of Capito is in a very real sense the story of Capito and the Reformation. The important questions about Capito's life derive from his having been a convert in an age of conversion. Under what circumstances and influences did he change from humanist to reformer? How deep was his conversion, and what sort of reformer did he become? In seeking answers to such questions, there is the danger of turning the categories "humanist" and "reformer" into objective realities against which Capito can be measured. But the intention here is to write biography, and therefore to allow Capito's career to define the categories. The details of his domestic and private life, and of his thought and deeds, serve, then, only to document the nature of his transition and the factors that played a role in shaping his life. Much that is found in traditional biography is missing from this study. All that is germane to the central motiv of Capito's life is present, and that motiv is his conversion from humanist to reformer.

CHAPTER ONE

A HUMANIST'S BEGINNINGS

Like so many who attain some prominence later in life, Wolfgang
Capito seemed to enjoy recalling the poverty of his origins. Over
fifty years after his birth as Wolfgang Köpfel in 1478 in Hagenau,[1]
near Strasbourg, he declared, "I was born of poor parents in a little
peasants' hut, and I was never really able to appease my hungering
belly with gruel and day-old peasants' bread; even today white bread
and honey are bitter and undesireable to me." [2]

There are good grounds for suggesting that this reminiscence is a
little exaggerated. In the first place, it contrasted sharply with the
comfortable circumstances of the wealthy prelates at the Council of
Basel, whom he was condemning even as he recalled his own beginnings. Secondly, his father, Hans, was not a peasant. He was a smith,
and for a time a member of Hagenau's city council. Such a position
was not normally open to those with much claim to truly small
means. Capito seems also to have been proud of his father's trade, for
he assumed the middle name "Fabricius" after Hans's death in 1500.
The family was thus rather typically bourgeois for the late middle
ages, and probably rather better off than many. On the other hand,
although Johannes Sturm likely exaggerated, too, when he described
the Köpfel's as the most honest burghers in the city, he was probably
right when he wrote that Hans and his wife Agnes worked hard to
support themselves and their children.[3]

Sturm also wrote that father Hans was exceptionally pious.[4] If
so, his piety was not of the sort that received official sanction, for
here too he was rather typically bourgeois. Hans Köpfel was deeply
anti-clerical. He commanded his son not to become a priest, and he
repeated the injuction on his death bed. In his view, entering the

---

[1] Sturm, *Luctus ad Camerarium*, sig. [Bvii(v)], noted Hans' death in 1500 when
Capito was twenty-two. A posthumous likeness of Capito, presently in New
St. Peter's in Strasbourg, carries the inscription "obiit 4 Nov. Aetat. 60. 1541,"
probably an estimate.

[2] *Das Concilium zu Basel satzung und constitution* ([Strassburg, 1530]), sig. Lii(v).
For the full titles to Capito's works, which are abbreviated in the notes and for
which no author will be designated, consult the bibliography.

[3] Sturm, *Luctus ad Camerarium*, sig. [Bvii(v)-Bviii].

[4] *Ibid.*, sig. [Bvii(v)].

clerical estate amounted to committing oneself to a life of idleness and sin.[5] According to his son, even Hans's formal beliefs may have been open to question. As a reformer Capito had often to respond to the charge that he was nothing more than a follower of Hus. On one such occasion he replied, "He has always existed and remained among the older laymen of the German nation. Even I heard many stories in my childhood years. I was amazed, for at that time I could not understand how it carried on." Perhaps Hans's anticlericalism was fueled by a romanticized version of Hus's career. In any event Capito also wrote that his beloved father knew salvation by grace alone before he died. "In my dear deceased father I have myself seen that God is known to those who have despaired. Thus, when a monk who lived nearby in Hagenau annointed him and said to him, 'Dear Master Hans, think on all the good works you have done,' he turned to the cross and said, 'What good works have I done? Oh, my Lord and God, be merciful to me, a sinner!' " With approval his son added, "Even though he had not been spiritual in an ordinary manner during his life, he still came to doubt himself and would not have faith in any of his good works, but called upon the name of God. . . ."[6] The picture is suspiciously stereotyped—a poor but honest and pious father who trusted to the grace of God alone. And yet the Köpfel's may have led a restive religious life. Perhaps religious ideas that were more earnest than orthodox circulated about the family table.

Capito also remembered the poverty of his intellectual beginnings. But here the tone was one of strident criticism rather than sentimental pride in their basic integrity. Hans may have been a frugal man, one disinclined to spend his gains on white bread and honey, but he was sufficiently prosperous to send his son at a tender age to the famous Latin school at Pforzheim to study under "the masters of letters," as Sturm put it.[7] Capito did not think so highly of his grammar school teachers. In 1519, at the peak of his fame as a humanist scholar, he remarked in the dedication of a translation of Chrysostom to

---

[5] Capito to Bonifacius [Wolfhart], [mid-1521]. Kirchenarchiv Basel, 25a, fol. 245. "Etenim pater moriens multis obtestabatur, ne in sacerdotium me temere conijcerem, quod doctrinam et vita praeluceret, et qui atrocem et violentum affectum moderetur." The text of this letter is partially published by J. V. Pollet, *Martin Bucer. Études sur la correspondance avec des nombreux textes inédits* (Paris, 1959), II, 267f.

[6] *Antwurt auff Bruder Conradts Vermanung* (Strassburg, 1524), sig. Giii(v)-H; I(v)-Iii.

[7] Sturm, *Luctus ad Camerarium*, sig. [Bviii].

Albert, Archbishop of Mainz, "As a young boy I was handed over to teachers who were unable to teach anything except those things that should be forgotten." [8] How different his memories were from the fond recollections of Philip Melanchthon, another of Pforzheim's famous pupils!

Northern humanists found it fashionable to complain about the failings of their early teachers, but there was more to the matter in Capito's case. The school at which he studied before 1495 differed from the school that Melanchthon recalled with such pleasure. It was then, and remained, a municipal institution that was unrelated to the city's ecclesiastical foundations. The city council contracted a schoolmaster on an annual basis. It provided the master with the barest accommodations and paid half his salary, with the remainder coming from student fees. But the master was more the school's superintendent than he was a teacher. "Laureates," or university graduates who had attained the B. A., provided most of the actual instruction in reading and writing Latin. They claimed the remainder of student fees, which were graded according to the student's age, his ability to pay, and whether his family resided in the city. Students were also required to bring a candle and a stick of firewood for winter classes, unless they could pay someone to do so for them. [9] Considering Capito's penny-wise father, young Wolfgang probably brought his own candle and firewood.

There was room for abuse in an arrangement under which the quality of instruction and student life depended so heavily upon the master's zeal and competence in supervising the miserably-paid teachers. Shortly after Capito departed for university, the Pforzheim city council investigated its school. He had legitimate grounds for his complaints, if the problems, that the new charter of 1500 sought to correct, actually existed. In their new order the councilmen instructed the master to supervise the laureates more closely and to insure that they did not defraud their charges by failing to provide the instruction for which they were so miserably paid. He was also ordered to check the riotous behavior of the older, vagabond students, who differed from the laureates only in their relative lack of attainment. According to the charter, the master was also to exclude students

---

[8] *Paraenesis Prior Divi Joh. Chrysostomi* (Basileae, 1519), fol. 7.

[9] Eberhard Gothein, *Pforzheims Vergangenheit. Ein Beitrag zur deutschen Städte- und Gewerbegeschichte.* IX, *Staats- und socialwissenschaftliche Forschungen* (Leipzig, 1889), pp. 29-31.

from cities that had been stricken by the plague and those who supported themselves by begging. The system still depended upon the master who controlled it, but this time the city council found the right man. Georg Simler, who became a confidant of the eminent Reuchlin, was the master whom Melanchthon so honored, but he became superintendent only after Capito completed his grammar schooling.[10] Student life was generally harsh in the late middle ages, but it was probably especially so at Pforzheim during Capito's enrollment. Poor instruction and rough treatment made a negative impression, and the memory of it lingered on.

He nevertheless acquired the rudiments of Latin sufficiently at Pforzheim to enable him to pursue successfully his university studies in the following years. Whether he even enrolled in a university immediately must remain a matter of conjecture, for there is no contemporary evidence regarding his life from about 1495 to 1500. Baum reports that he followed his father's wishes and earned a doctorate in medicine at Freiburg in 1498 and then studied law briefly at Basel.[11] But he did not claim the title "Doctor" until 1515, and he was not recorded in subsequent matriculations as having earned the degree. In any event, the death of his father in 1500 ended his presumed medical career. Hans's dying command was that his son should not "rashly" become a priest. What then can be said of Capito in the year 1500? He may have shared his father's earnest faith, but there is nothing to suggest that it had as yet matured into a desire for church reform. He was twenty-two years old, but he had not begun the humanistic studies in languages, grammar, and rhetoric upon which he later focused all his powers. In sum, there is no evidence that he differed from any other beginning university student at the dawn of the turbulent sixteenth century.

Hereafter Capito's life becomes more accessible. He enrolled in the arts faculty at Ingolstadt in 1501. He earned the B. A. by 1505 when he matriculated in arts at Freiburg im Breisgau. There he received the M. A. in 1506.[12] He then left Freiburg and returned to his home

---

[10] *Ibid.*, pp. 83-85, for the charter. Ottmar Sexauer, "Pforzheim zur Zeit Reuchlins. Ein Kulturbild," *Joannes Reuchlin, 1455-1522. Festgabe seiner Vaterstadt Pforzheim zur 500. Widerkehr seines Geburtstages*, Manfred Krebs, ed. (Pforzheim, 1955), p. 167.

[11] Baum, *Capito und Butzer*, pp. 7-9. Adamus, *Vitae*, pp. 88-89, suggests Basel for the medical degree. Gerdesius, *Introductio*, I, 115, agrees and cites a lost letter to a certain Bonifacius Augustanus.

[12] Hermann Mayer, ed., *Die Matrikel der Universität Freiburg im Breisgau von 1460 bis 1656* (Freiburg, 1907), I, 161-162.

town where he served for a time as proofreader for Henricus Gran, the publisher. This was an important period for his future development. The following three years were his first association with the humanist movement. He probably knew Jacob Wimpheling personally, and perhaps other members of the Rhenish humanist sodality, such as Beatus Rhenanus or Sebastian Brant. He and Wimpheling appear in fact to have been rather well acquainted, for in 1523 Wimpheling paternally exhorted him to remain loyal to Rome.[13] And in 1507 Capito published an afterword to Gran's edition of Conrad Summenhart's commentary on the physics of Albertus Magnus, to which Wimpheling contributed a preface.[14]

Yet, during these three years Capito acquired no more than a taste of the new learning that he later devoured. In the first place, the Strasbourg humanist sodality was one of the most conservative in Germany.[15] Wimpheling, the leader of the group and its most important member for Capito, was typical. He attacked ecclesiastical abuses and clerical immorality with special zeal, but always with the thought of improving the status of the clergy in the eyes of the laity. He could maintain, in a celebrated dispute, that Augustine was never a monk, but his own religious ideas were impeccably orthodox. Like Brant, he was particularly devoted to the cult of the Virgin Mary. Much the same ambivalence characterized his attitude toward the good learning of the antique world. He desired especially to reform grammar schools, which he believed should teach good morals, as well as elegant Latin. He did believe that there was an intimate connection between good learning and right living, and he urged students to read the authors of classical antiquity, but he excluded Ovid, Juvenal, and Catullus on the grounds that their works were too racy. Nor did he share the wholehearted disgust for the schoolmen that characterized humanists such as Erasmus. Just before Capito joined the Strasbourg group, Wimpheling became involved in a literary brawl on the side of an Ingolstadt professor who insisted that the scholastic theologians were better reading for Christians than the ancient authors. Capito

---

[13] Th. B., II, 33.

[14] *Conradi Summenhart Commentaria in summam physice Alberti Magni* (Hagenoiae, 1507), sig., [A(v)]; AA5(v).

[15] On the Strasbourg circle and Wimpheling, see Charles Schmidt, *Histoire littéraire de l'Alsace à la fin du XVe et au commencement du XVIe siècle* (Paris, 1879), I, 57-67, 132-150, and Lewis W. Spitz, *The Religious Renaissance of the German Humanists* (Cambridge, Mass., 1963), pp. 41-57, for Wimpheling's religious ideas.

left Ingolstadt for Strasbourg just after this fight; Wimpheling may indeed have come to his attention as a man of the new learning who nevertheless respected the learning of the universities.

All that can be known about Capito's own intellectual preferences during these years comes from his brief afterword to Summenhart's commentary. There he faithfully mirrored the conservative views of Wimpheling. On the one hand he tried to correct the text in the best humanistic fashion. "You have now, most candid reader," he wrote, "the learned commentaries of the theologian, Conrad Summenhart, which have been refurbished from the corrupted text as thoroughly as I considered possible." [16] To this praise for his own labors, he added a poem in which he lauded the scholastic work itself.[17] In the third line he suggested that there was a better form of learning then Summenhart's explication of Albertus Magnus by means of Aristotelian logic. But in the last three lines he clearly told the reader that great wisdom was to be gained from Summenhart, who was one of the last of the schoolmen. Emend the manuscript as much as he might, Capito was still comfortably within the late medieval learned tradition. At twenty-nine he was not a humanist. He had not thrown logic over for grammar, nor the schoolmen for the ancient authors.

On the other hand, the three years with Wimpheling's group did mark a genuine, albeit finally inaccessible, turning point in Capito's life. The Rhenish humanist sodality was particularly pious, and it included not only scholars and literati but also the great reform preacher Geiler von Kaysersberg.[18] Sturm even suggested that Geiler was a powerful example for the young Capito, who may have heard him preach from the stone pulpit in Strasbourg's cathedral. At the very least, Geiler was a living contradiction of the pious anticlericalism of Capito's father, for no German burgher ever excoriated the moral failings of the clergy with greater vehemence than did Geiler. A powerful change overcame Capito, as he recalled it in 1521: "Indeed I held in my memory this last command of my dead

---

[16] *Summenhart Commentaria*, sig. AA5(v).

[17] *Ibid.*, fol. AA5(v). "Optime lector habes fundamina vera sophiae/ Qualia ętas pristina contribuit./ Sunt meliora, reor, dictamine toto./ Quod sensus pulchros perplexitate tenet/ Ex his difficilem poteris perdiscere solus/ Naturam rerum. Sedulus, oro, legas."

[18] On Geiler, see Schmidt, *Histoire littéraire*, I, 337-461. The best and most recent work is E. Jane Dempsey Douglass, *Justification in Late Medieval Preaching. A Study of John Geiler of Keisersberg*. I, *Studies in Medieval and Reformation Thought* (Leiden, 1966).

father, and I often repeated it to myself, not heeding so much his words as his thoughts and judgments. And at the same time the task of the Gospel occurred to me as really glorious; I silently weighed its majesty and deemed its heralds worthy of the highest honor." [19]

Capito was deciding to become a priest. Geiler may have been a positive example, one drawing him to the priesthood, but other pressures also played a part. He appears to have been a young man who always took religious questions seriously, and while he was working for Gran he experienced a religious crisis of sorts. In 1525 in the early stages of the sacramentarian controversy, he wrote Luther's colleague, Johannes Bugenhagen, "Now I am accustomed to remembering with what severe doubt I was striken in my adolescent mind when I imprudently read Wyclif's condemnation concerning [transubstantiation]. Driven thereafter into the priesthood by a rashness that was certainly ill-advised, I was distracted by astonishingly great troubles." [20] He may not have become a humanist while with the Strasbourg circle, but he did take the decisive step of rejecting his father's dying command. He was but one young man in the early sixteenth century to put aside his parents' wishes, and to enter the clerical estate out of fear for his own soul.

In 1509 he returned to Freiburg, took minor orders, and was ordained a priest with Luther's later opponent, Johannes Eck, officiating. Wimpheling himself probably urged him to take this step, and he kept himself apprised of the progress of Capito's studies. He was an able and industrious theology student. As was his right as a Master of Arts, he was admitted by the arts faculty on December 6, 1509 to a lectureship, with the note that he followed the *via moderna*—the nominalist way of Scotus and Occam. He was a member of the arts faculty senate during winter semester 1511-1512. He became a *Biblicus* on December 10, 1510, and he received the licentiate on May 17, 1512. Like all advanced students at Freiburg, lecturing was a part of his studies, as well as a means of providing for his needs. In December 1510 he began a series of lectures on the Old and New Testaments, in which he treated Sophonias, Haggaeus, Zacharia, and Malachi, and then the second and third letters of John, and Jude.

---

[19] Capito to Bonifacius [Wolfhart], [mid-1521]. Kirchenarchiv Basel, 25a, fol. 244(v). "Equidem vero mortui parentis ultimum hoc mandatum memore mente asservavi, sepiusque mecum perpetravi non tam verbis illius quam animis atque iudiciis advertens. Atque simul eximium ferme occurrit Evangelii negotium; hujus majestatem tacitus expendi, praecones eius honore summor dignabar."

[20] O. Vogt, ed., *Dr. Johann Bugenhagens Briefwechsel* (Stettin, 1888), p. 37.

In October 1511 he began to lecture on the standard medieval theology textbook, the *Sentences* of Peter Lombard. Such a sequence was
common to most theology students in the late middle ages, but in
early 1512 Capito received a special honor—he was named a professor
of theology *extraordinarius*. This position entitled him to a half-salary
of twenty-five florins annually.[21]

Capito was a nominalist during his student years at Freiburg. He
did study the Bible, for the *cursus Biblicus* was the core of Freiburg's
theology curriculum. But he expounded the Scriptures by means of
Aristotelian logic rather than through the use of languages and
history. His first teacher, Gregorius Northofer, was a Scotist, and
when a soldier murdered him in the streets in April 1509, another
Scotist, Antonius Beck, took his place on the theology faculty. The
most influential professor during Capito's period of study was Johannes Brisgoicus, who lectured on Gabriel Biel, the nominalist theologian at Tübingen, and on Occam. In winter semester 1509-1510 Eck
too lectured on Biel and Occam as *extraordinarius* before he left for a
professorship at Ingolstadt. Because Capito was later promoted to
Eck's position, it is likely that he too lectured on Biel, as well as on
Scotus in the arts faculty.[22] He was therefore immersed in the same
theological tradition that Luther studied. He probably sought what
Luther later called the theology of glory, that required man to do
what was within him in order to achieve salvation.

Later, as a self-conscious humanist, Capito recalled his years at
Freiburg with loathing. He bemoaned "the trickery of the sophists
and the Scotist nausea with which I deafened the miserable auditors
while I was giving lectures for pay." His humanist biographer,
Sturm, was similarly inclined about the value of Capito's formal
theological training. He passed by the Freiburg period with the
remark that "In a few years he had made such progress in letters and
religion that he became a priest and gave public lectures." To Sturm's
mind all that he accomplished of merit was to read Augustine.[23]
For both biographer and subject these studies had an essential quality

---

[21] Mayer, *Matrikel Freiburg*, I, 161-162. Heinrich Schreiber, *Geschichte der
Albert-Ludwigs Universität zu Freiburg im Breisgau* (Freiburg, 1857), I, 97-99.
Johannes Joseph Bauer, *Zur Frühgeschichte der Theologischen Fakultät der Universität
Freiburg i. Br. (1460-1620). XIV, Beiträge zur Freiburger Wissenschafts- und Universi-
tätsgeschichte* (Freiburg, 1957), pp. 118-122, 188.

[22] *Ibid.*, pp. 74, 117-122.

[23] Capito cited, Gerdesius, *Introductio*, I, 116. Sturm, *Luctus ad Camerarium*,
sig. [Bvii(v)]-C(v).

in common with those Capito pursued at Pforzheim—they were best forgotten.

Such distaste born of subsequent achievement only obscures Capito's attitude toward his studies while he engaged in them. Little can be known about his early religious thought—the extent to which he was a nominalist or just what sort of nominalist he was—but even while excoriating his education, he revealed just how enthusiastic he was as a theology student. In 1521 he recalled, "Ah, how often I begged in my prayers for that faculty of speaking that would be adequate for a clergyman; how often I bemoaned the fraud, immersed in Scotist commentaries. How often I devoted my efforts to the rest of the hodge-podge of the theological disputants." [24] In dedicating a translation of Chrysostom to Albert of Mainz in 1519 he remarked that he thought his entire university education was designed more to teach "stubbornness" than "to refine the talents and smooth the way to piety." [25] These were the fashionable criticisms of a humanist who had just accepted a position as adviser and chaplain to Germany's most powerful ecclesiastical prince, and who scorned the base degrees by which he did ascend. At least during the earlier portion of his studies he was an avid follower of the *via moderna*. As late as 1519 he offered the judgment that Scotus was "the first among the more recent theologians." [26] And during the same period, while lecturing on Romans, he actually used the theological categories of Biel. [27]

On the other hand, there may be a small element of truth to his assertion that he "bemoaned the fraud of doubtful commentaries" even while he was a student. There is some evidence that he continued to flirt with more distinctly humanistic studies, just as he did during his brief association with Wimpheling and the Rhenish humanist sodality. For example, he was so impressed with Gregor Reisch's *Margarita Philosophica*, an immensely popular compendium of the seven liberal arts, that he enthusiastically recommended it even after

---

[24] Capito to Bonifacius [Wolfhart], [mid-1521], Kirchenarchiv Basel, 25a, fol. 244(v). "Quoties tum votis expetivi eam dicendi facultatem quae sufficeret ecclesiasti, quoties gemui fraudem immersus scoticis commentariis, quoties reliquae farragini disputatorum theologorum navavi operam."
[25] *Paraenesis Prior Divi Joh. Chrysostomi*, fol. 7. See also an almost identical remark in the letter to Wolfhart about two years later, "tantum enim ad pugnam et impudentiam asseverandi non intellecta instruebamur." Kirchenarchiv Basel, 25a, fol. 244(v).
[26] *Epistola de Formando Theologo* (Basileae, 1517), sig. Aii.
[27] Rom. Lec., fol. 69(v). "Ex condigno et congruo meritorium opus. . . ."

2

he had moved to Basel. [28] Reisch was the glory of Freiburg's arts faculty. He was also prior of the Carthusian chapter in Freiburg and sometime adviser to Emperor Maximilian. But his book had little to recommend it to the true humanist. Some editions did contain brief Hebrew and Greek grammars, and Reisch did consider dialectic merely one of the liberal arts rather than the only certain way to knowledge. But he remained in the old tradition. He did not consider classical and Christian antiquity normative for his own time. Most importantly, he presented grammar from the viewpoint of philosophy, and he followed Donatus and Alexander in both organization and method. In pictorially representing the spheres of learning, he placed Peter Lombard in the commanding position, at the apex of theology.[29] Capito's later praises may have been no more than fond but cloudy memories of a beloved textbook that he was recommending to the beginner. At the very least, however, his enthusiasm for such a modest work reveals how little the humanist he was as a student. He seems to have brought with him from the Strasbourg sodality Wimpheling's conservative, transitional approach to the new learning.

Capito did have one more acquaintance with German humanism during his formal theological studies. This was his presumed association with Ulrich Zasius, who was in the eyes of the German humanists the restorer of legal studies. But here too the evidence is mixed. He knew Zasius, and perhaps studied under him at Freiburg, but even later he disliked the subject of Zasius' humanistic labors. On the one hand he praised him as the man who "put the pettifogging lawyers into full flight" with good Latin. On the other hand he included "the lawyers" among those teachers "who were able to teach only those things that should be forgotten." [30] Capito's brief legal studies appear to have had no positive affect upon him. At Freiburg he was a zealous theology student who followed the *via moderna*. He took part in the disputations and he employed dialectic as the most important tool for theology. He continued to dabble in

[28] *Hebraicarvm Institvtionvm Libri Duo* (Basileae, 1518), sig. E(v)-E2, I2-I2(v).

[29] On Reisch see Friedrich Prantl's article in *Allgemeine Deutsche Biographie*, XXVIII, 117; Schreiber, *Geschichte der Universität Freiburg*, I, 63-67; and Terrance Heath, "Logical Grammar, Grammatical Logic, and Humanism in Three German Universities," *Studies in the Renaissance* (New York, 1971), XVIII, 33-34; 54.

[30] *Institutivncvla in Hebraicam Linguam* (Basileae, 1516), sig. aa4(v). *Paraenesis Prior Divi Joh. Chrysostomi*, fol. 7. Zasius referred to Capito as "Iovis meus Wolfgangus" in a letter to Boniface Amerbach. Alfred Hartmann, ed., *Die Amerbach Korrespondenz* (Basel, 1943), II, 170-171.

the liberal arts, but he was becoming a professional theologian in the traditional manner.

In 1512 the external circumstances of his life suddenly changed. That spring Philip von Rosenburg, the Bishop of Speier, called him to become canon and preacher at the Benedictine foundation at Bruchsal, on the Rhine midway between Freiburg and Mainz. When he resigned his extraordinary professorship in May, he explained that he was leaving for financial reasons. Other factors probably played a part in his decision. Just as he announced that he would accept Philip's call, the arts faculty senate was investigating his involvement with Eck in publishing poems in which they libelled another professor. The previous year Eck had left for a professorship at Ingolstadt, and Capito may have found it wiser to move than to face the investigation.[31] Moreover, the position he expected at Bruchsal had its own attractions for a young scholar who had not yet found himself. The Benedictine canonry was one of those that provided an honorable means of pensioning off the progeny of Germany's numerous and penurious nobility. It was not known for the zeal of its religious practices. Capito could expect to find time to continue his studies while he served as preacher to the noble canons.

The vigorous manner in which he pursued his calling at Freiburg made him stand out among his fellow students. The circumstances under which he decided to become a priest and theologian naturally gave him a seriousness and a sense of high purpose that other students may not have shared. In 1525 when he was recalling the anxieties he had about transubstantiation, he wrote Bugenhagen that "after several years I beautifully persuaded myself to believe through the faith of the Catholic Church what I did not believe for a moment from the heart." [32] Accepting the given faith of the church as one's own was a typically nominalist position, but it did not last much longer for Capito than it did for Luther. The solitude of Bruchsal provided the occasion for Capito's doubts about the Mass to return.

In October 1512 Conrad Pellican, the eminent Hebraist, interrupted a trip to Speier on business for the Franciscans to spend a night with Capito. "When he had taken me to a private place," Pellican reported forty years later, "he secretly inquired what I thought concerning

---

[31] Bauer, *Zur Frühgeschichte*, p. 76. Schreiber, *Geschichte der Universität Freiburg*, II, 168. Sturm, *Luctus ad Camerarium*, sig. C(v)- Cii, dated the call "decem annos Friburgi," an estimate.

[32] Vogt, *Bugenhagens Briefwechsel*, pp. 37-38.

the sacrament of the eucharist and the body of Christ." Pellican knew immediately what concerned Capito. "I will acknowledge the truth and hide none of my secrets from you," he replied. "The fiction of transubstantiation that presently rules indiscriminately in the church plainly does not deserve my faith. . . ." Pellican recounted Scotus' three possible ways of viewing the elements and then declared, "I would adhere more willingly to the first than to the third. Knowing the bread and wine to be a sacred thing, I sacrificed the Sacrament of the body and the flowing blood, that is the sacred sign, knowing it to be the visible form of invisible divine grace in Christ and nutriment for the soul, spiritually and through faith. . . ." Pellican flatly rejected the doctrine that had been so worrying Capito. "I declare the body and blood of Christ to be truly in the sacrament," he added, "and that this is perceived by believers, not indeed physically or really . . . but sacramentally. . . ." [33]

"When he heard this Capito responded that no other view seemed proper to him, and that he could not comprehend any other." He was not alone in his doubts about transubstantiation, and so he no longer needed to fear them. "Magnificent Pellican," he replied, "you have flooded me with delight. . . ." [34]

It is most likely that Pellican's account is true in substance if not in detail. It is true that he told this story forty years after it happened, and that he was then somewhat bemused over the irony that Capito spent the declining years of his life trying desperately to secure aggreement between the Swiss and the Lutherans over the nature of the elements, that he had indeed agreed to some sort of physical presence in the Lord's Supper. It is more important, however, to note that there is nothing anachronistic in Pellican's story. He did not deny, nor did he have Capito deny, that the eucharist was a sacrifice, even if only symbolically. After he became a reformer, Capito did reject the doctrine that the Mass was a sacrifice and that attendance at Mass was therefore a good work, meritorious for salvation. But all this came later. Here Pellican had Capito adopt a Wycliff-like spiritual view of the elements. Although it was dressed up in one of Scotus' alternatives, it was precisely the teaching that Capito himself reported caused him so much anxiety as a young man.

---

[33] Bernhard Riggenbach, ed., *Das Chronikon des Konrad Pellikan* (Basel, 1877), pp. 42-43, and Johannes Fabricius Montanus, "Oratoria Historia," in *ibid.*, pp. 185-187. Montanus' account came from Pellikan. *Ibid.*, p. 43 n. 1.

[34] *Ibid.*, pp. 43, 187.

More importantly, this conversation with Pellican really did solve Capito's spiritual crisis. He never again had such deeply personal concerns about the nature of the elements. In 1525 he wrote Bugenhagen how shocked he was to discover that he and Luther were insisting upon Christ's real presence in the Lord's Supper. "No one, as far as I know, ever heard a sermon in which I tried to persuade him to believe that the real body of Christ was in the bread, unless," he added ironically, "it may of course have slipped out once at Basel . . ." between 1515 and 1520.[35] As far as it concerned the nature of the elements, the issue of the eucharist seems to have been settled for Capito in 1512. While lecturing on Romans six years later he did refer to the Mass twice. Once he observed that it was foreshadowed in Jewish sacrifices and in the rites of purification. Then, after arguing at length that such ceremonies could not lead to salvation, he asked "But who should receive the eucharist?" and answered, "One is first to be justified before he can presume to receive [this] gift of God." There was no discussion of the elements here, although Capito was treating a text that spoke specifically of the blood of Christ.[36] Pellica calmed Capito's tortured conscience during their walk through the garden.

The Bruchsal period was also important for Capito because it marked his decisive turn toward humanistic studies. In 1541 Sebastian Münster wrote in the preface to his oft-issued Hebrew grammar, "And then in about the year of Christ 1513 Wolfgang Capito, who had been made preacher in the town of Bruchsal and who obtained a certain Jew who was baptized Matthew (Adrianus, evidently), began to Hebraize happily, and on his own, for it is all the same under a surely teacher." Adrianus, who came from Spain, lived with the Amerbachs in Basel until 1513 and then moved to Heidelberg. Capito probably travelled the short distance from Bruchsal for the lessons. Later he was joined by Johannes Oecolampadius, a life-long friend who became the reformer of Basel. Capito may in fact have been the author of Münster's low opinion of Adrianus' pedagogical skills. "The Spaniard," was useful, he reported while reminiscing on the occasion of Oecolampadius' death, "even if he gave us knowledge

---

[35] Vogt, *Bugenhagens Briefwechsel*, pp. 37-38.
[36] Rom. Lec., fol. 66, "Hostiae et purificationes ad Sacramentum Evcharistiae cuius figuram praetulerunt relati sunt," and fol. 71(v), "Sed quis suscepturus Evcharistiam? Ivstificati debet, priusquam donum dei praesumat accipere."

of the sacred language grudgingly and not in the best manner." [37]
However poor his language instruction was, these studies were the
beginning of Capito's career as a humanist, for he shortly became
known as one of Europe's most accomplished Hebrew scholars.
As he studied the ancient languages, he also began to insist with the
humanists that only they were the proper tool for theology, for they
alone allowed the scholar to return to the ancient sources.

Capito's three years at Bruchsal also started him down a path that
he never wanted to tread. This was the way of ecclesiastical politics,
a way that later led not only to preferment but also to the active life
of the reformer. He was called to Bruchsal to undertake occasional
missions for the Bishop of Speier, as well as to preach to the noble
canons. He stayed in Heidelberg "for several days" in 1513 as an
episcopal agent. It was on this trip that he became acquainted with
Oecolampadius. But the mission that led to this happy development
was only one of many such tasks that Bishop William thrust upon
him. In time, he wrote the famous knight-errant and poet Ulrich von
Hutten in 1519, "the infinite mass of duties drove me away from
there." [38]

Bruchsal should nevertheless have provided Capito with fond
memories, for it was there that his career finally began to take definite
shape. His spiritual struggles before 1513 were less profound and
less productive than Luther's. Where Capito pondered the nature of
the eucharist, Luther wrestled with he righteousness of God. Where
Capito adopted a relatively common late medieval heresy, Luther
broke through to a new understanding of the way to salvation. It
is clear that Capito took both his personal faith and his calling
seriously. His father's repeated warnings not to become a priest
"rashly" perhaps reveal worry for an eldest son who, in the parental
mind, always was too sensitive about religious concerns. In Bruchsal,
Capito began to formulate his own religious views. And at Bruchsal
he began to acquire the tools of humanist learning, and to value them
more than the scholastic tradition in which he was educated. He
became a humanist slowly and through many starts and stops, but
he prepared well for a sudden rise in Basel to the position of a scholar
of European eminence.

[37] Sebastian Münster, *Opus grammaticum consummatum. ex variis Elianis libris
concinnatum* (Basileae, 1556), fol. 2(v). *BAO*, II, 745. On Adrianus, see Ludwig
Geiger, *Das Studium der Hebräischen Sprache in Deutschland vom Ende des XV bis
zur Mitte des XVI Jahrhundertes* (Breslau, 1870), pp. 41-48.
[38] *BAO*, II, 745. Capito cited, Gerdesius, *Introductio*, I, 116.

CHAPTER TWO

THE HUMANIST AT BASEL

In the sixteenth century's second decade Basel boasted as fine a group of northern Europe's intellectual avantgarde as could be found anywhere. No city was more congenial to the humanists and no university provided more positions in which they could exercise their talents. There one found the publishers, Froben, Cratander, and the Amerbachs, who competed in printing humanist treatises and editions of classical and Christian antique sources.[1] There one found a reform-minded patron in the Bishop, Christoph von Utenheim. There one also found, from time to time, the "ornament of Christendom," as Capito called him, Erasmus of Rotterdam,[2] to say nothing of a host of his eager followers, Beatus Rhenanus, Conrad Pellican, Johannes Oecolampadius, and others. When Bishop Christoph called him in 1515 to become Basel's cathedral preacher, Capito quickly fled the cares of the intellectual backwater at Bruchsal, for, as Sturm remarked, he "was extremely apt for learning and wished to be among many learned men." [3]

In Basel, he received not only the stimulus of like minds but also the powerful example of Erasmus, the man who combined learning and piety with a facility that was admired and emulated throughout Europe. The humanists' emphasis upon rhetoric and languages as against dialectic, and their urgent desire for moral renewal, found their highest expression in Erasmus. The *philosophia Christi* provided a complete intellectual and religious program for Capito. Erasmus' successful use of the ancient languages in theology suited well his growing distaste for the rigorous and, to his mind, minutia-ridden dialectic of the nominalists. And Erasmus' assurance that good studies would create inward piety and reform Christian morals found a hearty response in a man whose own spiritual life had been deeply troubled by what he came to call "an outward thing." The influence of Erasmus made of Capito a Christian humanist who dedicated him-

---

[1] Friedrich Luchsinger, *Der Baslerbuchdruck als Vermittler italienischen Geistes, 1470-1529*. XLV, *Basler Beiträge zur Geschichtswissenschaft* (Basel, 1953), pp. 9-19, refers to the presses of Froben and Amerbach in particular as centers of Basel's intellectual life.

[2] *Paraenesis*, fol. 7. Also in Rom. lec., fol. 19(v), "orbis decus Erasmus."

[3] Sturm, *Luctus ad Camerarium*, sig. Ciii.

self equally to good learning based upon the sources of Christian and classical antiquity, and to a reform of Christendom that would express itself in a new age of peace and love. Such was the humanist program in the north.[4]

Capito's five years in Basel during the city's halcyon days at the beginning of the sixteenth century marked a turning point in his life in another way. He was such a little-known man when he arrived at the age of thirty-seven that it seems miraculous that Bishop Christoph had even heard of him. Perhaps Pellican or Oecolampadius was instrumental in securing the call to become cathedral preacher. But when Capito left Basel in 1520 for the court of Germany's most powerful ecclesiastical prince, he was a Hebrew scholar of European eminence and a compatriot and defender of the illustrious Erasmus, who thought him a better Hebraist than Reuchlin himself.[5] "Our Capito," Beatus Rhenanus fondly called him in a letter to Erasmus. Johannes Faber hailed him as a preacher who served that art in the same manner that Nicholas Cop served medicine and Budé and Zasius law. No less an authority than Zasius acknowledged Capito as a proficient Latinist, while for Oecolampadius, he was "that learned leader of ours." [6] Although it is impossible to reconstruct many details of his personal life between 1515 and 1520, it is evident that he became one of the most highly regarded members of the Basel humanist sodality.

Throughout the remainder of his life, except for his three-year tenure as adviser to the Archbishop of Mainz, Capito pursued the

---

[4] The argument is, then, that the case of Capito fits will the view of Paul Oskar Kristeller, *Renaissance Thought. The Classic, Scholastic, and Humanist Strains* (New York, 1961), pp. 3-23, that humanism was not a philosophical but predominantly a literary movement. On the other hand, he also reinforces the discussion of William J. Bouwsma, *Venice and the Defence of Republican Liberty* (Berkeley, Calif., 1968), pp. 1-11, according to which most humanists did share skeptical assumptions about the possibility of knowing the truth of general philosophical propositions. For such truths, as Spitz, *Religious Renaissance*, pp. 4-5, argues, they substituted the cultural norms of classical and Christian antiquity. That such intellectual values could influence religious, as well as secular, concerns and still remain humanistic seems obvious. Thus, humanists could free politics from the constraints of philosophical propositions and religion from those of systematic theology.

[5] To Fisher, 5 June 1516. *EE*, II, 244. "Capito . . . vir Hebraice longe doctior Reuchlino," but it must be added that here Erasmus was advertising his own *Novum Instrumentum*.

[6] Adalbert Horawitz and Karl Hartfelder, eds., *Briefwechsel des Beatus Rhenanus* (Leipzig, 1886), p. 94. *BAO*, I, 89; 68. Hartmann, *Amerbach Korrespondenz*, II, 146.

dual vocations of preacher and scholar that he took up in Basel. These activities were the natural foci of both the Renaissance and the Reformation in the north. Although none of his sermons are extant, his pulpit soon became the city's most popular and influential. There is evidence that he was a distinguished academician as well. On July 3, 1515, he received the doctorate in theology from Freiburg and became a professor of Old Testament at the University of Basel. He had good students, for he was one of the examiners who appointed his friend Oecolampadius to the licentiate in October 1516, and he reportedly chaired Caspar Hedio's doctoral disputation in 1520. Like so many good professors, he also served time as a university official. He was rector from May 1 to October 17, 1517, and dean of the faculty of theology a year later.[7] All the available evidence indicates that Capito's private life and his public life were one during these years. He was a theologian who brought the values and methods of humanism to the service of his profession. He preached and taught and lived the life of the mind.

The dual positions of cathedral preacher and professor certainly entitled him to associate with the humanists in the Basel circle. But the high esteem in which men like Oecolampadius, Pellican, and Beatus Rhenanus held him depended finally upon his own considerable intellectual achievements. His first efforts were modest. He became best known as a Hebrew scholar, but his brief *Institutio in hebraicam literaturam* attracted so little attention that it was lost to the historian. In 1516 Froben also published a joint effort that Capito undertook with Pellican, who edited a Hebrew Psalter to which Capito appended a short grammar. This work too had little abiding merit, although one copy did have the distinction of becoming a gift from Johannes Lang to his friend, the young professor, Martin Luther.[8] Had he known of this event, Capito probably would still have preferred the reception of the grammar's first complete edition, which appeared in 1518.[9] Conrad Resch, an expatriate member of the Basel circle, urgently wrote Boniface Amerbach to send him 200 copies in Paris.

---

[7] Hans Georg Wackernagel, ed., *Die Matrikel der Universität Basel* (Basel, 1951), I, 326; 334-335; 370. Schreiber, *Geschichte der Universität Freiburg*, I, 98. *BAO*, I, 31. Baum, *Capito und Butzer*, p. 42.

[8] Capito recommended the 1516 *Institutio* in *Institutivncula*, sig. [aa8]. Siegfried Raeder, *Die Benutzung des masoretischen Textes bei Luther in der Zeit zwischen der ersten und zweiten Psalmenvorlesung (1515-1518)*. XXXVIII, *Beiträge zur Historischen Theologie* (Tübingen, 1967), p. 1.

[9] *Hebraicarvm Institvtionvm Libri Duo* (Basileae, 1518).

"They are clamoring for Capito's grammar here," he exclaimed; the royal lecturer in Hebrew planned to use it. Resch begged Amerbach not to forget his request, for he had put up ten crowns earnest money as a guarantee of delivery. As Glarean put it in a letter to Amerbach's brother, Bruno, Capito's grammar was now part of "the pristine glory of the city of Basel." During his years there, Capito was an adroit practitioner of the humanist program "*summa eloquentia cum sapientia*—the highest eloquence in the company of wisdom," as he himself characterized it.[10]

Nothing can be detracted from his own achievements in Basel as preacher, professor, and humanist scholar. Yet he finally owed his position in some measure to Erasmus, who first came to Basel in 1514, and then stayed through winter 1515-1516 while he completed the famous 1516 edition of the New Testament in Greek. Apparently as a new acquaintance,[11] Capito joined in the work on the *Novum Instrumentum*, aiding Erasmus with the Hebrew names. When Erasmus published a letter that he originally wrote to Henry Bullock in August 1516, he added a note in which he confessed that the assistance of Capito and Ludwig Ber was invaluable. "With these witnesses the book was done," he wrote.[12]

From such a fortuitous beginning, Capito felt Erasmus' influence in both senses of the word. First, he was the beneficiary of Erasmus' public esteem, an endorsement that could hardly fail to increase his own modest reputation, especially before the publication of the 1518 grammar. In September 1516, after Erasmus had returned to Louvain, he summoned his best Latin style to write his master a long letter:

> I live right well, most excellent Erasmus, if living well is suffering sadly a sense of loss for the most desireable Desiderius. . . . I plead, I urgently beg, Erasmus, author of my puny talents, to whom I rightfully owe whatever I might someday become, I pray . . . that you may present the most zealous Wolfgang of yours with other letters.[13]

---

[10] Hartmann, *Amerbach Korrespondenz*, II, 146-148. *EE*, III, 9.

[11] His personal association with Erasmus was not very extensive, even during this period, for he wrote Erasmus in September 1516 that "duties and adverse health" occupied his time. *EE*, II, 333. The most recent discussion of Erasmus in Basel is by Roland H. Bainton, *Erasmus of Christendom* (New York, 1969), pp. 129-151.

[12] *EE*, II, 326.

[13] *EE*, II, 333.

In his response, Erasmus almost made the younger scholar his *alter ego*, proclaiming,

> You have a whole life, one that flourishes and thrives; you have a sound body, capable of exertions; you have a fortunate disposition, sharp judgment, and an uncommon knowledge of the three languages, combined with eloquence sufficient not only to sustain but even more to illumine the work. Your breast beats with ardor, but not of any craving for anything that serves well the general run of mankind. Your good fortune, if not the most abundant, is certainly respectable. ... Above all, you have character so unblemished, reputation so unimpaired, that no one could be so much of a slanderer that he would not be ashamed to speak badly of Fabricius.[14]

Erasmus' words must have made heady reading for Capito, but perhaps he found the published version of Erasmus' letter to Bullock even more exhilarating. There Erasmus declared that he was "not meanly learned, in addition to the other disciplines, in the three languages, Greek, Latin, and Hebrew," and that he was moreover "in life so very upright, in morals so holy that I have never seen anyone more unspoiled." [15] Such encomia, although a convention of the day, probably went far toward establishing Capito's European reputation and his position of leadership in the Basel circle.

As is commonly true, such rewards did not come easily. For Capito they required not only his own productivity as a humanist scholar but also continued vigilance in defence of Erasmus. The Greek New Testament was produced hastily and naturally contained errors for which other scholars rightfully chided Erasmus. Although Capito too reproved Erasmus for sloppiness,[16] his reaction to public criticism of the master was almost autonomic. When "a certain Franciscan," possibly Pellican, argued in spring 1517 that there were errors in the translation, Capito led an immediate counterattack for which he claimed success in three months. Part of his zeal in this instance was probably related to the nature of some of the criticisms, which were directed at the Hebrew names for which Capito himself was responsible.[17] But his personal attachment to Erasmus was genuine and at least once had a detrimental effect upon his own work. Wilhelm Nesen, for example, complained to Bruno Amerbach that

---

[14] *EE*, II, 490-491.
[15] *EE*, II, 326.
[16] *EE*, II, 335.
[17] *EE*, II, 512-513; 519-520; III, 9.

he obscured "the sense of Hebrew grammar" by his frequent digressions in the 1518 *Institvtionvm* to buttress Erasmus' New Testament.[18]

Capito nowhere more clearly exhibited his loyalty to Erasmus than in the famous controversy with Edward Lee, who attacked the *Novum Instrumentum* in 1520.[19] Lee not only charged that it contained errors but he also seemed to call into question the propriety of applying the humanist's tools to the Scriptures, especially if it meant deleting references to the Trinity when there was no basis for them in older texts. Lee's attack was no sooner in print than Erasmus began soliciting his friends for letters of support "Not even Orestes could write more insanely," he wrote Capito. Erasmus charged that it was obvious Lee was seeking personal reputation, because he used the first rather than the second edition.[20]

Capito's response was all that Erasmus could have wished. He noted that he had already written in Erasmus' defense four days earlier. Now he suggested, "If you would be open to advice from Capito to Erasmus (this is a pig teaching Minerva), it would seem better . . . to overlook everything and to smile unconcernedly. Things have certainly not come to the point that you should worry that a tasteless book . . . would harm your reputation with influential and learned men." He agreed with Erasmus' judgment of Lee. "The poor little thing thirsts for fame," he wrote.[21] He was so eager for the defence that he attached a piece that he had written against Lee, with a note that Erasmus could use it as he thought best. Erasmus chose not to publish this essay, but he did pass Capito's letter on to Nesen, who included it in an edition of other such letters Erasmus had received. But Capito was still dissatisfied. In a letter to Zwingli of April 1520, he called Lee "an ignorant man, but one who thirsts mightily after glory," and concluded, "I am considering writing in this regard on the way . . ." to Mainz. He may indeed have added a new essay to the lost edition of Erasmus' three apologies that Scheffer published at Mainz in June.[22]

Many young German intellectuals joined Erasmus' defence against Lee. Many, who later became reformers, prided themselves on having

---

[18] Hartmann, *Amerbach Korrespondenz*, II, 121.
[19] On the development of the dispute, see Wallace K. Ferguson, ed., *Erasmi Opuscula. A Supplement to the Opera Omnia* (The Hague, 1933), pp. 225-234.
[20] *EE*, IV, 198-201.
[21] *EE*, IV, 210-212.
[22] *ZW*, VII, 299.

the slightest association with Erasmus as young men.[23] And yet
Capito may be taken as paradigmatic for them all, for it was he to
whom Erasmus publicly passed the torch to carry on the work of the
"Christian restitution," [24] as they called it. But the question remains:
were they such strong defenders of Erasmus merely because he was
so famous and because they had turned their backs on the scholastic
learning of the universities, or was there also some genuine con-
gruence between their world of thought and his? Capito is one of
the few for whom the question can be answered with any precision,
for, a little older than most, he left solid evidence of his own intellectual preferences before the Reformation. Where Zwingli, Bucer,
and Melanchthon left a few letters and poems,[25] there are several complete works from Capito, as well as a set of lectures on the first five
chapters of Romans.

   From 1515 to 1522 he was an Erasmian intellectually. Speaking
of his students in Basel, he wrote Erasmus in September 1516, "I
encourage and in fact I command them to study Erasmus, to ponder
Erasmus daily and to have him at hand nightly. Moreover, I can
accomplish nothing more from the ability of most of the lesser talents
than that they should know a piece of Erasmus, the overflowing
ocean of universal teaching and the vindicator of true letters." Like
so many young Germans, Capito was most attracted to Erasmus'
skillfull combination of good letters and sacred letters. "For me,"
he added, "utility is consistent with pious letters; truly I will be of
benefit to literary matters; and do not consider the remark insolent,
because I serve letters at the same time as piety, and I serve copiously,
namely inviting the unlearned of our lands to Erasmus." Henceforth,
he declared, the simpler works of Erasmus should be in the home of

---

[23] See, for example, the call for research on the indebtedness of Bucer, Bugenhagen, Zwingli, and Melanchthon to Erasmus' work on the New Testament by
Ernst-Wilhelm Kohls, *Die Theologie des Erasmus* (Basel, 1966), II, 136.

[24] The judgment of James D. Tracy, *Erasmus. The Growth of a Mind*. CXXVI,
Travaux d'humanisme et renaissance (Genève, 1972), p. 66. See *EE*, II, 490, ". . . age
accingere, Fabrici optime, et hanc lampadem a nobis traditam accipe."

[25] The best treatment of the young Bucer is Martin Greschat, "Die Anfänge der
reformatorischen Theologie Martin Bucers," *Reformation und Humanismus.
Robert Stupperich zum 65. Geburtstag*, ed., by Martin Greschat and J. F. G. Goeters
(Witten, 1969), pp. 124-140. For recent works on Zwingli and Erasmus, see
Ulrich Gäbler, "Zwingli-Forschung seit 1960," *Theologische Literaturzeitung*,
XCVI (1971), 482-488. The most recent study of Melanchthon is Wilhelm Maurer,
Der junge Melanchthon, 2 vols. (Gütersloh, 1967-69), who is forced to infer Me-
lanchthon's own thought at Tübingen from the intellectual preferences of his
associates.

every child so they might be instructed in good letters and piety at the same time.[26]

Such remarks were more than mere flattery, for Capito shared Erasmus' view of good learning. Above all he disliked the schoolmen's exclusive reliance upon dialectic in theology. In 1517 he dedicated a new edition of Summenhart to Rudolph von Halwill, the dean of the cathedral, whose nephew he was then tutoring. "Somehow, and certainly not long ago, Johann Rudolph," he began, ". . . a small part of Aristotelian philosophy snared the universal teaching of theology: dialectic, of course, as well as a little metaphysics and the minutia of physics." He complained in particular about the followers of Scotus, who included his own teachers, and with whom, he charged, "you are completely entangled by the quantity of arguments." [27] In 1519 he wrote with special bitterness about the effect the nominalist theologians had upon himself. After recounting the horrors of his grammar schooling, he remarked,

> And now I am bearded and I must try, too late, I fear, to learn by heart those things a child should know. The vigor of talent that should be nourished by the beneficial reading of authors was wasted, blocked by the arid arguments of disputations and two-times-a-thousand nonsencical chatterings. Just as a sheep is shorn of its wool by a thornbush, I was stripped of my talents, which were once not entirely bad, by the subtleties of conclusions, of corollaries, of propositions, of summations.[28]

As a man who came into his own at a late age, he could speak with special authority against the intellectual tradition that he felt had so retarded him.

Yet, his attitude toward the scholastic theologians was a bit more ambivalent than Erasmus'. Where Erasmus put them utterly beyond the pale, Capito did recommend at least one of them—Summenhart—to one of his own students. In the dedicatory letter to the new edition of Summenhart he remarked about Halwill's nephew, that

> we decided he should be sent first, faithfully, I suppose, to all studies, and that in the present age it is necessary that he come upon philosophy through a short-cut, if you like. Moreover, the chief (such is my opinion) in this type of theologian comes from the commentaries of Conrad Summenhart, most well versed, unless I am deceived, one

---

[26] *EE*, II, 334.
[27] *Epistola de formando theologo*, sig. [A(v)].
[28] *Paraenesis*, fol. 7-8.

who freed the teachings of Scotus from the great layers of arguments of the more recent theologians, especially the Scotists, to, as they say, evident conclusions.[29]

Granted that he regarded learning a little philosophy as a concession to the times, there was nevertheless a form of theology, founded upon dialectic, of which he approved, however backhandedly. He intended, in fact, to be part of the young Melanchthon's ambitious proposal to do a purified edition of Aristotle with the help of "the most illustrious men of Germany." [30]

What, then, was Capito's objection to the traditional way of doing theology? He consistently declared that theology founded upon dialectic and practised by means of disputations was designed more to teach "stubbornness" than "to refine the talents and smooth the way to piety." [31] He recalled his own university experiences with the remark that "we were being taught so much of arguing strenuously for the sake of a fight and impudence, rather than understanding." [32] He objected to scholastic theology on what can only be called moral grounds. Even while recommending Summenhart, he observed that the scholastic theologians "not only accomplish nothing but . . . they propound the art of painting over a cause of offense." Rather, he urged his student, "Always let the memory occupy itself with some piece of Scripture; always let it boil down with assiduous thought." There is no evidence that he concerned himself with the truth or falsehood of specific theological teachings. His objection to the schoolmen was not that they taught falsehoods, but that they taught too much, and encouraged harmful wrangling. They were "well endowed neither with religion nor by nature, but bountifully supplied with doctrine." He was recommending Summenhart to the beginning theologian, he wrote, in order "to recall from obscure and remote digressions those who have gone off the track, to lead them back, and, as it were, to bring them together to a short-cut." [33]

Capito must have had some vision of a different sort of truth that could be obtained without the strenuous argumentation of the scholastic theologians. In 1517 he replied to the publication of one

---

[29] *Epistola de formando theologo*, sig. Aii.

[30] Melanchthon to Bernardus Maurus, [May 1518], *CR*, I, 26.

[31] *Paraenesis*, fol. 7.

[32] Capito to Bonifacius [Wolfhart], [mid-1521], Kirchenarchiv Basel, 25a, fol. 244(v). ". . . tantum enim ad pugnam et impudentiam asseverandi non intellecta instruebamur."

[33] *Epistola de formando theologo*, sig. [A(v)] -Aii.

of Erasmus' laudatory letters in just this vein. "My Erasmus, you do not so much praise your Fabricius as you motivate and marvelously goad him on to the image that he had projected, so he will accomplish his studies." [34] These were the very studies Erasmus himself proposed. "For the theologian," Capito wrote in September 1516, "let there first be acute judgment instructed with full preparation by the reading of good authors. Then there may be the rich skill and happiness of handling sacred things." [35] The "good authors" he had in mind were the essayists, the poets, the orators, and historians of classical antiquity. In theology itself he far preferred the Greek and Latin Fathers to the theologians of the *viae*. In a letter to his young student, Halwill, Oecolampadius remarked, "Wolfgang Fabricius Capito, that learned leader of ours, and by no means a counterfeit theologian, disregards nothing in the proper ordering of your mind." Oecolampadius reported that Capito had Halwill read Basil, Chrysostom, Origen, and Gregory of Nyssa.[36] True to his admonition, Halwill's teacher was well-read in the learning of Christian and classical antiquity. In a single letter he could allude eruditely, as was the custom among the humanists, to Venus, Vulcan, Mercury, and Hercules. He was at least acquainted with the work of the Italian humanists, for he once cited a letter from the younger Pico to Baptista Mantuanus on a point of Hebrew grammar. Zwingli reported that at one time Capito had in his possession copies of Lucian and Aristophanes.[37] As a humanist in Basel, his erudition went beyond the Christian writers and the "safe classics." So too did his teaching of the young Halwill. "Moreover," he charged in the letter to Halwill's uncle, "let him at the same time be sent ahead to music, arithmetic, geometry, and the other arts that they call liberal. . . . We will then abandon one who is trained in the arts and philosophy (in so far as it is necessary) to taking hold of a theology of quibblings." [38]

Such continued preference for an understanding of human affairs in all their particularity was characteristic of the humanists. Capito reduced the grave questions of professional theologians and philosophers to "quibblings," to "two-times-a-thousand nonsensical chatterings." He sought to replace doctrinal assertions and counter-

---

[34] *EE*, III, 10.
[35] *EE*, II, 337.
[36] *BAO*, I, 168.
[37] *Institvtionvm*, sig. [A2]-A4; G3(v)-[G4]. *ZW*, VII, 190.
[38] *Epistola de formando theologo*, sig. Aii.

assertions with the *Verstand*, the understanding, the *savoir faire* of the
liberal arts, and he founded them in turn upon as wide as possible a
grasp of the ancient world.[39]

He was also one with the other humanists in his insistence that
the only sure way to grasp the liberal arts was through the ancient
languages, Latin, Greek, and Hebrew. He himself was among the
few to wear the tiara of the three languages, and he wished others to
follow his example. "And so now," he summarized the preface to the
1518 Hebrew grammar, "I would commit to you the three languages,
which are the foremost and the greatest supports to the whole world
of learning." Zasius, he wrote, "put the pettifogging lawyers into
full flight" with good Latin. "Likewise, certainly the three languages
do nothing different for theology, for all memory of the Christian
religion is held by them. . . ." Perhaps he was quoting Erasmus'
preface to the New Testament unconsciously when he proclaimed
that it could not be understood without Hebrew, for the Apostles
wrote "according to Hebrew custom," although in Greek.[40] But his
literary dependence was appropriate, for he was repeating one of
Erasmus' distinct themes, especially when he declared, "these are in
every way incomparable riches; instructed by them, you will spring
from the poor house of the commentaries . . . into the open sea of
the Scriptures. . . ." In the preface to the 1516 grammar he summarized the place of the ancient languages in his education program:

> I wish that you would accordingly procure from such a small book
> of Psalms the sacred way of speaking, by which key alone, as it were,
> the door is opened to mysteries, and that you would copy them again
> and again, as I have been fond of saying, with a zealous hand, and
> then you would learn them by heart more accurately, and, moreover,
> in their own language. Ever after, as from the clearest fountain,
> the truth would doubtlessly pour into you liberally. Ever after, you
> would welcome the first spring and the pure vein of the most beautiful
> wisdom. . . .[41]

---

[39] On Erasmus see especially Tracy, *Erasmus. The Growth of a Mind*; the
excellent introductory chapter in Bouwsma, *Venice and the Defence of Republican
Liberty*, pp. 1-52, lays the groundwork for a fruitful comparison of Italian with
Northern humanism, if those with religious interests are not on that ground
excluded from the ranks of the humanists.

[40] *Institvtionvm*, sig. a3-a4, G(v)-G2. Erasmus, who knew no Hebrew, remarked,
"et cum Graece scribunt, multum referunt ex proprietate sermonis Hebraici."
Hajo Holborn and Annemarie Holborn, eds., *Desiderius Erasmus Roterodamus
Ausgewählte Werke* (Munich, 1933), p. 158.

[41] *Institvtivncvla*, sig. aa4(v); aa3-aa4.

Capito was at one with his mentor, Erasmus, in judging that with the three languages the scholar truly went *ad fontes*, to the very fountain of wisdom.

But it was wisdom, rather than knowledge of universal philosophical or theological propositions, that one sought. The true fruit of learning was thus moral, rather than intellectual, virtue. Capito began the dedication of his 1518 Hebrew grammar by remarking that young Halwill's uncle held "uncultured you" in high esteem and was concerned for his education. He reminded his charge that "no splendor of birth exalts you," but promised that he would be able to boast "nobility of the soul" if he did his lessons well.[42]

Teachers have commonly used such inducements to goad a lethargic but promising young student to more zealous labors. But there was more to the matter. Capito also believed that the cultural status of Christendom determined the moral and religious status of Christianity. He attributed the decline of piety and morals in his own age to the barbaric schoolmen and their search for a form of knowledge that did not lead to good living.

> In their desire to do nothing else their whole life long, they are creating so much trouble, so much wearisome prolixity by their interminable treatises that they are inflicting the greatest harm on Christendom. This is because in the meantime the writings of the ancients will perish—the Gospel, the Pauline epistles, the records of the growing faith; and in place of them we have that profane author, Aristotle. . . .[43]

But Capito was confident; echoing Erasmus' letter to him of 1517, he proclaimed,

> Now that God is at last taking pity, men are coming to their senses in regard to the better creations of the Gentiles. For the first time, they are everywhere embracing civilized literature and the scholarly languages, those tools of learning. Therefore I trust that at the same time we shall see the return of the ancient virtues and the pristine purity of the Christian faith.[44]

Here was the true mark of the Christian humanist, the naive belief that his cultural program, based upon the sources of classical and Christian antiquity, carried with it the *restitutio Christianismi*.

Capito's view of good learning thus bore an unmistakably Erasmian imprint. But there were also differences between the two men in both

---

[42] *Institvtionvm*, sig. [A2]-A3.

[43] *Epistola de formando theologo*, sig. [A(v)].

[44] *Institvtionvm*, sig. A4. Compare *EE*, II, 490.

temper and substance, and never more so than when it came to questions of church reform. In brief, Capito was dedicated to the reform
of the church with a dour zeal that was unknown to the urbane
Dutchman. Like Luther, some matters were so dear to him that he
felt tears rather than laughter were the appropriate response to their
perversion. He did not shrink from criticizing Erasmus himself for
improper levity, even in his solicitous letter of September 1516.
After urging him to compare more diligently the Greek and Latin
texts for the next edition of the *Novum Instrumentum*, he declared,

> And because I began the duty of an inept admonisher, I dare to bring
> forth my stupidity even more impudently. I accordingly implore
> you to say nothing either more vehemently or more frankly about
> the superstitious choice of foods among Christians, about a certain
> prescribed number of prayers, or about these common things that
> either credulity or faith assumed from the public practice of our
> age. . . . You know, Erasmus, what customs, what spirit the false persua-
> sion of doctrine and religion has dressed us in. Unless surrounded by
> that marvelous evasiveness of yours, you ought not have added a
> single word concerning penitence, the sacrament, the superstitious little
> rules of the monks. . . .

If Erasmus' contact with the religiously zealous Basel sodality did
imbue him with greater earnestness in the cause of reform, at least
Capito did not approve the manner in which Erasmus chose to
express his commitment. If he were not more careful, Capito remarked, he might find himself "cursed" and "damned" as an enemy
of the Christian people on account of his wit. "And accordingly I
plead and I beg your prudence, my Erasmus, that you would be a
slave to the defences you long ago occupied; that is, that you would
restrain the fullest impulse of your eloquence with the check of
modesty." [45]

Erasmus' friend, Martin Dorp, was not alone in urging the "Prince
of the Humanists" to forego for the sake of reform cheap, albeit
eloquent, satire of nonessentials. On the other hand, Capito was
still fully the Erasmian even in his criticism of Erasmus. He was not
blindly defending orthodoxy. He urged Erasmus not to satire the
practices of popular piety for tactical reasons. Although he declared

---

[45] *EE*, II, 335-336. James D. Tracy, "Erasmus Becomes a German," *Renaissance Quarterly*, XXI (1968), pp. 221-228, thus errs in ascribing Erasmus'
greater sharpness after 1516 to the Basel group and to Capito in particular. Rather it
seems the Basel group apprehended Erasmus the particularly *Christian* humanist,
as in the work of Gerhard Ritter, *Erasmus und der deutsche Humanistenkreis am
Oberrhein. 23, Freiburger Universitätsreden* (Freiburg im Breisgau, 1937), pp. 8-14.

such things as penitence, the eucharist, veneration of the saints, and monastic regulations "the false persuasion of doctrine and religion," he clearly considered them "externals" that did not in and of themselves merit serious attention. Moreover, it was his very zeal for reform that caused him to urge Erasmus to be silent on such matters. For his part, Erasmus graciously recognized Capito's greater earnestness. "We have accomplished what is permitted, considering our shortcomings," he replied; "in your case, there is nothing that seems necessary for this most beautiful work that is not abundantly supplied." [46]

It is understandable that Capito should take a rather more calculating attitude toward the subject of reform than did Erasmus. He was, after all, a professional theologian, and one who thought even Erasmus, amateur that he was, might do well to acknowledge the work of professional theologians.[47] Moreover, he worked for reform in his own diocese of Basel. In 1517 he pirated the French humanist Jodocus Clichtove's *Elucidatorium Ecclesiasticum*, to which he added a blunt call to reform in the dedication to his bishop. "How did it happen," he demanded, "that we, forgetful of duty, slid down the trough into a wickedness fouler than that of a brothel-keeper, excuse the word?" He knew where guilt lay.

> During the past two years that I have held the office of preacher in the most elegant cathedral of Basel, over which you, Reverend Father, so wondrously preside, I have often and seriously pondered from what source such a progression of all the vices once took possession of the clergy. The first thing to occur to me was the neglect of those who are sitting in the government of the faith, seeing that connivers at whatever impious things you might want to name promote licentiousness and the custom of wrongdoing, things which could have been extirpated with a relatively modest effort. . . .

Bishop Christoph might have been excused had he taken offense from the dedication, for he was both a patron of the humanists, and of Capito in particular, and he had sincerely attempted administrative and moral reform within his jurisdiction. He held a diocesan synod for that purpose in 1503 only to see it collapse under his own clergy's opposition. Reflecting perhaps on this earlier failure, Capito conceded the difficulty of the task. "It nevertheless seems to me," he charged,

---

[46] *EE*, II, 490.

[47] Capito to Erasmus, Sept. 1516, *EE*, II, 336. "Quandoquidem nullum theologum Nouum celebrat Instrumentum. . . ."

"that the progress of which we are capable should be earnestly attempted and insisted upon forever." Improvements could be made, he insisted, "if only we are firm, if only we rebuke opportunely, harshly. Otherwise," he warned, "by carelessness and a lack of concern on our part for our task, we will certainly bring forth an avenger of wickedness who will properly call for the full prosecution of the law." [48]

Capito took his calling as a theologian so seriously and he so desired reform that he risked offending both his patron, Bishop Christoph, and his mentor, Erasmus. Yet, his vehemence notwithstanding, Capito's reform program in 1517 was similar to the demands for reform "in head and members" that were voiced throughout the Middle Ages. In the book that Capito republished, Clichtove declared that clerical laxness and the decline of piety among the laity derived from the clergy's ignorance of the liturgy's true meaning. He accordingly sought, in good humanistic fashion, to explain the service with reference to older texts, in the belief that fresh understanding would induce in the priests more fervor in performing their offices, and that this zeal would communicate itself to the laity. Here was an instance of Capito's assumption that learning and piety were intimately related. In the dedication to Bishop Christoph he described Clichtove's book as a good means of accomplishing the reforms that failed in 1503. Now, he declared, "I am not ashamed that the goal may be, one way or another, in spite of everything, to obtain in this age some bishops, in whose number your dignity is also counted, who are true cultivators of piety and religion, whom injury to Christ torments, and who will indignantly attack the crimes of the raging crowd, and certainly of the priests." [49] When he thought of reforms, he did not foresee doctrinal changes but a deeper, more inward comprehension of what existed. He viewed the structure of the church similarly. He did not foresee destroying the hierarchy, but filling its stalls with abler and more zealous churchmen. He was part of that

[48] *Elvcidatorium Ecclesiasticum, Ad Officium Ecclesiae Pertinentia Planivs Exponens* (Basileae, 1517), sig. [Aa]. The letter is dated August 11, 1517. On Bishop Christoph see the articles by J. F. Villiger in *Lexikon für Theologie und Kirche* (Freiburg, 1965), X, 584-585, and by Bernd Moeller in *Die Religion in Geschichte und Gegenwart* (Tübingen, 1962), VI, 216.

[49] *Elvcidatorium*, sig. [Aa]. On Clichtove and his book, see Jean-Pierre Massaut, *Josse Clichtove. L'humanisme et la réforme du clergé.* CLXXXIII, *Bibliothèque de la Faculté de Philosophie et Lettres de Liège* (Paris, 1968), II, 284-317; 332-334, and the judgment of Augustin Renaudet, *Préréforme et humanisme à Paris pendant les premières guerres d'Italie (1494-1517)* (Paris, 1963), esp. pp. 616-617.

tradition of "pre-reformers" whose plans were passed by in the German Reformation.

Within less than a year of Capito's letter to Bishop Christoph, an angry call to reform resounded across Germany from a different source. Erasmus' zealous younger followers took Luther's side the moment they heard of the Wittenberg professor's attack on the indulgence preaching of Johannes Tetzel. Leo X may have judged the Indulgence Controversy "a monks' quarrel," but all over Europe the young humanists considered it another round in the battle between the proponents of good learning and the schoolmen. In their judgment this was a battle that had already been joined between Reuchlin and the Dominicans, Erasmus and the theologians at Louvain. The news of Luther's affair accordingly spread quickly through the network of humanist literary friendships. It was the humanists who turned Luther into a popular hero and who raised his controversy with Tetzel into a national religious *cause célèbre*.[50]

For his part, Capito corresponded with Luther at least as early as summer 1518. In September he wrote Luther that he was delighted with "the sermons on penitence and forgiveness," which were probably delivered at about the time Luther posted the Ninety-five Theses, and were first published in early 1518.[51] With the aid of other members of the Basel humanist sodality, Capito translated the sermons and other works of Luther into Latin for publication by Froben in October.[52] In February 1519 he declared that all the Basel humanists were ready to support Luther with funds and with their pens. "Whatever we are capable of doing by way of support we will do anywhere," he pledged. And he was good to his word. He reacted swiftly when

---

[50] The standard survey is by Bernd Moeller, "Die deutschen Humanisten und die Anfänge der Reformation," *Zeitschrift für Kirchengeschichte*, LXX (1959), 46-61.

[51] *WABr*, I, 197. The opening line of this first extant letter reads, "Proximis tuae charitati ex Argentina respondi. . . ."

[52] E. Freys and H. Barge, "Verzeichniss der gedruckten Schriften des Andreas Bodenstein von Karlstadt," *Zentralblatt für Bibliothekswesen*, XXI (1904), 156-158, have the better of the argument with Riggenbach, *Chronikon*, p. 75, in maintaining that Capito, rather than Beatus Rhenanus, was primarily responsible for publishing Luther's works. All Beatus Rhenanus could say in a letter to Zwingli on December 6, 1518 was, "As yet we know nothing certain about Luther," and three weeks later he reported only that a bookseller had arrived from Bern with more of Luther's works. *ZW*, VII, 113-114. On September 4 Capito had already read the sermons that were published in October, and on February 12, 1519, he wrote Luther, "We published your works that are enclosed. . . ." *WABr*, I, 198; 336.

Erasmus tried to stop Froben from issuing more of Luther's works. "I speak from the heart," he wrote Erasmus on April 8, 1519. "I implore you not to disparage Martin's work in public." He promised that "we will keep Germany and Saxony dutiful to you," but he stoutly maintained that Luther was justly famous at this time. "Thereby the will shall be given the remaining youth to dare anything for the liberty of Christ." Capito added that "for my part I hope for much in him." [53]

Anonymously publishing Luther's works and intervening for him with Erasmus were relatively safe activities, but Capito did more. By 1520 his sermons took on what his contemporaries thought to be a Lutheran character. Pellican declared to Luther that "W. Fabricius Capito, preacher to the people, breathes your learning . . ." and offered to take up the work when Capito left for Mainz.[54] Boniface Amerbach reported to Zasius on March 1, "Our Capito wishes you good fortune. At this time he is declaring the Gospel of St. Matthew to the people with great success." [55] About two weeks later Hedio ratified Amerbach's judgment in a letter to Zwingli. "The common people are still fully capable of evangelical doctrine," he exulted. "They progress well in judgment and they support the Christian rebirth extraordinarily." Regarding Capito he too reported, "He accordingly preaches the Gospel according to St. Matthew daily to a packed crowd. The doctrine of Christ is very effective; it penetrates and inflames souls." [56] The practice of preaching through an entire book in the New Testament was common among the reformers, and Capito himself admitted, "There are those who accuse me of favoring Luther's cause, although I conceal it purposely." [57] By concealment he probably meant that he did not refer to Luther as support for his sermons, but hearers connected the two men nevertheless. In October 1519 Amerbach wrote Zasius that Eck's account of the Leipzig Debate "talked an uncommon amount of nonsense to Capito. . . ." Zasius replied with an admonition: "Tell Wolfgang I disagree with Luther when he turns good works into sin, and when he does not properly accept

[53] *Ibid.*, I, 336. *EE*, III, 527, and 445-446; 590 for Erasmus' relations with Froben on the matter. See Maurer, *Der junge Melanchthon*, II, 37-38, for the judgment that Capito was the central spokesman for Luther to Erasmus and his young humanist followers.

[54] *WABr*, II, 66.

[55] Hartmann, *Amerbach Korrespondenz*, II, 231.

[56] *ZW*, VII, 279.

[57] Capito cited in Scultetus, *Annalium Evangelii*, I, 67.

that authority, *'Tu es Petrus.'* " [58] As for so many of the younger humanists, some of Capito's standing friendships began to weaken on account of his support for Luther.

Such public and private defence of Luther constituted only one-half of Capito's relationship to the Saxon reformer. Just as with Erasmus, he was bold enough to offer Luther unsolicited advice on the best manner of accomplishing reform. In September 1518 he urged Luther to be less vehement in his denunciations, just as he earlier admonished Erasmus to be less witty in his criticisms.

> The Apostles surely urged nothing rashly, nothing without reserve; they observed propriety and refinement everywhere. It was in this consideration that Paul walked with solicitude in the letter to the Romans. . . . He pretends, he dissembles, he persuades, he draws out, he shows the rich goods from afar and immediately conceals them; in short he holds his language surely in balance, and neither displeasure nor indignation spring up one after another. The Acts of the Apostles are overflowing with examples of his genius. Thus the divine Paul would merely respond with evasiveness in an uproar: he would not say, 'I say nothing against the Law,' but, 'I am convinced of the resurrection' all the while returning the proper method of speaking about the Law with splendid prudence.

Had Luther followed Capito's advice in the controversy with Prierias, he would have been a very different Luther:

> You should relate the birth and increase of religion, the custom of the ancients, the reason for the hardening of error, and the various decrees of popes and especially of councils, drawing, as it were from the fountain of truth. Then, in kidding, you may bring up a few pieces of nonsense. You should studiously avoid offending the Pope; you should turn aside everything invidious. . . .[59]

When it concerned reform, a matter he held so dearly, Capito preferred the calm voice of sweet reason to either Erasmus' biting sarcasm or Luther's prophetic denunciations.

Capito's attitude toward Luther did in fact closely parallel his judgment of Erasmus. "Look at the extent to which I am carried by the heat of friendship!" he exclaimed in the same letter. "Forgetful me, I prescribe rules to you like a teacher! But it can be condoned; all of it is in every instance my solicitude for you." And for the cause of reform, he might have added. Just as with Erasmus, he was offering Luther tactical advice. "Believe me," he wrote, "you will

---

[58] Hartmann, *Amerbach Korrespondenz*, II, 215-217.
[59] *WABr*, I, 198-199.

succeed by small, repeated strokes, where you would not have been able to accomplish anything by violence." The opposition was powerful, he added, "for, you see, they occupy a castle strengthened on all sides. They snore on ... surrounded by a triple wall: that is, by papal authority universally over the church, by the power of tyrants, and of all scholars who are unified in stubbornness. You will never rupture this utterly base rope of dung easily." In sum, he advised care, lest the strenuousness of the effort destroy the chances for success. "I have been wishing so much," he wrote in words reminiscent of an earlier letter to Erasmus, "that you would always preserve a big loophole through which you might, unattacked, avoid even argument." [60] A powerful desire for reform led Luther to intemperate outbursts of righteous indignation, while Erasmus belittled his opponents. Not so Capito. He was one of those individuals whom deep dedication to a cause inclines toward careful tactical calculations. As a preacher and professor in Basel, he already possessed a politician's sixth sense. It served him well when he became a more public figure.

The similiarity between his relations with Erasmus and those with Luther suggests that he did not distinguish sharply between these two giants of the sixteenth century. It has become, in fact, a commonplace to speak of early humanist support for Luther as being an historically "productive misunderstanding." [61] For his part, Erasmus' standoffish attitude was founded upon the recognition that Luther's affair and the cause of good letters were not identical, and upon the fear that they might well be confused, with damage to good letters ensuing. In Capito's case it is possible to characterize the confusion that actually existed, for he certainly did regard Luther as another, albeit somewhat bumptious, follower of Erasmus. In the preface to Froben's edition of Luther's works, he praised Luther for attacking "the theologians who neglect the Gospel and the Pauline theology along with the old commentaries, and who are caught up in amplifications, restrictions, terminologies, and the nonsense of mere logicalities." [62] To his mind, here was another man who was going to the sources and serving the *restitutio Christianismi*, in much the same manner as Clichtove.

Capito thus hailed Luther's preference for the Fathers and the

---

[60] *Ibid.*, I, 198-199.

[61] Moeller, "Deutsche Humanisten," *ZKG*, LXX, 54-55.

[62] Reprinted from the second ed. by A.-L. Herminjard, *Correspondance des reformateurs dans les pays de langue française* (Genève et Paris, 1866), I, 61-62.

Scriptures over the theologians of the *viae*. But it is important to note also what he did not do. He did not show any appreciation for the doctrinal issues that were at stake even in Luther's early writings. This failure is the central clue to Capito's own theological position before 1522. In brief, he had no more interest than Erasmus in formulating and defending precise doctrinal statements.[63] In April 1520, he wrote a preface for Oecolampadius' index to Erasmus' edition of Jerome. There he went out of his way to argue that the index should not be used for "the murky business" of piling up quotations with which "to beat back adversaries." For him it was rather a tool for "distinguishing arguments, fine phrases, the exegesis of Scriptural passages, and all other questions." [64] His supposedly "Lutheran" sermons probably followed the same pattern of ignoring doctrinal issues in favor of moral ones. In 1518 Oecolampadius wrote a treatise in which he attacked the practice, known as the "Paschal laugh," of preaching an amusing sermon just after Easter to break the deadly earnestness of the Lenten season just past. Capito contributed a preface in which he charged some preachers with frivolity because they played to their audience with "obscene stories." Referring to homiletic custom during Lent itself, he observed that many preachers created superstition by trying to frighten their congregations with gruesome tales of hell-fire and damnation. On the contrary, he charged, regardless of the season, "it is fitting that a serious and pious priest should preach sincerely and modestly, and from a theme. . . ." [65] He was probably true to his advice. Although his sermons are not extant, in 1521 he recalled his feelings, and perhaps his words: "Sometimes I exclaimed, 'Oh! Faithful common folk, whom [Christ] reaches to inflame with his torch to the love of immortality, to integrity and innocence of life, to a tolerance of evils, when being abused do not retaliate, so the innocent may live among you, so one may not offend another.' " [66] Strictly understood, there was

---

[63] See Tracy, *Erasmus. The Growth of a Mind*, pp. 131-132, for the judgment—true in Capito's case—that Erasmus "inclined to the view that any preoccupation with dogmatic issues could detract from the necessary attention to moral behavior."

[64] *BAO*, I, 115.

[65] *BAO*, I, 44-57. On the practice and on Oecolampadius' treatise, see Ernst Staehelin, *Das Theologische Lebenswerk des Johannes Oekolampads*. XXI, *Quellen und Forschungen zur Reformationsgeschichte* (Leipzig, 1939), pp. 84-87.

[66] Capito to Bonifacius [Wolfhart], [mid-1521], Kirchenarchiv Basel 25a, fol. 244(v). "O, felicem, cui contigit inflammare plebem suo igni ad amorem

no doctrinal point to these sermons. At stake rather were the daily life and the moral regeneration of the Christian people. Although one of Luther's strongest supporters after 1517, he was still an Erasmian by religious values.

At least in Capito's case there was a solid reality to the "productive misunderstanding" that lay behind early humanist support for Luther. This misunderstanding, or rather, basic disagreement, is never more evident than in a comparison of Capito's recently discovered lectures on Romans with his strong promotion of Luther. The lectures could hardly have been given at a more propitious time for historical comparison. He began them one year after Luther finished his famous lectures, and shortly after the publication of Erasmus' paraphrase. But while Capito was republishing Luther's other writings and defending Luther to Erasmus, he was treating this key text in a manner very different from Luther. Where he stood in relation to the two scholars is put nicely in his opening remarks to his students, ". . . I will be subject to the paraphrase from Erasmus, that is, the Pauline argument in clearer words." [67]

Capito's religious values were in fact so like Erasmus' that the unwary reader can easily find Luther-like passages in his lectures. A hasty glance at his remarks about faith and works could lead to the conclusion that he had arrived at Luther's famous position on the subject. The lectures are filled with such statements as, "And therefore only faith suffices, even if no works were performed," or, "We believe faith is the cause of salvation," or, "He who attributes all things to faith excludes trusting in works." [68] Capito could even speak of faith itself as a gift of God. "For in fact the gift of a different faith is granted from the same spirit, by whom it is revealed, which faith is given through grace. And the converse. It is given to you from God, not solely that you may believe in Christ, but that you would submit to him." [69] It appears at first glance that Capito even linked faith and grace to the promises of God in much the manner of Luther, as in

---

immortalitatis, ad synceritatem innocentiamque vitae, ad malorem tolerantiam vt inter se vivant innoxii, alius alium non ledat, laesi ne retalientur.

[67] Rom. lec., fol. 1(v). ". . . subiiciam ex Erasmo Paraphrasim, Hoc est, clarioribus verbis Paulinam sententiam."

[68] *Ibid.*, fol. 63(v)-64. "Ideoque sola fides ad Justificationem sufficit, etiamsi nihil operis fuerit explitum." "Fides igitur credimus causa salutis est." "Qui fidei omnia tribuens, fiduciam excludit operum."

[69] *Ibid.*, fol. 76(v). "Nam alii enim datur donum fidei ex eodem spiritu, vbi ostenditur, que fides per gratiam datur. Et rursus. A deo vobis datum est, non solum vt credatis in Christum, sed vt patiamini pro illo."

declaring, "If they are bound to human merit or ceremonies, the promise would not have been firm, but it is firm through the one grace, just as in regard to Abraham." [70]

To place much weight upon such statements is to miss the point of Capito's understanding of faith and works. He was not contrasting them in anything like Luther's treatment of the Gospel and the Law. Whenever Capito used the word *"opera"* in the Romans lectures, he referred to the works of the Mosaic or, more precisely, the ceremonial law. Where Paul declared that Abraham was saved by faith "without the works of the Law," Capito explained "In this place he calls the law of works the works themselves of the Law—ceremonies, sacrifices, and the keeping of the Sabbath." His understanding of Paul's discussion was exclusively, even narrowly, historical and literal. It had no application to popular piety in his own time. According to him, when Paul wrote "the boasting of works is excluded," he referred only to the works "by which the Pharisee, being ostentatious in the temple, perishes." Abraham would have something of which to boast, Capito explained, "if he was justified by works, that is, by circumcision. . . ." [71]

Obviously, he was following Erasmus in arguing that Paul was contrasting faith only with the works of the Law, with "the Law" conceived as narrowly as possible. [72] Faith underwent a similar interpretation. In brief, it became a work necessary for salvation. He transmuted Paul's discussion of heirs of Abraham according to the spirit into the assertion that Paul "says the Jews are not children of Abraham according to faith." [73] Thus, for a community founded upon the Mosaic Law, he said Paul substituted one founded upon a

---

[70] *Ibid.*, fol. 77(v). "Non esset firma promissio, si hominis meritis aut Ceremoniis debent, sed per vnam gratiam firma est, quemadmodum in Abraham, Paulus Loquitur."

[71] *Ibid.*, fol. 63. "Quo in loco legem operum, ipsa Legis opera, Ceremonias, hostias, et sabbatismum nominat;" fol. 64(v): "Excluditur, inquit, gloriatio de operibus: quibus phariseus se jactans in templo periit;" fol. 67: "Nam si ex operibus justificatus est, hoc est circumcisione, habet gloriationem, videlicet apud se;" see also fol. 57, "Ideoque subdit, quod ex operibus legis, hoc est Ceremoniis et sacrificiis, quibus Judei fidebant. . . ."

[72] See, for example, Erasmus' paraphrase of Romans 1:17. *Erasmi Opera*, VII, 781B. "Cum enim antehac aliis in rebus alii sitam esse justitiam existimarent nunc Euangelio Christi palam fit omnibus justitiae, non Mosi, sed ipsius Dei, quae non sita sit in superstitioso cultu simulacrorum, aut legalibus Judaeorum ceremoniis, sed ex fide contingat. . . ."

[73] Rom. lec., fol. 66(v). "Vt fortassis dicat Judaeos non esse filios Abrahae secundum fidem," because "non est iustificatus ex operibus et circumcisione."

new law. The Jews cannot boast of having done the works of the
Law, he explained, because such boasting "is excluded by the Law
of faith." In sum, according to Capito, Paul "says the law of faith
is by no means in the law of works." [74] There were in reality four kinds
of law: "a written law of ceremonies and sacrifices," a "law of the
mind, which is of nature," a "written law that comprises the Law of
Moses, in as much as it concerns ceremonies, and morals, and all
things," and finally a "Law of faith." [75] The first chapters of Romans
concerned the substitution of the *Lex fidei* for the *Lex Moysi*. It was
this law that Capito had in mind when he wrote in 1517, "Let the
Bible and certainly the Law of Christ always rule in theology," or
when he commented on Romans 3:27, Paul "calls faith, which is
without the Law, the Law itself of faith." [76]

What was necessary for salvation, then, was to believe, and to
believe that Christ was the Messiah. [77] But how could Capito maintain
both that faith was a gift, and that faith was necessary, and that
Christians were not predestined, indeed that they had free will? [78]
In other words, how could it be that faith was both the gift of
salvation and a requirement for salvation?

Capito solved the problem by adopting not only the concepts but
also the language of the nominalist theology he learned from Gabriel
Biel, and perhaps heard from Geiler von Kaysersberg. The clue to
his procedure lies in his comments on Paul's quotation, at Romans
4:3, of the words "Abraham believed God, and it was reckoned to
him as righteousness." Here he explained that "According to Paul,
therefore, faith is two-fold. The one is partial. . . . The other is
perfected by Christ." [79] The distinction he had in mind was analogous

---

[74] *Ibid.*, fol. 64 ". . . inanem esse gloriationem Judaeorum de operibus legis,
quae est exclusa per legem fidem;" fol. 63(v) "Et legem fidei in lege operum
nequaquam esse dicit."

[75] *Ibid.*, fol. 74-74(v), "Lex scripta sacrificiorum et caeremoniarum;" "Lex
mentis, quae est naturae;" "Lex scripta, quae continet Legem Moysi, quantum
ad caeremonias et mores et omnia;" "Quarto est Lex fidei."

[76] *Epistola de formando theologo*, sig. [A(v)]. Rom. lec., fol. 63, "Sed et Legem
fidei ipsam nominat fidem, quae sine Lege est. . . ."

[77] See *Ibid.*, fol. 62 ". . . Christum esse propiciatorem et hostiam et sacerdotem
in sanguinem. . . . Quid fit per fidem."

[78] *Ibid.*, fol. 62, where he concluded the discussion in n. 77 above with, "Nulla
enim praedestinatio in id cadit. . . ." See also fol. 62 and the discussion of Romans
2:27, "Hic vides apparente duas circumcisiones, alteram quae est ex nata, alteram
quae ex libertate arbitrij constat, qum anima purgat affectibus. Item duas circumcisiones, in carne unam et unam in mentes."

[79] *Ibid.*, fol. 68. "Est igitur in Paulo Fides du[ple]x. Altera ex parte. . . .

to the one Biel drew between a partial merit (*meritum de congruo*) and genuine merit (*meritum de condigno*) in the presence of God. Just as Biel could maintain that God graciously accepted partial human merit in place of genuine merit, so too Capito declared that "imperfect faith arises, so long as we concern ourselves with articles, but it is not at all easy to maintain life in all of them, except by the occurence of the gift of God, which they tell me is acquired and infused faith." [80]

The "they" Capito had in mind were his nominalist theology teachers and Biel in particular. With them he was arguing that all men could know, and even believe, most truths about God, and that they could know them naturally. Accordingly, no one was excusable in the sight of God, and the freedom of the will was protected.[81] But the faith that men could acquire naturally was insufficient for salvation unless God himself added to it and turned it into more than mere assent to true propositions about God. Regarding Abraham's faith being imputed to him as righteousness, Capito explained, "that is, not only credulous but certain of the power of the promising, he staked everything on that faith." [82] The critical distinction was between Abraham's being credulous (*fides acquisita/ imperfecta/ ex parte*) and his being certain (*fides infusa/ Christo perfecta*). Not only could all men believe, they must believe. And if they did believe, as was within them, then God would be gracious and impute it to them as righteousness.[83]

It is true, then, that late medieval nominalist theology had an influence on the religious values of the Northern humanists, at least if Capito is taken as one of their number.[84] To be sure, he did

---

Altera Christo perfecta. See also fol. 70(v), "Qua ingeniose Paulus duplicem fidem astruat. Vna enim ex parte est, altera perfecta," and fol. 76(v) for the terms "fides imperfecta" and "fides iustificata."

[80] *Ibid.*, fol. 77, "Itaque fides imperfecta, dum in articulis nos exercemus, exoritur, sed in omnes vitam tueri haud facile est, nisi dono dei accidente, quod mihi dicunt Fidem acquisitam et infusam." On Biel see Heiko Augustinus Oberman, *The Harvest of Medieval Theology: Gabriel Biel and Late Medieval Nominalism* (Grand Rapids, Mich., 1967), esp. pp. 71-74 for Biel's understanding of *fides acquisita* and *fides infusa*.

[81] Rom. lec., fol. 25(v), ". . . deus est autor istius scientiae salutaris per exteriora, vt Thomas ait. Hoc est, ni fallor, per opera, mundique machinam, cui toti affudit sapientiam suam," and fol. 28, "Et Graeci facti sunt inexcusabiles, propterea cognoscentes per creaturam Deum. . . . Sed idolis his honorem tribuerunt."

[82] *Ibid.*, fol. 80(v), "Hoc est, omnes in illam fiduciam posuit, non modo credulus, sed certus de potentia promittentis."

[83] *Ibid.*, fol. 70, "Videlicet fidem esse ad iusticiam citra operam Imputandam."

[84] See the suggestion of Oberman, *Harvest of Medieval Theology*, p. vii, "that

not clutter his lectures with disquisitions on the absolute and ordained power of God—that would surely be too disputatious. But these notions were present—indeed Capito's remarks about faith make sense only in the context of the typical nominalist distinction between the *potentia absoluta* and the *potentia ordinata* of God.[85]

Consequently, seen from one point of view, salvation was *sola gratia,* because it came only when God graciously accepted human partial faith as if it were the genuine article. But from another point of view, salvation was *solis operibus,* because humans could and must accomplish the essential first step of having partial faith, which God would then impute to them as righteousness. Salvation was, in any event, by faith alone, but this was not the *sola fide* of which Luther spoke. He began to attack nominalist theology ever more trenchantly during just the years that Capito was affirming the essence of Biel's teaching on faith, according to which faith itself became a merit. In the background of Capito's warm endorsement of Luther lay, unbeknownst to both men, a flat denial of Luther's central theological position.

Yet, even Capito's disagreement with Luther about the nature of faith will be misleading if it obscures his own intentions. Did his chief interest, even in the Romans lectures, lie in teaching true doctrine, or did it have more to do with enlightened piety? Direct evidence is hard to come by, but his exegetical principles offer a strong clue. Like Erasmus and Luther he insisted that the chief failing of the scholastic theologians lay in their neglect of the Scriptures. Like Luther, he deviated from Erasmus by insisting upon interpreting them according to a single sense. Thus, he wrote Erasmus, who did recommend allegory, especially on the Old Testament,

> Surely, while explaining the Scriptures according to the four-fold sense, it is not rare that we do not grasp even one, and that we misuse words because we often do not penetrate to the meaning of the Prophets, and this applies to moulding character or to explaining the Church, or other things of this nature. . . . Then, when truth protests, or when we are convicted of error, we take refuge in our fortress—

nominalistic thought . . . deeply influenced the Reformation, the Counter Reformation, and—as future studies of the period may establish—the religious climate of the Renaissance north of the Alps."

[85] The same sort of dependence may be evident in Erasmus' paraphrase of Romans 4:3. *Erasmi Opera,* VII, 788C, "statimque ob fiduciae meritum justus est habitus, non ex circumcisione, quam nundam acceperat, sed ex credulitate: et habitus est utique non apud homines sed apud Deum, quo uno teste hoc negocii tum agebatur, et a quo illi hoc imputatum est ad justitiam. . . .''

the various senses—asserting not the literal sense, but the anagogical
or tropological or allegorical, and, as hunters, we lose ourselves in
snares of that sort.

On the other hand, he admitted, "I know, of course, the nature of
the Scriptures; I know how they may entangle the sweetness of
truth in metaphors and allegories; I know how they may not escape
enigmas, or rather summon them from elsewhere; they may import
them and accumulate, as it were, at the heart, as if the works that have
been given might conceal the abstruse truth of another." [86] Although
Capito, like Luther, opposed the four-fold method, perhaps because
it opened the door to dialectic, he remained far from the mature
Luther's assertion that the Scriptures had one clear sense, which was
Christ.

Capito seems to have found no single doctrinal point in the
Scriptures. Where Luther solved the problem of Scriptural mysteries
with the assertion that their sole content was Christ, Capito suggested
only, "I think this labyrinth is to be retraced with different threads.
First let there be acute judgment, instructed with full preparations
by the reading of good authors. Then there may be the rich skill and
happiness of handling sacred things. . . ." In practice he seems to
have found the law of love. Only the Scriptures were finally reliable
in theology, he explained, because "the law, explained by the
gospels (lex evangeliis explicata) straightens out the turns, equalizes
circumstances, elevates the lowly, and draws the bonds of mutual
love completely together." [87] In the lectures on Romans, where Paul
declared "grace and peace" to his readers, Capito explained peace at
some length but ignored the subject of grace. A little earlier he
interrupted his discussion of the text with an excursus on "the
princes of the earth," the point of which was that "the Law of the
Gospel makes all things equal." And he concluded his lectures with
an exhortation to the young theologians in his class: "Listen carefully:
Christ, who put aside the sword, does not want you to disagree
with your neighbor, and he does not like contentious people." [88]

However many doctrines one may find in the Romans lectures,

---

[86] *EE*, II, 337. On Erasmus' hermeneutics see John B. Payne, "Toward the
Hermeneutics of Erasmus," *Scrinium Erasmianum* (Leiden, 1969), II, 13-49, and
portions of Tracy, *Erasmus. The Growth of a Mind.*

[87] *EE*. II, 337.

[88] Rom. lec., fol. 8(v)-9; 7(v). "Nam omnia Lex Euangelii paria reddit. . . .",
and fol. 82(v), "Audi diligenter: Christus, qui gladium missit, non vult vt proximo
repugnes, non amat contentiosum."

and they are there, Capito himself seems to have been unwilling to fight about—or die for—any of them. Perhaps this distaste for dogma lay behind not only his narrowly historical understanding of Paul's treatment of works but also his failure to draw lessons from Paul that related to doctrine and practice in his own time. Positively, he may even have entertained some of Reuchlin's notions about the hidden meaning of Hebrew words, which would indicate that his interest lay in the wisdom of daily living rather than in the knowledge of true doctrine. He interrupted his discussion of Hebrew nouns in the 1518 grammar, for instance, to point out that Absalom meant *pater pacis* and Bethlehem *domus panis*. He then declared that there was "much significance" in the Hebrew names and promised to discuss it in a "third book," the uncompleted Hebrew lexicon.[89] Perhaps such exegetical practice was an instance of "acute judgment." In any event, as a professional theologian he was true to his views about good learning in general. He sought an enlightened piety that led to good living, rather than true doctrine, which, to his mind, led to quarreling.

The case of Capito nevertheless suggests the need to appeal to more than a "productive misunderstanding" and a shared zeal for reform as explanations of early humanist support for Luther. To be sure, Capito's understanding of faith was very different from Luther's. And he disagreed with Luther on the even more basic question of what constituted the task of the theologian. Yet, it cannot be assumed that he, and the other young humanists, foolishly misunderstood Luther in the face of good evidence about him, or that they would have wholeheartedly supported an obvious heretic, no matter how dedicated they were to reform.[90]

Strictly speaking, then, there was no "misunderstanding" between Capito and Luther. To be sure, Capito did not know Luther's innermost thoughts, but neither did anyone else. He did not hear or read

---

[89] *Institvtionvm*, sig. Ee3(v)- Ee4, [Ff(v)]. See also Rom. lec., fol. 24(v), where he referred to the Pseudo-Dionysius and the Cabala.

[90] The argument of Moeller, "Deutsche Humanisten," *ZKG*, LXX, 46-61, implies that the humanists were fools who supported a man with whom they disagreed. This unfortunate implication can be avoided with the recognition that even to the learned public there was no such thing as "Luther's theology" during the years 1517-1519. Consequently, the insightful, and almost sociological, discussion by Lewis W. Spitz, "The Third Generation of German Renaissance Humanists," *Aspects of the Renaissance*, ed. by Archibald Lewis (Austin, Tex., 1967), pp. 105-121, may relate more to the young humanists' final conversion to the Reformation than to their initial support for Luther.

Luther's early Biblical lectures. And he surely was not privy to the gradual development of Luther's theological ideas that has been revealed by modern scholarship. But then, neither was anyone else in the sixteenth century. All Capito could know of Luther was contained in what Luther published. And here there were good grounds for thinking he was another partisan of the new learning. There was nothing in them that was truly revolutionary. In the Ninety-five Theses Luther did not purport to take from the Pope the right to issue indulgences. And his denial of papal and conciliar authority at Leipzig reached Capito and other German intellectuals in garbled partisan reports that he might well have disbelieved. Positively, Luther sometimes sounded like an Erasmian, especially in the sermon on indulgences and grace of which Capito thought so highly. Luther's point was that indulgences were worthless in the sight of God, who insisted that sinners trust him alone. But Erasmus himself could have declared, "He who sincerely contributes to the building of St. Peter's . . . for God's sake acts much more securely and better than he who buys indulgences for it, because there is the danger that he may make a contribution for the sake of the indulgence, rather than for God's sake." But these were the words of Luther, who also added the fine "Erasmian" counsel that "before all things (either the building of St. Peter's or the highly-regarded indulgence), you should give to your poor neighbor, if you want to give something." [91] There was good reason for Capito and the others to claim Luther as one of their own during the early period of Luther's public emergence as a reformer.

No conversion was necessary for Capito to support Luther, if only because to his mind reform did not have to do with universal doctrines and right practice but with enlightened piety. Given that his criticism of the scholastic theologians centered upon the very complexity and multiplicity of their doctrines, which he put down to their use of dialectic, it was natural for him to embrace another scholar who seemed to work from the ancient sources. Moreover, where Luther did become disputatious, Capito was quick to warn him of the necessity to proceed cautiously. Indeed, his reaction to Luther is another instance of the truth that humanism—even in the north— was not a philosophical school but a cultural movement that was bound together by basically skeptical assumptions regarding the

---

[91] *WA*, I, 243-246.

question of what could be known. Had humanism been a philosophical or theological school properly conceived, then early humanist
support for Luther would pose a problem. But it was not. The
factor that unified Capito's work was the rarely stated assumption
that knowledge took the form of wisdom rather than universally
applicable general truths. That this was nevertheless a vitally important assumption is evident in the difficulties he had with Luther
while he was adviser to the Archbishop of Mainz.

CHAPTER THREE

THE COURTIER AT MAINZ

A large crowd of Baslers gathered on April 28, 1520, to wish Capito farewell as he boarded ship for Mainz. His humanist friends, with their traditional distrust of the active life, regretted the move. Hedio feared that his teacher would be "led astray" at Mainz. "Oh, my Capito, what are you giving up?" lamented Christoph Hegendorf, an official of the Basel cathedral. Andreas Cratander, the printer, announced the new position to Boniface Amerbach in concerned tones on November 13. "I nevertheless fear for the otherwise so learned and upright Capito," he wrote; "he may wrap himself up too much in the labors of the court, which are usually the most virulent plagues for all zealous and candid talents." Amerbach replied less restrainedly two weeks later, "What, I ask, is there for Capito at the court—the upright with the dishonest, the speaker of truth among the flatterers, a free man among slaves?" [1]

His friends' worries were partially justified. Even Erasmus' judgment, "Capito is wholly of the court and is taking on its characteristics," [2] was not entirely unwarranted. He was appointed to preach in the Archbishop's place, but he was quickly employed as one of Albert's regular advisers and was soon relieved of the cathedral preacher's duties. These Hedio assumed in October on Capito's recommendation. When Hedio wrote Zwingli to announce his own new position, he reported that Capito was in Aachen with Albert for the coronation of Charles V.[3] Erasmus was right; Capito had become an "*aulicus*, a man of the court." Between 1520 and 1523 he was so engrossed in ecclesiastical and Imperial politics that he produced only a second edition of his Chrysostom translations.

It is understandable that his humanist friends should fear the death

---

[1] *ZW*, VII, 280; 305-306. Th. B., I, 91-91(v). Hartmann, *Amerbach Korrespondenz*, II, 265; 271. Others sought to lure him back to the life of study. See Peter Mosellanus to Mutianus Rufus; Karl Krafft and Wilhelm Krafft, eds., *Briefe und Dokumente aus der Zeit der Reformation im 16. Jahrhundert, nebst Mittheilungen über Kölnische Gelehrte und Studien im 13. und 16. Jahrhunderte* (Elberfeld, [1875]), p. 149.

[2] *EE*, IV, 376-377.

[3] *ZW*, VII, 355. Protocolls of the Mainz cathedral chapter in Herrmann, *Evangelische Bewegung, Beilage I*, 208-209.

of a scholar as he moved to the court. Some were anxious even about his soul. "Farewell in Christ," Pellican wrote in March 1521, "and, entangled in secular labors, see that you do not cease to be a soldier for God." But that was just what he himself intended to be. He brought to his new post all the enthusiasm for reform, and for Luther's cause, that filled his years at Basel. He announced the move to Luther with the declaration,

> My Luther, you do not know how much you have accomplished in human terms, to the extent that you could take a stand apart from popes and mendicants. For my part, like Hushai for the sake of David, until now I have undermined the advice of Ahitophel. Then, truly, I, who could escape notice, am afraid. A foul Englishman wrote something against Erasmus; the Midasses of Louvain and Cologne condemned some of your theses. I am therefore compelled to enter the arena. . . .[4]

Not quite a year earlier, in June 1519, he vowed to Georg Spalatin that, like "Pigmeus among the Athletes, I will fight on foot against the arrogance of obstinacy. . . ." [5] And he prepared to carry out his intentions. In November he wrote Hutten, "I will undertake a doctorate in papal law, as they call it, in order, namely, to establish my authority." [6] Even if he had not intended to defend Luther, he could scarcely have avoided religious concerns in his new post. In mid-1521 he wrote a letter defending it, in which he approvingly quoted Albert: "I supervise all ceremonies and the general outward appearance of worship. . . ." He then observed that he was especially close to Albert as both personal chaplain and adviser.[7] It was therefore an honorable undertaking. However that may be, his position did assume critical importance between 1520 and 1523, and he was naturally propelled into decisions on what was to be done with Luther and the burgeoning reform movement. Capito could not avoid hard decisions at Mainz, about public religious policy, and about his own faith.

Luther replied warmly to Capito's announcement of his new

---

[4] Th. B., I, 149. *WABr*, II, 71.

[5] The letter to Spalatin is printed in Jo. Fredericus Hekelius, *Manipulus Primus Epistolarum Singularium* (Plaviae, 1695), p. 37.

[6] Edvardus Böcking, ed., *Ulrichi Hutteni Equitis Germani Opera Quae Repervi Potuerunt Omnia* (Leipzig, 1859), I, 316.

[7] To Bonifacius [Wolfhart], Basel Kirchenarchiv, 25a, fol. 244-245. The suggestion of Baum, *Capito und Butzer*, p. 51, that he was chancellor comes from Adamus, *Vitae*, p. 89. But Capito described himself as having been "ein vngeschickter rhat." *Von der kirchen lieblichen vereinigung* (Strassburg, 1533), sig. iij.

position. "I truly hope you will enter the arena skillfully and brilliantly," he wrote. His reaction would probably have been a little different had he known that his self-appointed defender had more than reform in mind when he became Albert's adviser. He was also hunting for a prebend.[8] The prize was the provostship of the collegiate church of St. Thomas in Strasbourg, and he had a rival in Jacob Abel, a papal protonotary. But Capito too had powerful friends. Besides his own Bishop in Basel, both the warlike Cardinal-Bishop of Sitten, Matthias Schiner, and the papal legate to Switzerland, Antonio Pucci, were pushing his candidacy. In his own behalf Capito travelled to Strasbourg in 1519 in regard to the chapter election, or in other words, to make certain "the monks work no mischief," as Hedio put it in a letter to Zwingli.[9] Initially he hoped he could persuade Albert to grant immediate possession by exercising the *preces regales* as Chancellor of the Empire during the interregnum between Maximilian's death and the election of Charles V. During the preceding months Albert had fallen under the influence of the humanist group at his court—Ulrich von Hutten, Heinrich Stromer, and Frowen von Hutten. They wanted to install a fellow humanist in the Mainz cathedral and Capito appeared just as the death of Bartholomeus Zehender, an opponent of Reuchlin, created an opening. Hutten recommended Capito to Albert as a man of "true erudition with a knowledge of both ancient and recent theology," and Albert appointed him over Cajetan's objections. On August 31, 1520, Capito wrote the canons of St. Thomas, requesting his election and warning them against Abel. The next day Albert wrote Leo X, requesting that Capito, "my most faithful counsellor," be awarded the provostship *ex plenitudine potestatis*.[10] Capito did accept his position at Mainz with the intention of furthering reform, but also with the understanding that Albert would work for the prebend while he served at court.

Yet, he was also true to his declaration to Luther that he would further the cause of reform from his new post. In December, Hedio wrote Zwingli that Capito continued to preach occasionally even after he became Albert's adviser. His sermons contained only "the

---

[8] *WABr*, II, 94. The account of the negotiations for the prebend follows Kalkoff, *Capito*, pp. 7-16.

[9] *ZW*, VII, 227.

[10] See in addition Herrmann, *Evangelische Bewegung*, p. 73. For the letter to the canons, Th. B., I, 101; for Albert's request to Leo X, Kalkoff, *Capito, Beilage I*, 133-134.

pure doctrine of Christ and the Gospel," Hedio proclaimed. In the beginning the canons of the cathedral opposed their new preacher, but Capito took a personal hand in their instruction so that "now they also exert themselves to proclaim the Scriptures." The text was the Letter to the Romans, Hedio reported, and large crowds were listening to it enthusiastically. And yet these sermons illustrate the difficulty of interpreting Capito's behavior while he served Archbishop Albert. The "doctrine of Christ" that Hedio identified was probably the same message of inward piety and brotherly love that Capito proclaimed in Basel. At least there was nothing about his sermons to raise doubts in the very suspicious mind of Johannes Cochlaeus, who is remembered as Luther's most scurrilous biographer. In June he reported to Willibald Pirckheimer, the Nuremberg humanist, that Capito's "sermons are receiving the highest praise here . . ." in Frankfurt.[11]

The praise these sermons received, both from Hedio, another defender of Luther, and from Cochlaeus, suggests the danger of drawing conclusions about Capito's religious beliefs solely from his reported behavior. During the early 1520's, many knowledgable people felt that the lines between what was acceptable and what heterodox were not surely and unalterably drawn. A variety of reasons led individuals to support Luther or, in some cases, merely to oppose proceeding against him with force. There were, to be sure, genuine "Lutherans", but, as the example of Hutten suggests, older attitudes motivated even some of Luther's most passionate partisans. Capito tried to avoid passion in religious matters, but his support for Luther resembled Hutten's in that it derived from pre-Reformation religious values.[12]

Anticlericalism, directed against the monk in particular, was one older attitude that played an important role in generating early backing for Luther. In detesting monasticism, Capito was at one with not only his father but also many fellow humanists. In the middle of May 1520 he sadly reported to Melanchthon that their friend Oecolampadius had entered a Brigettine monastery. "A man otherwise cautious and prudent, who burdened a melancholy spirit

---

[11] *ZW*, VII, 376.

[12] Kalkoff, *Capito*, p. 2, calls him an Erasmian, which would be an accurate description, but he also (p. 55) approvingly quotes the later judgment of Cochlaeus that he was "Lutheranissimus," which is not true. Herrmann, *Evangelische Bewegung*, pp. 77-78, found Kalkoff's study "outstanding."

with unaccustomed labors in the cause of religion, acted indiscreetly,"
he judged, but, he added, "it must be endured, since it cannot be
changed." Endure it he might, but he did not like it. He criticized
monasticism for its false discipline, "as if Christ enjoyed our sorrow,"
and for its uselessness, "as if the cultured Christian were freely to run
away from public view." He worried for Oecolampadius' health
because he would be required "to afflict an infirm body with absolute
silence, vigils, fasting." Above all, he objected to the Brigettine order
itself, because "women have authority over men, which is a perverted
rule."[13]

Capito felt nothing could be done about Oecolampadius' decision,
but he was willing to act upon his convictions about monasticism if
he were given the opportunity. In the impenetrable maze of ecclesiastical wirepulling, he helped his future colleague Martin Bucer
secure release from his vows as a Dominican. The two men probably
met during summer 1519 when Bucer traveled to Basel to celebrate
his ordination. After returning to the monastery he sent certain
"propositions" to Capito for an opinion. And he turned first to
Capito when he began to consider shedding his habit. Although he
did not leave the monastery until November 1520, he already referred
to him as "my sole patron" in a letter to Spalatin on September
19.[14] When Capito did not respond quickly, Bucer enlisted Hutten
to pressure him into action. By late November he had written Capito
twice on Bucer's behalf. A month later Bucer was frantic. He had fled
the monastery and found refuge with Maternus Hatten in Speier.
Now he begged Capito to help him: "Your kindness to me is so
great and has been so clearly shown for such a long time that I dare
anything. . . . I implore you in Christ to endure such trouble patiently,
bearing in mind my utter misery. . . ." He wanted a letter of recommendation to a protector "who has been released from the terrible
fear of our party." [15]

Capito continued to drag his feet. He at first opposed Bucer's
plan to have the case transferred to Anton Engelbrecht, who also
became a Strasbourg reformer but was then the Suffragan Bishop of
Speier. Capito suggested instead that Bucer seek dissolution of his

---

[13] *CR*, I, 163-164.

[14] Horawitz and Hartfelder, *Briefwechsel des Beatus Rhenanus*, p. 166. Rudolf
Staehelin, ed., *Briefe aus der Reformationszeit* (Basel, 1887), p. 9.

[15] *Hutteni Opera*, I, 428. Staehelin, *Briefe aus der Reformationszeit*, p. 11. None of
Capito's correspondence on this matter is extant.

vows in Rome. Bucer demurred on the basis of the trip's length, but he was bold enough to complain that Capito had done nothing to secure him a more reliable host. In January 1521 Hatten visited Capito to hear his decision, and Capito apparently changed his mind, for on February 2 Bucer wrote, "I appreciate, I acknowledge the perseverance and solicitude of your heart by which you leave no stone unturned that might at last set me free." He reported that the appeal was on its way to Rome and asked Capito now to influence Engelbrecht to a favorable judgment. By the end of March, Bucer was anxiously awaiting the bull of dissolution in the castle of Franz von Sickingen,[16] the leader of the Knights' Revolt. By the middle of the summer, Bucer was no longer a monk.

Bucer's case was one example of Capito's skill in employing personal influence, and of the way in which his own reform ideas accidentally reinforced the evangelical movement. At the same time he was paying attention to the fate of a far more important figure than Bucer. During the second half of 1520 and early 1521 Germany's temporal and ecclesiastical authorities faced the critical problem of dealing with Luther. This was an issue that bore especially heavily upon Capito's master, the young pluralist, Albert of Mainz. In June in the bull *Exsurge Domine*, Leo X gave Luther sixty days in which to submit to Rome. He also appointed Jerome Aleander special legate with authority to publish the bull against Luther throughout Germany. Albert's agent in Rome, Valentine Tetleben, wrote on July 5 to inform the Archbishop of Aleander's mission and of how irritating Rome found the literary attacks of Hutten and Luther. A warning was well advised, for a week later Leo X's secretary, Jacopo Sadoleto, wrote Albert with the same complaint. He informed the Archbishop that the curia was astounded to discover that some of Hutten's attacks on the Holy See were being published in Mainz. Writing in Leo X's name, Sadoleto smoothly concluded that he was sure Albert was unaware of Hutten's activity and that the pope was confident the Archbishop would put a stop to it, and, moreover, that Albert would cooperate with Aleander.[17]

Capito's desire to further Luther's cause, or what he understood it to be, was thus tested severely just three months after he arrived at court. He had already secured the Archbishop's confidence, for Albert turned to him to draft a reply to the curia's demands. This was

[16] *Ibid.*, pp. 11; 13. Th. B., I, 133; 144.
[17] *Hutteni Opera*, I, 360-361; 362-363.

the first of several official dispatches Capito wrote for the Archbishop. On this occasion, he tried to placate Rome and at the same time to lay the groundwork for postponing vigorous action against Luther. He began by acknowledging that he was expected to provide every support for Aleander's mission. Then he transisted directly to the subject of Hutten's and Luther's books. He had Albert declare, ". . . I labored with great persistency not only to take Hutten's infamous books from the hands of readers. . . but I also was zealous to suppress the most seditious furies of Luther, which are even now springing up. . . ." In Capito's words the Archbishop of Mainz proclaimed that he "moved every stone. . . so that this evil may be prevented from growing worse."

Capito was protesting too much. He also had Albert assert, "Then I decreed that no one may sell or acquire within my dioceses writings that are slanderous or that depreciate the authority of the Holy See of Rome." But he almost gave the real story away when he reported that Albert's officials were "prohibiting them in the same manner for over a year," although the edict itself had only recently appeared. How, a zealous curial official might ask, could Hutten's books have been published at Mainz if their mere possession had been prohibited for over a year? The edict in question was in fact a general proscription of libel and slander that did not mention either Hutten or Luther by name. When Aleander passed through Mainz a few months later and conducted a burning of Luther's books, he was horrified to observe the executioner refuse to light the fire when the crowd roared, "No," to the question whether they had been rightly condemned.[18] It appears that the Archbishop did not enforce his decree against books "that are slanderous or that depreciate the authority of the Holy See of Rome."

Enforcement was the critical issue, in regard to censorship, to be sure, but especially as it concerned *Exsurge Domine*. One passage in Capito's letter could well have given a close-eyed Roman official grounds for concern about Albert's intentions on this score. He returned to the subject of Aleander's mission at the end of the letter:

> Therefore, most sacred Father, concerning the present commands to publish the bull against Luther in the dioceses of Mainz and Magdeburg and of my sacred constituents, weighing not so much words as understanding (*non tam verba quam mentem perpendens*), in common

---

[18] *Ibid.*, I, 364. On the bookburning see Hedio to Zwingli, 21 December 1520, *ZW*, VII, 376-377, and Herrmann, *Evangelische Bewegung*, pp. 81-82.

cause with my lords the nuncios, I am devoting attention to obtaining for us the favor of the secular princes, without whom we would have labored in vain and our entire undertaking would finally be severely limited.[19]

On the surface these words were innocent enough. Albert seemed to promise he would secure the assistance of the secular authorities in bringing Luther to heel. But a close reading reveals that Capito was in fact notifying the curia that Albert would not simply carry out Aleander's instructions and publish the bull. He intended to play an independent role. He was delaying action by insisting upon consulting the princes.

Taking Capito's advice, the Archbishop of Mainz did refuse to publish *Exsurge Domine*. In October, Hedio wrote Zwingli, "You would scarcely believe what [Capito] may be able to accomplish in that position. Luther would already have been destroyed in this district and the Lutherans excommunicated if he had not persuaded the Prince differently." [20] This was only the beginning. Capito made Aleander's life miserable as he tried to carry out his mission in Albert's territories. Thanks in large part to Capito's grip on the malleable Archbishop, Luther's burning of *Exsurge Domine* was more than bravado. The bull was dead as a device for halting the spread of Luther's protest.

In fact, the plan to give Luther a hearing, before declaring him an outlaw, was already taking shape in the response to Leo X. Through Albert, Capito played an important part in thwarting Aleander's instructions, which did not allow a confrontation such as occurred at Worms. Hedio may have been exaggerating the value of Capito's efforts in persuading the Archbishop not to publish the bull, but during late 1520 and early 1521, he did exert influence in the religious question out of proportion to his official position. It is impossible to detail all his activities, but he was with Erasmus during the famous interview with Frederick the Wise in Cologne after the coronation of Charles V. In December 1521, during a particularly stormy period of their relationship, Capito reminded Luther of all he had done for him. Erasmus "counselled for the middle way at Cologne," he reported, "so I could take care that the case would be postponed . . . which the moment required." This was no small task, for the new Emperor, Charles, was a devoted son of the church who was never enthusiastic

[19] *Hutteni Opera*, I, 364-365.
[20] *ZW*, VII, 355.

about bringing Luther to Worms, but finally acceded to the wishes
of the princes. Capito could rightly take pride in his labors. "What
did I not maintain? With what support, by what possible manner,
might I have acted for your benefit?" he demanded from Luther.
His exact efforts at Cologne and elsewhere are unrecorded, but he
may have introduced Erasmus to Frederick and he probably persuaded the advisers of other princes to favor delaying Luther's
case.[21] After all, what harm could there be in bringing Luther to
a hearing if the "most faithful counsellor" of the Archbishop of
Mainz, whose own pocketbook was hardest hit by Luther's protest,
favored delay? Bucer thus wrote Capito with some justice in November, declaring, "Good learning in all Germany seems now to have
settled in your hands. . . ." [22]

During the first months as Albert's adviser, Capito made a healthy
downpayment toward redeeming his pledge that he would "fight on
foot" in Luther's behalf. To an outside observer he remained one of
Luther's most loyal supporters. And yet, Bucer's easy identification
of Capito's defence of Luther with the cause of "good learning"
points to the true source of his efforts. He was still the humanist
who commanded his students at the close of his lectures on Romans,
"Take care, then, lest you exercise anger against the neighbor under
the pretext of piety." [23] There was no room for righteous indignation
and denunciation in his understanding of genuine reform. Consequently, during the same period that he was working to bring
Luther to a hearing, rather than allow him to be condemned out of
hand, he was becoming increasingly critical of the movement that
Luther's protest released, and of Luther himself.

Hutten was the first to lose favor with Capito. In his case the
shift in thinking was decisive. In 1519 Capito praised Hutten to
Albert. He associated him with Erasmus as "our Hutten, who was
most happily taught from childhood, and seeks the goddesses of
both languages. . . ." [24] But in response to Leo X for Albert, Capito
wrote, "I banished from me anyone I sensed to be alienated from a

[21] *W ABr*, II, 416. In April, Bucer reported to Beatus Rhenanus that Erasmus
and Capito had met with "the hero," probably Frederick. Horawitz and Hartfelder, *Briefwechsel des Beatus Rhenanus*, p. 273.

[22] Staehelin, *Briefe aus der Reformationszeit*, p. 10.

[23] Rom. Lec., fol. 82(v). "Cave, itaque, praetextu pietatis iram in proximum
exercias."

[24] *Paraenesis Prior Divi Joh. Chrysostomi*, fol. 7. "Huttenus noster, qui felicissime
institutus a paruulo, atque utriusque linguae Veneres aucupatur. . . ."

zeal for your sanctity, which is apparent in regard to Ulrich Hutten, previously most precious to me, whom I immediately excluded from my circle. . . ." [25] Whether Capito personally had a hand in Hutten's banishment is unclear, but he did use it as evidence of Albert's devotion to Leo, and he did nothing to help Hutten, who wrote him on July 1520 that he had intercepted a threatening papal letter and begged him to intervene on his behalf at court. On August 8 he wrote again and claimed that he had seen an order from Leo to Albert to capture him and send him bound to Rome. "Well, then," he exploded, "so the way will have to be forced through. Thus far I have been gentle. Now I see the Roman lions thirsting for blood. And unless everything fails me, they themselves will be the first to bleed and the first thrown into prison. . . ." He told Capito, "Write Erasmus and the others what interests are at stake," but there was no response.[26] Hutten had reacted in precisely the manner to assure Capito's further estrangement. By late 1520 Capito the follower of Erasmus decided that the man who secured him the post at Mainz spoke too quickly of war.

Hutten was one thing; Luther presented a different problem. During summer 1520 Luther publicly revealed most of his reform program. There no longer could be any doubt that he desired fundamental changes in religious life. Moreover, it appeared to many observers that he was allying himself with some of the most bloodthirsty elements in Germany. On more than one occasion he seemed, like Hutten, to call for war against Rome and against all Germans who remained loyal to Rome. For Capito the most important of his publications in 1520 was the *Address to the Christian Nobility*, in which he called upon the temporal authorities to reform the church. The reforms that he mentioned in this work included the most common demands of German laymen and humanists alike, in sum, that the church return to apostolic simplicity. And the rhetorical appeal he made was equally popular to a nationalist sense of Roman exploitation. The abiding religious tone and theological significance of the pamphlet lay in Luther's use of the doctrine that all believers were priests, but a reader in 1520 might be excused for overlooking it,

---

[25] *Hutteni Opera*, I, 364.

[26] *Ibid.*, I, 367; 400-403, and Staehelin, *Briefe aus der Reformationszeit*, p. 9. See also Hajo Holborn, *Ulrich von Hutten and the German Reformation* (New York, 1966), pp. 145; 150-151.

especially if he considered doctrines unworthy of a fight in any event.[27]

In September, one month after the publication of the *Address*, Bucer reported to Spalatin that "Capito . . . was astounded by the first rumor of this book. But when he reads it, he will act so he may be what is fitting a true theologian, a champion and interpreter of the truth, not at all false and not at all timid." [28] Bucer was too optimistic, for Capito saw in Luther's tract precisely what many people saw, an appeal to force. "Accordingly," he wrote Luther in December, "even if I might perhaps appreciate the reason for your plan, which in my opinion is almost another matter, by suggesting armed camps and force you severely discourage those who are committed to you." He observed that public opinion was becoming increasingly polarized between those who questioned how "a mere private man could impudently call the decretals into doubt" and those he still termed "the more sane" who considered it "impiety to destroy the decrees of Christ with human decretals." But he was seeking a middle path. He condemned Eck and Hochstraten as "barbarians, fools, atheists, rubes without learning, without grace, without faith, even utterly without human talent," and Hutten for "blowing the trumpet of war among us." According to his reading of the work, Luther must moderate his appeal for reform. "We must pray for peace in our time through Jesus Christ. . ." he concluded.

Before assuming his post in Mainz, Capito urged Luther to be cautious in pushing his reform program. Because he was now the central adviser to Germany's most powerful ecclesiastical prince, within whose jurisdiction Wittenberg lay, it is understandable that he should be even more anxious to moderate Luther. But on this occasion he was giving more than merely tactical advice, which, if Luther would only follow it, would make Luther more effective. It is apparent that he genuinely feared not just theological wrangling but war itself.

> You may sense what I remain silent about: recall an earlier time and consider carefully that cruel tyranny created bloody wars. I want Christ to flourish again; perhaps you have surmised that patience will flourish again during warfare. Religion was born, was nourished, and was strengthened by the peaceful; with tolerance the defenceless shattered the control made by soldiers. I have not observed whether

---

[27] See the discussion in *ibid.*, pp. 139-141, and the literature cited.
[28] Staehelin, *Briefe aus der Reformationszeit*, p. 9.

a people bloodied by war fever necessarily receives true religion, although I do know well that an old law... has been more often maintained with the clenched first, and that this has also been attempted by those of our party; I do not say how happily or piously, because in the meantime our cause has disappeared.

Earlier in the letter Capito declared flatly, "There are those who fear that every semblance of piety may be obliterated by that uproar of yours." [29]

The same concern for enlightened piety that was the object of his studies in Basel lay behind both his defence of Luther and his growing criticism of Luther. In this regard his letter is just as revealing for what he ignored as for what he discussed. The year 1520 saw the publication not only of the *Address to the Christian Nobility* but also of the two seminal essays *On the Freedom of a Christian* and, above all, *The Babylonian Captivity of the Church*. All the profound theological and practical issues that divided Luther from Rome had been in public view for at least three months when Capito sat down to write him in December. And yet he ignored Luther's destruction of the sacramental system, of the special order of the priesthood, and of the Christian's obligation to perform meritorious deeds in order to attain salvation. In the one letter Capito wrote Luther during this period, it must be assumed that he addressed what he regarded to be the most critical issue. For him, then, peace, rather than doctrine, was the overriding concern, because piety could survive only during peace, both political and doctrinal. The advice he now gave Luther was the same advice he gave his students as he closed his lectures on Romans: "do not extinguish plebeian devotion with too much earnestness; do not preach the word of Christ by reason of contention but of love." [30] Capito could not understand how Luther could become

---

[29] *WABr*, II, 222-224. Herrmann, *Evangelische Bewegung*, pp. 82-84, views the letter merely as a tactical attempt to moderate Luther in order to prepare the way for a successful hearing at Worms, while Kalkoff, *Capito*, ignores the questions the letter poses. Herrmann's mistake (and by implication Kalkoff's) derives from ignoring Capito's own religious values and his development during his years at Mainz. Moreover, the letter does not once approach the tone of the admittedly tactical advice he gave Luther in 1518. Consequently, Capito provides a counter example to the argument of Ernst-Wilhelm Kohls, "Humanisten auf dem Reichstag zu Worms," *Der Reichstag zu Worms von 1521: Reichspolitik und Luthersache,* Fritz Reuter, ed., (Worms, 1971), pp. 257-270, that Luther's refusal to compromise *during* the Reichstag caused the first and enduring division in the ranks of the humanists.

[30] *WABr*, II, 224, "ne extinguas nimia sedulitate plebeiam devotionem; ne praedica per contentionem sed per charitatem verbum Christi." Surely this was the

so careless of public order in his insistence upon doctrinal issues that
he found essentially indifferent. His religious concerns remained
typically Erasmian during his first year of service to the Archbishop
of Mainz. They led him to become deeply critical of Luther, as well
as to defend him.

And yet, he was genuinely caught in the middle. The same principles that led him to beg Luther to be more moderate also compelled
him to insist that Luther's movement must not be put down with
force. He wrote the letter to Luther in the midst of preparations for
the Diet of Worms, while Aleander was still trying to persuade
Charles V simply to ratify Luther's excommunication and declare
him an outlaw. Capito had to walk with special deftness in the
shadowy no-man's land between the two sides, for he desired at the
same time to frustrate Aleander's mission and to enlist Aleander in
his campaign for the envied provostship of St. Thomas. His success,
on the latter count in particular, was as much a tribute to Aleander's
short-sightedness as it was to Capito's powers of dissimulation.
More importantly, no episode more clearly illustrates Capito's
ambivalent position than his dealings at Worms in early 1521.

Initially he sought to convince Aleander of his basic loyalty to
Rome. Aleander arrived at Worms full of suspicions about Capito and
Albert's other advisers, as he reported to Rome in mid-December on
Albert's trustworthiness:

> If his inclinations and good intentions are above doubt, then certainly
> his zeal slackens too easily; he is, namely, unable to disregard the
> influence of the crowd of old and high-ranking advisers who surround
> him and who are radical Lutherans in their hearts; to be sure they
> speak against Luther as enemies, but they act as friends.

Two months later Capito had given Aleander cause to revise his
judgment, at least sufficiently to secure the desired end. On February
6, Aleander wrote a long report requesting prebends for influential
Germans, which he concluded with a paragraph about Capito:

> Finally I am forwarding another request from the Doctor of Theology
> Capito, who is in the service of the Archbishop of Mainz. Although
> the common opinion is that he has been a Lutheran sectarian all
> along, he has now been converted by his patron, or at least acts that

---

practical precipitate of the general remark at the end of Rom. Lec., fol. 82(v),
"Audi diligenter: Christus, qui gladium misit, non vult ut proximo repugnes,
non amat contentiosum. Cave, itaque, praetextu pietatis iram in proximum
exercias."

way. In spite of everything he continually returns in conversation to his old sickness, and when I come to speak with him about it, he does not deny it, but explains that he only wants to test the inclinations of others by that means. . . . If anything can be done, the Pope should accommodate him, for he is learned and eloquent and as much in a position to be used as to harm.[31]

Capito was capable of duplicity for the sake of his prebend. Although he could imply to Luther that Aleander was really a Jew,[32] he was also willing to work for the legate. He travelled to Frankfurt in late March to interview Cochlaeus and Nesen on Aleander's behalf, and he so charmed Cochlaeus that this ardent foe of Luther guaranteed his credit in asking Pirckheimer to acquire Aldus' portable edition of Cicero's works.[33] Erasmus was right when he wrote that Capito had become a "man of the court."

The double game with Aleander came to a speedy end. For Aleander, loyalty to Rome meant unquestioning obedience, particularly to the instructions he was carrying, and Capito, however much he desired a benefice, was unwilling to see Luther condemned, especially without a hearing. Aleander's February dispatch indicates that Capito did try to cover his tracks in promoting the plan to bring Luther to Worms, but by mid-March the nuncio no longer had any doubts. He nevertheless came to a curious conclusion regarding the prebend. Replying to the papal Vice-chancellor, he wrote,

I have read Doctor Capito the section of your letter in which your lordship gives him such good hopes, and I request now that the disputed matter be brought to a decision in his favor, for he is one of the important spokesmen of the intellectuals who oppose us, even if he does not hazard to go over to that side openly on account of his relationship to the Archbishop of Mainz. The affable Cardinal, however, has allowed himself to be so ensnared and to be led astray into such blunders that I was unable to convince him with my arguments. We must therefore find another way to shackle Capito, and I think it best to attempt at the outset to win him by a few favors from Rome, and especially through the questioned provostship; and even if we cannot make him entirely ours with these lures, he will still harm the

---

[31] Paul Kalkoff, ed., and trans., *Die Depeschen des Nuntius Aleander vom Wormser Reichstage. 1521* (Halle, 1886). pp. 19; 41.

[32] *WABr*, II, 223, "Exsibilatur a popula ceu Iudaeus. . . ." Erasmus may have been the author of this rumor. See Tracy, *Erasmus*, p. 185 n. 113.

[33] Cochlaeus to Aleander, 25 March 1521. Walter Friedensburg, "Beiträge zum Briefwechsel der Katholischen Gelehrten Deutschlands im Reformationszeitalter," *Zeitschrift für Kirchengeschichte*, XVIII (1897), 109. (Hereafter cited as Friedensburg, *ZKG*.) *Hutteni Opera*, I, 359. On the mission to Frankfurt, see Kalkoff, *Capito*, pp. 45-54.

Catholic cause less, for his interests would then demand the maintenance of the provostship, while the Lutherans want to eliminate all ecclesiastical benefices.

Where Capito's duplicity failed, his official importance succeeded, for, Aleander continued, "Inasmuch as he has thrown sand in the eyes of the Archbishop, he occupies a highly influential position—the preacher of the Church of Mainz, and the teacher of nearly all the theologians and pastors who are presently the main spokesmen of the most important churches in Germany." [34] Capito succeeded with one of his objectives almost in spite of himself.

To be sure, double-dealing and trickery characterized Capito's relationship with Aleander before, during, and after the Diet of Worms. Yet, a basic consistency underlay his activities. As someone who was not a committed evangelical but a proponent of a more amorphous reform of piety and morals, he wished neither Aleander nor Luther nor the Church of Rome harm. Consequently, even after his failure to convince Aleander of his impeccable loyalty to Rome, the two men were able to continue to cooperate on the thoroughly political basis of mutual usefulness. Still holding that preferment might quench the Germans' hatred of Rome, Aleander wrote the Vice-chancellor on April 5, "I commend Capito's request anew, for he is of great importance to us. . . ." For his part, on June 21 Capito warned Aleander, "Ulrich von Hutten has artfully and characteristically declared war indiscriminately against all the Pope's followers wherever they may be . . . . I wanted Your Kindness to know this so you would not thoughtlessly encounter some mercenary in this affair." He repeated the warning on July 13.[35] At times, even while seeking Aleander's aid, he frankly confessed his true position. In reporting his mission to Frankfurt he declared, "Everything that concerns a patron belongs to you, for you are willing and able to have improved my poverty. I am always working to make recompense, and, as far as I know, I have faithfully discharged the mission at Frankfurt these days." He then reported his discussions with Cochlaeus and described himself as one "who is not so much learned as in love with grammarians, and who, as you know, does not at all wish Luther evil. . . ." [36] Capito understood himself better than Aleander understood him.

---

[34] Kalkoff, *Depeschen*, pp. 105-106.
[35] *Ibid.*, p. 120. Friedensburg, *ZKG*, XVI, 496-499.
[36] Kalkoff, *Capito, Beilage II*, pp. 134-135. See also Capito to Luther, 4 Decem-

Capito was less successful at Worms in warding off the ban against Luther than he was in securing Aleander's help in acquiring the provostship of St. Thomas. Luther did nevertheless have a hearing of sorts and Capito was surely instrumental in bringing about the historic moment. But there were not enough followers of Luther—or even Capito—there to counterbalance Charles V's determination to act as a loyal son of the Church. Capito was filled with foreboding on May 29 as he described to Spalatin the burning of Luther's books that heralded the official condemnation: "They exhibited the Imperial Decree more out of hatred than prudence. For that reason they are at ease with an encamped army; but in that there is the risk that the thing may raise feelings on both sides, and, having been discussed with words, it may be ended with arms and blood; I see nothing more calamitous than that evil. May our Christ well prevent it." [37] And so Capito's efforts to preserve a fluid situation went up in smoke along with Luther's books. The lines were drawn. Luther was excommunicated and he was an outlaw.

What was Capito to do now? He remained convinced that any attempt to crush the evangelical movement with force would end in war, and that war must be avoided at all costs. Perhaps much to his surprise, the promulgation of the Edict of Worms still left room for maneuver. Just as Luther could be "kidnapped" on the road to Wittenberg, so there were opportunities for other equally effective, if less dramatic, countermeasures. In its immediate consequences the Edict of Worms was much like *Exsurge Domine*—it had only moral force. Both Emperor and Pope were too far removed from the seats of effective power in Germany to be able simply to decree, and then to watch their will be enforced. Thanks in part to Capito's efforts, it was not. As an effective measure against Luther, the Edict of Worms went the way of *Exsurge Domine*, with which it was linked.

Capito's fight against enforcing the Edict was foreshadowed in a small episode before the Diet met. In late November or early December, Aleander, in accordance with instructions from Rome, ordered the Provincial of the Minorites in Albert's territories to instruct members of the order to preach against Luther. In the middle of December, he reported that he "subsequently discovered" that Albert did his best to see that this order was followed. Aleander was

ber 1520, *WABr*, II, p. 222, where he described himself as "hominem, ut scis, pacis et tranquillitatis observantissimum."

[37] Hekelius, *Manipulus Primus*, p. 60.

either lying or misinformed. On May 2 Balthazar Geier, one of Albert's secretaries, wrote the Provincial that the Archbishop was very displeased to discover that a member of the order was attacking Luther from the pulpit. According to Geier, Albert thought it "would seem fitting that he preach nothing against Luther in his sermons for fear that the tumult amongst the populace may have been encouraged by his attacks." He added the warning that "if these monks venture to declare hatred for Luther in public, they will create notoriety for themselves ... and incite the populace against the clergy." [38] Capito's advice probably lay behind Geier's letter, for the arguments that Geier employed against the project accorded with his thinking. Two days later Charles V announced his decision about Luther, but Capito was already taking effective measures against it.

The most deflating of Capito's shafts into the Edict was his success in turning Albert of Mainz against it. Aleander was disappointed that Luther had been accorded a hearing, because this was properly an ecclesiastical matter in which the civil authorities ought not to have meddled. But once all was said and done, Aleander was prepared to carry out the remainder of his instructions without pause. In order to prosecute Luther speedily, he came to Germany with another bull, *Apostolicae sedis* of January 3, 1521, in which Leo X named the Archbishop of Mainz inquisitor general for all Germany. With the aid of Aleander, Carracciolo, and Eck, Albert, as legate, was given full canonical authority to punish heretics, to absolve the penitent, and to construct the apparatus necessary for the task. Albert had long coveted the legateship to add to his list of dignities in Germany, so Aleander tendered the office to him with some confidence in early May, when it became apparent that Luther would be condemned. But in his dispatch of May 18, the papal nuncio was forced to confess, "The Archbishop of Mainz wished to hear nothing about the distribution of the bull in which he himself, Caracciolo, Eck, and I are entrusted with complete authority to proceed against the Lutherans. ..." He hastily added that Albert did not refuse the assignment because he favored the Lutherans but because "he fears to call down the wrathful hatred of all Germans upon himself if he alone is named among all German prelates and consequently be brought forth as the sole leader of an undertaking of this type." Above all, the Archbishop disliked the title "inquisitor" and insisted that at the very

---

[38] Kalkoff, *Depeschen*, p. 12. Kalkoff, *Capito, Beilage IV*, p. 158.

least it must be shared by all German bishops before he would consent.[39] By refusing the commission, Albert assured that there would be no German equivalent to the Spanish Inquisition. If the Edict of Worms were to be enforced, it would be done on a piecemeal basis, the same method that had already proved ineffective in the case of *Exsurge Domine.*

Aleander was frankly bewildered by Albert's refusal, for he gave the back of his hand to an office that would have made him indisputably the most powerful person in Germany next to the Emperor. Had he thought more carefully, Aleander would have pointed in his dispatch to Albert's timerity and to the hoard of "Lutherans" who were his advisers, for a memorandum from Capito lay behind Albert's uncharacteristic refusal to add another title to his already encumbered name. Capito had in his patron a ready subject upon whom to work his wiles. Albert was so frightened by the appearance in Worms of the *Bundschuh*, the symbol of the peasant rebels, that he and others pressured Charles V into reconsidering the whole matter in a special committee of the Diet. And Capito played upon precisely this sort of selfish fear when he advised Albert to decline the inquisitorship. "Whoever wishes to advise my most gracious Lord whether he should accept the Legation at this time," he wrote, "should consider what such a charge would contain in burdens, inconvenience, work, and cost, and whether such an acceptance by His Electoral Grace would carry commensurate honor and profit. . . ."

Stating the issue in this manner led inevitably to Albert's refusal. The memorandum contained thirteen main points with various subpoints in support of each. "First," Capito began, "never in human memory has there been established in Germany a legation from Rome more dangerous than this would be." Then he argued that it was well-nigh impossible to quash the reform movement by any means. Toward the end of the memorandum he returned to the main point:

> *Seventh*: My lord can expect very little or no honor from the legateship, on the contrary shame and public hatred.
> *Eighth*: I do not know what profit is to be expected from it, although I clearly see definite losses and expenses that it will not be easy to recover.

---

[39] *Ibid.*, p. 30, and Kalkoff, *Die Entstehung des Wormser Edikts. Eine Geschichte des Wormser Reichstages vom Standpunkt des Lutherischen Frages* (Leipzig, 1913), pp. 248-249. Aleander to Albert, ca. 15 May 1521. Adolf Wrede, ed., *Deutsche Reichstagsakten unter Kaiser Karl V. Deutsche Reichstagsakten, Jüngere Reihe* (Gotha, 1896), II, 640. Kalkoff, *Depeschen*, p. 200.

1. It is well-known what expenses are incurred for reputable men of learning. For one would require not fewer than four or five learned theologians, or more, who know well how to write and speak not only from books but also from history and experience. 2. In the same manner some jurists, secretaries, and others who know and have mastered Roman customs, all of which people require expensive maintenance. 3. And then, at least at this time, there is not much profit from resources and concessions, and even if they were in consideration, at the present time they do not yield a third of what goes to Rome. *Ninth*: It is easy to comprehend what reason for war and attack upon my gracious lord might be created from such a legateship.

Capito closed by suggesting that there might be other means of ending the religious controversy, but he did not specify them. He concluded that it would be wiser to enlist all Germany's secular and ecclesiastical authorities in enforcing the Edict of Worms than to accept sole responsibility for the task.[40] And so Capito had Albert return to just the sort of considerations that made it impossible a year earlier to enforce *Exsurge Domine*.

Capito knew his man. There was no appeal here to transcendent duty or service, and Albert gave just the selfish reasons he learned from Capito when he refused the office. Aleander was checked again. Albert in fact wished to disassociate himself completely from the Edict of Worms. An edict of this nature normally required the signature of the Archbishop of Mainz as chancellor of the Empire, but Albert never signed it. It appeared rather over the signatures of the vice-chancellors for Germany and Burgundy. Capito's hand can be seen here too. "Today Luther's books were burned. . . in a public fire," he reported to Spalatin on May 29. "My prince left; he cautiously wishes to have no part in this tragedy." [41] Capito lamed the Edict of Worms before it was publicly pronounced. He assured there would be no central enforcing apparatus by turning the Archbishop of Mainz against it.

Room to maneuver expanded the farther that Capito and his patron travelled from Worms. At the Diet, he was but one adviser to one prince, however important that prince was. But upon returning

---

[40] "Ratschlag, ob die Legation mein gnedigsten Hern, dem cardinal erzbischof und churfursten von Mentz, sy anzunemen. . . ," edited by Herrmann, *Evangelische Bewegung, Beilage V*, pp. 212-216.

[41] Wrede, *Deutsche Reichstagsakten*, II, 640 n. 3. Hekelius, *Manipulus Primus*, p. 60. In his dispatch of May 26, Aleander declared that Albert signed the Edict twice! Kalkoff, *Depeschen*, pp. 206.

to Mainz, or to his other residence in Halle, Albert was insulated from competing voices. The question now remained whether the Administrator of Halberstadt and the Archbishop of Mainz and Magdeburg would publish and enforce the Edict of Worms within his own considerable territories. In June, Cochlaeus, who was belatedly becoming suspicious of Capito, wrote Aleander from Frankfurt, "The Imperial Edict has not yet been published here" in a city scarcely a day's ride from Mainz itself. But a few weeks later Aleander received a letter from Capito in which he declared, "The Prince has convened his counts and vassals; he is working through representatives with the temporal princes and intends to act with his whole heart. . . ." According to Capito some negotiations already had been concluded successfully. "The Counts of Mansfeld, who have been very much favoring Luther to this point, have promised every effort, and that whoever they catch from that faction will be punished with the utmost severity." If this letter were to be believed, even Capito had experienced a sudden awakening of a sense of duty. He reported that Albert commissioned him to treat with the city council of Magdeburg, which he "persuaded to promise nightly vigils and a secret search with great diligence to track down the authors" of an outburst of iconoclasm. "I am already thoroughly in this tragedy that I was formerly fleeing out of zeal for tranquillity," he proclaimed.

Any skepticism Aleander may have felt about Capito's professed change of heart would have been understandable, especially when he read the last paragraph of Capito's letter. There he received instructions to forward the letters of provision for the provostship of St. Thomas either to Strasbourg or to Mainz.[42] Distance seemingly encouraged Capito's tendency to duplicity in dealing with Aleander, for he had no intention of suggesting that Albert enforce the Edict of Worms even within his own jurisdiction. On August 4 he reported to Zwingli that Albert had repeated his injunction against the Minorites' attacking Luther from the pulpit, and had commanded them instead to "hold firm to preaching the evangelical truth purely and simply, without brutal slander."[43] At the end of the month he composed a letter to Charles V in which Albert flatly refused to publish the Edict of Worms itself. He said he had received it, and the accompanying instructions, but complained,

---

[42] Friedensburg, *ZKG*, XVIII, 112, 115; XVI, 497-499.
[43] *ZW*, VII, 465-466.

Now very few princes and authorities, in so far as I know, have
published the mandate, much less dared to enforce it vigorously
in practice. And now disloyalty, sacrilege, libellous tracts and well-
nigh public uproars and mass meetings of the opposition grow more
and more frequent. . . . Out of fear for that reason, were I to publish
and proclaim the edict of Your Imperial Majesty but he unable to
bring it to a conclusion and to obtain action in support of it (which
appears to me truly impossible) . . . then the high name and imperial
[dignity] of Your Imperial Majesty . . . would be diminished and our
enemies strengthened, which would deeply distress me as a loyal
Electoral Prince. I have also determined that this discord and licen-
tiousness cannot surely be ended with force and other such means
without shocking desolation. . . . I have accordingly decided to remain
silent in this matter. . . .[44]

Not even Leo X's direct command in October moved the Archbishop of Mainz. On this occasion Capito responded more artfully.
He had Albert recommend Johannes Faber for a benefice, because
he was "on the side of the church not only in appearances and words
. . . but also in deeds and with his pen, by which he lives not meanly." [45] Perhaps the irony of the commendation was not lost on Capito,
who composed both it and Albert's policy of studied inaction.

Capito's motives for continuing to protect Luther were the same
after the Diet as before it. On December 20, 1521, at the height of a
particularly stormy period in their relationship, he protested to
Luther, "While promising security to my prince, I accomplished everything on your behalf, so that anything against you was resolved
too late among the Germans." [46] Inasmuch as one man could "accomplish everything" in such an important matter, he was right. At the
very least, he and his pliant master made a shambles of Aleander's
mission to Germany. And yet he was not being merely clever by
emphasizing to Charles V what a dangerous undertaking it would be
to seek to enforce the Edict of Worms. The very thought of religious
warfare horrified him. He did not need to be a "Lutheran" in order to
defend Luther. He was in fact still an Erasmian humanist. On April
23, 1521, Hartmann von Halwill, one of his students in Basel, wrote
him, "Now at last I know your most prudent advice, for you wish to
become involved with neither faction, especially not with the side
that may have sinned . . . ." And which side was that? "If Luther's

---

[44] Edited by Kalkoff, *Capito*, *Beilage VI*, 140-141.
[45] Herrmann, *Evangelische Bewegung*, *Beilage VI*, 218-219. The request to help
Faber came from Johannes Brassicanus on February 7. Th. B., I, 34.
[46] *WABr*, II, 418.

affair tends toward tumult," Halwill continued, "what good and true Christian would encourage his party, when Christ himself decreed nothing more than peace, and charity toward the neighbor?" These apparently strange sentiments for one who was working at that moment to block every attempt to stamp out the young Reformation movement were Capito's thoughts. Halwill learned them from Hedio, who remained in Mainz during the Diet of Worms.[47] In 1521 Capito differed from his own mentor, Erasmus, only by virtue of being involved actively in the hard affairs of the religious dispute.

He in fact revealed the practical sort of reform he had in mind when he wrote Zwingli on August 4, 1521. He probably knew of Zwingli's activities in Zurich, and although he did not mention them, his letter amounted to a word of caution. "The memory of you . . . comforts me," he wrote, "when I have seen so many disturbances under the guise of faith. For you are truly among the rare Christians, ignorant of pretence." He deplored the direction that the reform movement was taking. "And now Luther's sycophants are splitting up and being torn into many pieces. The sophists introduce a new division: some question everything, turn everything into a contest of words; others, seized, reach out after frantic people, chiefly friars, so that a good part of the masses do their best for the barbaric monks more frequently. . . . Oh, ill-advised rashness; oh, bitter piety!" In Capito's judgment, the followers of Luther were doubly guilty of the same crime of which he earlier accused the schoolmen: they created divisiveness in a religion of brotherly love, and they drew the common people into their wranglings. He saw reform far differently from Luther. Throughout his letter to Zwingli he did not mention a single doctrinal point. His paramount concern was for the maintenance of peace and order, as he revealed while defending his post. "To be the one who must preserve the Christian community is, to be sure, an important position: the received ways are to be improved, not overthrown." [48] Capito still had in mind the program of moral reform and inward piety that he professed in Basel. That program required peace, and it led him to oppose the

---

[47] Herrmann, *Evangelische Bewegung, Beilage IV*, 211-212. Halwill included greetings from Hedio. Compare Capito to Luther, 4 December 1520, *WABr*, II, 222, "Sunt, qui verentur, ne ista turba omnis imago pietatis obliteretur. Nam tua forte sinistre, ut fit, accipiunt."

[48] *ZW*, VII, 465-466.

use of force against Luther, as well as to question Luther himself.

However badly things had gone from his viewpoint, Capito had still to suffer the genuine crisis of his years at Mainz. The Indulgence Controversy and the growth of the reform party had a disastrous impact upon Albert's finances. So, on September 8 he tried to replenish his treasury by opening at Halle a new relic collection from which the penitent could receive marvelous indulgences and he enormous profits. Luther was furious when he heard of it, and he was incredulous when Spalatin urged him to follow the moderate examples of Capito and Erasmus. "The opinion of neither Capito nor Erasmus moves me in the least!" he responded. He intended to reply to the renewed sale of indulgences with the treatise *Wider den Abgott zu Halle*, which he completed by October 7.[49] Capito was suddenly confronted with the possibility of an explosion from the Wartburg that would destroy his mediating policy when his patron heard of it.

His sole objective in the last months of 1521 was to prevent Luther from attacking Albert in print. In late September he wrote Luther a letter he never sent. Without mentioning the reliquary, he asked Luther not to attack erring and immoral ecclesiastical princes "by name." Even Christ, he wrote, criticized the Pharisees only as a general group and not as individuals. He even threatened to withdraw his support for Luther at court if he assaulted the Archbishop of Mainz. Although he concluded his letter by maintaining that he "would assuredly never have been against Luther" and with the declaration that all measures against his party had been "attempted half-heartedly thus far," he clearly warned that any outburst could force him to the other side. "In truth, the battle is becoming more and more violent daily . . . and you seem to act ever more intemperately, as if you were forgetful of duty and profession; for this reason, many—including those by no means a little hostile to Rome—confess to be deserting you."[50]

Perhaps he was trying to pressure Luther and then thought better of it. Rather than send this letter, he went to Wittenberg to plead his case with Melanchthon. He and the humanist physician Heinrich

---

[49] *WABr*, II, 387. On the reliquary see Albrecht Wolters, *Der Abgott zu Halle, 1521-1542* (Bonn, 1877), esp. pp. 14-22, and the excellent discussion of the entire incident from Luther's viewpoint by Gottfried Krodel, "Wider den Abgott zu Halle," *Lutherjahrbuch*, XXXIII (1966), 9-87.

[50] *WABr*, II, 393-394. On December 20 Capito wrote Luther they had not corresponded for "a long time." *Ibid.*, II, 416-419.

Stromer arrived on October 1 and stayed for two days.[51] Capito spent most of the visit in private conversation with Melanchthon, but the important exchange occurred in Stromer's presence. After being led to their quarters, Capito and Stromer discussed topics of general interest with Melanchthon and Jonas, until Melanchthon took them to his home for privacy. Then Capito came to the point. Melanchthon, he charged, must see that Luther did not attack Albert publicly. Melanchthon responded that he was unable to control his colleague, who was being led by the Holy Spirit. Moreover, he said, the impious could not avoid being hurt when they acted against the Gospel. Capito and Stromer replied with another appeal to moderation and asked if Albert could not be admonished "privately, in order to spare Mainz." If not, there could be a "catastrophe." Capito punctuated this thinly-veiled threat by showing Melanchthon a copy of the Edict of Worms, which he said might be published in Albert's territories. In his report to Spalatin, Melanchthon admitted that it "could be thrown against us forcefully." To Capito, he suggested that the "catastrophe" already existed in the person of Albert of Mainz.[52]

In spite of Melanchthon's bravado, the mission was a success. On the basis of Melanchthon's report of the meeting, Spalatin held up publication of the *Wider den Abgott zu Halle*, much to Luther's irritation. Spalatin was indeed skeptical about the gullible Jonas' report, on Capito's testimony, that Albert had mended his ways and was about to begin preaching in his own cathedral. But he still favored muzzling Luther.[53] Frustrated in his attempt to denounce Albert in print, Luther wrote the Archbishop a strong personal letter. He told Albert that he had already written twice about indulgences but would follow the Biblical injunction and write yet a third time, on this occasion in German. He demanded specifically that the Archbishop close the reliquary and leave the married priests in his territories free to preach. He bluntly added an ultimatum: if he did not receive a satisfactory reply within fourteen days, he would follow Paul's advice on evil doers and "let fly a game with the Cardinal

---

[51] The dates of the visit are established by Albert Burer to Beatus Rhenanus, 19 October 1521, Horawitz and Hartfelder, *Briefwechsel des Beatus Rhenanus*, p. 245, and from Felix Ulscenius to Capito, 5 October 1521, Th. B., I, 190-190(v). Burer and Ulscenius were students in Wittenberg.

[52] *CR*, I, 463-464.

[53] *WABr*, II, 402-403. *CR*, I, 486. Gustav Kawerau, ed., *Briefwechsel des Justus Jonas* (Halle, 1884), II, 79.

of Mainz of which there may be little mistake." [54] Luther was so
certain that Albert would respond badly or not at all that he took the
occasion of his hasty trip to Wittenberg in early December to press
once again for the publication of his treatise. On December 5 he
complained bitterly to Spalatin about the failure of a number of his
essays to appear, including *Wider den Abgott zu Halle*. But Spalatin
was by then convinced that Luther must be restrained, and he countered by reporting Capito's tales about Albert's plans to preach.
"I know the plans of Satan, my Spalatin," Luther replied. He would
believe that the Archbishop of Mainz was preaching when he saw
it and not before. He demanded that Spalatin allow the attack on
Albert to be published. [55]

Once again Capito had prepared the ground well. Luther entrusted
Melanchthon with the task of finding a messenger to bear his letter
to Albert, but Melanchthon had become part of the plot to prevent an
explosion. He found a courier on December 11, but he posted the
letter care of Capito, rather than directly to Albert. He especially
urged Capito to guarantee that the Archbishop read Luther's letter
privately, quietly, and when in good spirits. Above all, Melanchthon
added, Albert must respond well to Luther, for he was acting with
the hand of God in this matter. [56]

"I cannot admire your prudence sufficiently, you who sent such a
circumspect letter to me," Capito replied to Melanchthon; "you
could have done nothing more obliging." [57] Their precautions
notwithstanding, the mediating policy scarcely survived. Albert
stormed and raged when he first read Luther's letter. He was especially furious with Capito, who, he knew, maintained communications
with Luther and on whose advice he was risking the displeasure of
Pope and Emperor on Luther's behalf. Albert's final reaction hung
in the balance during the night of December 20. Fearing the worst,
Capito that evening composed a letter in which he tried desperately
to mollify Luther no matter what Albert did. "I am delighted by
your letter," Capito declared. "You may accomplish with it what
I had attempted this far." He urged Luther to remember, however,
that Albert was easily led astray because he "was born a prince and

---

[54] *WABr*, II, 406-408.
[55] *Ibid.*, II, 409-410; 412.
[56] *CR*, I, 464-465, properly dated in Otto Clemen, ed., *Melanchthons Briefwechsel*,
(Leipzig, 1926), I, 164.
[57] *Ibid.*, I, 174-175.

is young." He recounted that Albert opened the reliquary in his absence, and he maintained that incarcerating a priest who married "some whore" from Switzerland was necessary to maintain public order. But, now, he reported, Albert has "turned himself to reading sacred things, to hearing evangelical sermons, and to discharging the primary duties of a Bishop. . . ." Luther must think before he acted. "I beg so much, do not desecrate anything, do not make public what is going well, nor the fine beginning . . . quite the contrary, you would destroy what is occurring with a public outburst; do not sin because of strong and intractable zeal, and, for my sake, smoothly condone at least one thing . . . ." He even pledged at the end of his letter, "Finally, so I may reveal myself fully to you, if the courage and spirit of the Prince should not agree . . . then I would wear out the reason for my being at this loathsome court, nor would I be a slave to four minds any longer. . . . "[58]

The threat to resign his position saved the day. The Archbishop capitulated the next morning. He thanked Luther for the letter of reproval and assured him that the matters that caused him to write had "long ago been remedied." Albert also confessed that he was far from a model Christian and begged Luther to remember that "I do not deny that I am in need of God's grace, since I am a poor, sinful man who can sin and err and who sins and errs daily; I know well that without God's grace there is nothing good in me, and just as well that I am a worthless, stinking piece of dung. . . ." Capito's hand showed through in Albert's words, but he still worried for the future. He posted Albert's reply to Melanchthon and added a covering letter. "It will be your concern," he wrote, "that you do not extinguish a growing spirit by provoking the lover of peace and much leisure."[59]

Capito blundered once in this delicate affair. Rather than allow Albert's response to stand by itself, he sent his cover letter of December 20, with a short postscript in which he again begged Luther to be tolerant.[60] On January 13 Luther wrote Melanchthon that he had received the Archbishop's letter. He would have been happy if it had been alone, he reported, but Capito's letter made him suspicious.

---

[58] On the threat to leave Albert's service, see Andreas Cratander to Capito, 20 September 1521, Th. B., I, 188, and Capito to Erasmus, 14 October 1521, *EE*, IV, 596-598.

[59] *WABr*, II, 420-421. Clemen, *Melanchthons Briefwechsel*, I, 175.

[60] *WABr*, II, 419.

"I was wishing there would be an end to impiety, and that orator pleads the cause of impiety while he tells the Bishop to confess his personal sins. . . ." Luther closed with a simple command. "See that the book against the Bishop of Mainz is published and make it well known. . . ." [61] In spite of Luther's wishes, the book never appeared. The work with Melanchthon and Spalatin had been too well done.

Capito must have posted his and Albert's letters to Luther with a sense of relief. He had succeeded in getting Luther to admonish the Archbishop privately; he had ridden out the storm of the night of December 20; he had secured from Albert just the response to Luther that he wished. But his personal crisis was just beginning. In his letter of December 20 he placed the best possible construction on his own activities. "I acted (what would I gloss over in your presence?) deviously but piously," he wrote Luther, "and I brought human diligence to the enlargement of the ministry of the faith." He could not believe that he had done anything truly reprehensible or that his objectives were in the least ignoble. "I truly desire nothing other than the progress of the Gospel and the security of my undeserving Prince . . . and that all lawlessness in writing might be stopped, because I fear that the future will not be without an endless sacrifice in the blood of Christians," he explained.[62]

In this letter he gave Luther the fullest and most persuasive statement of his position. What he did not guess was that Luther recognized it, and that he would denounce it. He replied on January 17, 1522 in a letter in which he for the first time referred to Capito by his middle name—Fabricius, or artificer. "However much your Cardinal's letter may have raised my spirits, yours knocked them down again, my Fabricius," Luther began. "It is, my Fabricius, truly one thing to praise and extenuate vice, another to exercise care benignly and sweetly," was his response to Capito's urgings that he proceed with Christian charity. "The most important thing of all is to tell what is right and what is not right. . . ." Capito could not have read the letter without knowing that he and Luther were in fundamental disagreement. "Even the Gentiles wish evil on friends who flatter the vices of friends. . . . In fact, whom did Christ not offend, or whom did he not accuse? Yes, the spirit of truth accuses, it does not flatter. In truth, it accuses not just some but the whole world." There were, thus, matters of faith about which the truth

[61] *Ibid.*, II, 424; 427.
[62] *Ibid.*, II, 417-418.

could be surely known. "Assume everything from our charity, but certainly fear our faith everywhere," Luther wrote. "I wish you well, my Fabricius, and do not doubt my courage to be candid with you. The thing . . . is itself a great and sacred thing, which we are not allowed to accommodate, for fear that we would esteem brothers and sisters more highly than Christ." [63]

Luther's declaration that "The most important thing of all is to tell what is right and what is not right. . ." struck at the very foundations of Capito's policy of accommodation. Because Luther believed that the truth of essential articles of faith could be known, he could speak and let events take their course. Because Capito did not, he could not. During his visit to Wittenberg in October 1521 he and Melanchthon took a walk before dinner. Their discussion soon turned to the problem of authority. According to Melanchthon's report,

> Soon after, while we were discussing things pertaining to the papacy, he freely condoned Luther for what he had written against the Roman Pontiff. But all the same, he was claiming this: we should not have been taking away from the church the authority to define and to prescribe; otherwise in the future someone may interpret the obscure Scriptures according to his own whims. There would be as many teachings as teachers; nor would it follow any order.

Melanchthon reported that he gave Capito Luther's reply, that the Scriptures were perfectly clear on essential matters of faith. But Capito was insistent; "but it is impossible to deny that they are rich," he responded; "it would finally be the voice of disputation" that would settle controverted issues.[64] There it was again—the old humanistic objection to disputations. But here there was something more to it. He was objecting to the wrangling that the evangelical movement brought in its wake, to be sure, just as he objected to the wrangling of the scholastic theologians. But to his mind such disputatiousness was more than merely offensive; it was also foolishly so, because he doubted that the truth could be surely known in any event. Consequently, some authority—in this case, the Pope—was needed to settle issues and to keep the religious peace.

Can there be any surprise, then, that when asked whether he found

---

[63] *Ibid.*, II, 430-434. To Luther's query "whom did Christ not offend," compare Capito's description of Christ as "exemplum modestiae et pacis" in a letter to Melanchthon, 21 December 1521. Clemen, *Melanchthons Briefwechsel*, I, 175.
[64] *CR*, I, 464.

anything objectionable in Luther's teachings, Capito "said smoothly,
so as not to commit himself to objecting, that he approved of Luther's
teachings, except that there might be something on the free will that
would be open to dispute at the outset"? [65] During the conversation
with Melanchthon he anticipated precisely the two points upon
which his mentor, Erasmus, formally broke with Luther in the
Diatribe on the Free Will. And he anticipated them in precisely the
manner of Erasmus. Even in questioning Luther's views on the
freedom of the will, he spoke with a certain diffidence, for, just as
with Erasmus, this was not the point at all. As for so many humanists,
the real issue was whether general truths—even religious truths—
could be known with any certainty. In Capito's case, as in the cases of
many others, the basic skepticism of the humanist movement brought
with it, ironically enough, a tendency to affirm human freedom even
in the presence of God.[66]

The policy that Capito followed at Mainz thus grew naturally
from his Erasmian intellectual and religious values. If, as a reform-
minded, humanistic scholar at Basel, he condemned the scholastic
theologians for their divisiveness, he could hardly approve Luther's
intransigence. Luther's followers in particular drew his anger in late
1521. In October he wrote Erasmus,

> The Lutherans become more mad, more insolent, and more arrogant
> about everything; they snap like dogs at anything; they revile everyone
> to his face with barbaric impudence; they openly scorn every intel-
> ligence except their own. Some time ago, I interceded with them and
> begged them not to inveigh violently like that and not to defend
> their cause with insults; and I especially entreated them to refrain
> from captious criticism of petty points in the authors, for so much
> arrogance powerfully alienates from them the unbiased judgments of
> men.[67]

Through a student at Wittenberg, he was well informed about the
rising tumult under Carlstadt's leadership during Luther's absence.
Later that year he wrote Carlstadt,

> Where will all this lead? It is too much that, placed in a high castle
> in the most eminent erudition, you would, as it were, look out in

---

[65] *Ibid.*, I, 464.

[66] This is not to deny the oft-expressed view of Kristeller, *Renaissance Thought*,
pp. 3-23, that humanism was not a philosophical school one of whose main tenets
was the freedom of the will. It is rather to affirm the argument of Bouwsma,
Venice, pp. 1-11, that their aversion to general propositions almost necessarily
implied some degree of human freedom.

[67] *EE*, IV, 596-597.

despair and prohibit blundering people snatching at the pulpit, who by false pretext lost the true fruit of the Gospel, who disturb true and Christian peace, virulently corrupt the simplicity of the listeners with aberrations, disturb us servants of the Magistrate, call for the harrassment of our studies, our piety, our inclination to the functions of religion.[68]

The reference to Luther in the Wartburg was obvious. In Capito's judgment he had opened Pandora's Box and fled to safety while disorders destroyed true religion.

And yet Capito was so true to his principles that he could not join those who would put Luther down with force. In sum, he believed the advice that he was giving the Archbishop, that any forceful action against Luther would result in war. At just the moment his judgment of Luther and his followers was at its lowest, he wrote Erasmus, "Someday, far from now, the decree of Emperor Charles will be different. . . . Christ will undoubtedly make an end to these evils. Certainly no one can prohibit preaching and reading the gospels; nothing is accomplished by burning books." [69] He saw clearly that the violence of the reform movement encouraged violence in reaction. "There are those who wish the restoration of law everywhere," he wrote Carlstadt. "There are also the opposite, who on the contrary are zealous for betrayal and passion. . . ." [70] What Capito really favored was peace, within which piety and morals might be restored; what he really feared was force, in the presence of which piety and morals would be destroyed.

Self-serving though it sometimes was, Capito's policy at Mainz had its own nobility, if consistency be regarded as noble. Melanchthon concluded the report of his conversation with Capito with the remark that he was "a good man" but that "he is different from our kind of theologian." [71] How right Melanchthon was. In the end Capito's skepticism made of him a religious elitist who believed that the ignorant masses must be led by the more learned men of letters and the established authorities. "I do not say that the work of Christ

---

[68] Simler'sche Sammlung. S. 5., fol. 48. Reel 953, Foundation for Reformation Research, St. Louis, Missouri. The reports from Ulscenius began on January 13, 1521. By October 5 Capito was sending him money regularly. Th. B., I, 190(v). Some of the letters are published by Theodor Kolde, ed., "Gleichzeitige Berichte über die Wittenberger Unruhen im Jahre 1521 und 1522," *Zeitschrift für Kirchengeschichte*, V (1882), 325-333. Capito's responses are not extant.

[69] *EE*, IV, 597-598.

[70] Simler'sche Sammlung. S. 5., fol. 48.

[71] *CR*, I, 465, properly dated by Clemen, *Melanchthons Briefwechsel*, I, 159.

should be abandoned," he wrote Luther in 1520, "but much should be tolerated for the sake of the crasser common people." [72] In mid-1521 he approvingly reported Archbishop Albert's declaration that he spared "neither labor nor expenses" in the thought that public worship was "like a lure" that would draw people to "a true, more simple worship" in time.[73] Capito still had in mind the reforms that he recommended in 1517 when he republished Clichtove's *Elucidatorium Ecclesiasticum*, and these reforms had nothing to do with teaching the masses true doctrine. He came to Mainz as an Erasmian humanist, and he remained one through the epoch-making events of 1520 and 1521. But his humanistic religious values led him to foster Luther's reformation movement in spite of himself.

---

[72] *WABr*, II, 223.

[73] Capito to Bonifacius [Wolfhart], [mid-1521], Kirchenarchiv Basel, 25a, fol. 244. Quoting Albert, "Summatim exerceo caeremonias omnes et universam scaenam devotionis, neque laboribus neque sumptibus ferendis abstinens, quo tanquam illicebris quibusdam invitem ad verum cultum simplicium mentes."

CHAPTER FOUR

THE TRANSFORMATION

Through most of his tenure at Mainz, Capito did not believe that the theological issues at stake between Luther and his opponents were worth the rising struggle he saw about him. He was thus left to make such increasingly irrelevant appeals to moderation that Melanchthon on one occasion dismissed them as "a funny teaching." Events were rapidly outdistancing Capito's plan for a peaceful, undogmatic religious renewal on the model of Erasmus' *philosophia Christi*. He closed his letter to Erasmus of October 1521 with a warning against Aleander, and with a dictum that indicated his dismay: "*Devoranda nobis multa videntur*. The fates will find a way." [1] The lines between the two sides were hardening rapidly in late 1521, and one casualty was Capito's policy of accommodation. His fates decreed a conversion.

Melanchthon first, in private conversation, and then Luther, more insistently in a letter that was soon published, forced Capito to face the theological issues of the Reformation. He may well have felt aggrieved upon reading Luther's letter of January 1522. Its tone was certainly harsher than he thought he merited. Yet it appears that Luther struck a nerve when he condemned Capito's policy of accommodation, for on March 27 Albert Burer, a student at Wittenberg, reported an extraordinary encounter to Beatus Rhenanus:

> On the fourteenth of March, Fabricius Capito came to Wittenberg to reconcile himself, so they say, with Luther, whom something in his letters had offended to such an extent that they say he was called a virulent beast by Martin. Yes, there is already a beautiful harmony between them. . . . Those things that displeased Capito are beginning to satisfy him. He heard Martin preaching in the Wittenberg parish where we caught sight of him by chance. [2]

There is no record of the two men's conversations, but they probably centered on Luther's insistence that "The most important thing of all is to tell what is right and what is not right," and upon Capito's

---

[1] *CR*, I, 452. Properly dated mid-September 1521 by Clemens, *Melanchthons Briefwechsel*, I, 159. *EE*, IV, 598.

[2] Horawitz and Hartfelder, *Briefwechsel des Beatus Rhenanus*, pp. 303-304.

admonition to proceed moderately. As events proved, the two men were not far apart on the latter point.

Capito chose a particularly critical moment to visit Luther. Wittenberg was in an uproar in early 1522 as mobs roamed the streets, smashing images, harrassing monks, and even throwing stones at those who said devotions to the Virgin Mary. Luther returned in early March at the invitation of the city council. He donned traditional clerical vestments, mounted the pulpit, and exhorted his followers to remember their obligation to love the neighbor. Only established authority had the right to act coercively, he declared. No message could have been more appealing to Capito. And he told others of what he had learned. A month later, while en route to Basel to see another edition of his Chrysostom translation through Cratander's press, he encountered an acquaintance of Agrippa of Nettesheim, from whom he inquired what Agrippa thought about Luther. "Moved by such talk," he wrote Agrippa that evening, "I wanted to write to you while drinking in the tavern. . . . And it is what it concerns you to know, that is, the state of the Germans." [3]

This letter provides the first evidence of Capito's conversion to the evangelical movement that began with the visit to Luther in March 1522. To be sure, he still disliked Luther's followers, and he still deplored the divisiveness of the reform movement. He reported that

> The Wittenberg Lutherans have been instructing in this manner: First, whatever they may have been surmising from evangelical truth, they teach with loose words to be observed. Let me suggest a few: whoever, they say, does not eat meat and eggs and that sort of thing on Fridays shall not be a Christian. Whoever confesses during Lent shall have no part in the grace of God. Whoever thinks works of piety to be something excludes himself from the path of salvation, and much of that sort.

Yet he seems to have regained his approval for Luther. Speaking perhaps of himself, he wrote that

> Learned men had written to Luther; they urged that he remain openly steadfast. He is therefore now at Wittenberg; he preaches daily; he plucks at his men; he rebukes the rash innovaters who had not maintained respect for the simplicity of the people; nor does he, however, omit contributing what he contributed at first. Already the

---

[3] *Henrici Cornelii Agrippae ab Nettesheym armatae equitis aurati, et iuris utriusque ac medicinae Doctor Opera* (Lugduni, n. d.), II, 729-730.

people are flowing together into a procession and continuing on to the liberty of Christ.[4]

This refound approval for Luther was so powerful that Capito never again allowed his disapproval of Luther's followers to color his attitude toward Luther himself.

It is certainly true that Luther's firm stand against the disorders in Wittenberg accounts for much of Capito's new appreciation of him. Tactical considerations were still in his mind, as he wrote Agrippa, "and now the authorities everywhere may come to know what a light and easy thing Christianity is and how completely a patient Christian differs from a seditious revolutionary." [5] Yet the letter also reveals that, although his old concerns for peace and order remained, he was beginning to have a theological understanding of Luther. Thus, his criticism of the "rash innovaters" turned upon their disregard for the *libertas Christi*, as well as for peace. And he praised Luther not only because he reestablished order but also because "Already the people are flowing together into a procession and continuing on to the liberty of Christ." To Agrippa he also wrote that the great popular issues of the reform movement were the cultus and the position of the papacy, but he thought that learned men could relegate such matters to the realm of nonessentials. The truly critical question was what Capito now called simply "the Gospel," and on it he thought there was broad agreement, or at least that agreement could be secured. "There are those who do not work to have the Gospel torn away from men with rituals," he wrote; "nor do we of the Papal party intend to do so, with the exception that the rotting sycophants may have tried something." He reminded Agrippa, in regard to the Pope himself, "Now, while he may be the Antichrist and an enemy of the faith, just as Luther always makes Rome, he did not thereby deter you from the Gospel." To Capito's mind in April 1522, the sole problem with the reform movement was that "the common cause of the faith . . . was turned over to the judgment of the masses." [6]

He was, to be sure, still a religious elitist who thought that the learned should settle religious issues quietly among themselves out

---

[4] *Ibid.*, II, 730-731. The letter will not bear the construction placed upon it by Charles G. Nauert, Jr., *Agrippa and the Crisis of Renaissance Thought*. LV, *Illinois Studies in the Social Sciences* (Urbana, Ill., 1965), pp. 160-161, who argues that Capito completely opposed Luther.

[5] *Agrippae Opera*, II, 730.

[6] *Ibid.*, II, 730-731.

of respect for public order. Yet, with the visit to Wittenberg and this letter to Agrippa, he had taken a first step toward converting to the evangelical movement. He seems to have come to agree with Luther that it was possible to know the truth of theological assertions without the authority of pope, church, or tradition. The evidence of this one letter is too slim to establish the additional possibility that he had appropriated Luther's views on faith and the Scriptures. On the other hand, Burer's declaration that "Those things that displeased Capito are beginning to satisfy him" certainly did not refer to Luther's intemperance. Consequently, considering his subsequent actions, it is likely that in March-April 1522 he found himself for the first time willing to entertain Luther's theological views, as well as a general impulse toward reform of the church.

Capito's actions during the following year attest to his new theological understanding of Luther. Although he continued to consider himself a member of the "Papal party," he dedicated himself even more resolutely to Luther's defence. In June, while he was at the Diet of Nuremberg at Archbishop Albert's side, he learned that Jacob Stunica had attacked Erasmus as "the standard-bearer and prince of the Lutherans." He quickly wrote his old mentor a long letter in which he unconsciously revealed his own new position:

> They are talking here about a book from Erasmus against Luther. I have not yet seen nor do I believe you to have dared what you would have rebuked in me. My Prince advises you not to respond to Stunica, and I urge the same on you. Toward whichever side you might turn, the other will take offense. There are those who prefer that you turn aside to the better, rather than the more successful, party, because the latter wavers and may be faint-hearted; the former, on the other hand, with its roots resting securely upon Christ the rock, will proceed from strength to strength as time goes on; and yet it is more secure to be free and without public obligations and out of spear range, if indeed we look to ourselves rather than the common good.

Capito feared that if Erasmus responded to Stunica, he would turn against Luther. To his mind, Erasmus publicly neutral was better than Erasmus wrongly partisan.

A sense of confusion nevertheless pervades Capito's letter. On the one hand he could urge Erasmus to be silent for his own good. On the other hand, while cleaving to the "Papal party," he spoke of Luther's party as "resting securely upon Christ the rock." He concluded with the even more curious judgment that "In so far as it concerns religion, our world will either be Christian or it will shed the entire image of Christ; there is no third possibility." Does this remark mean that he was finally urging Erasmus to declare publicly for Luther? No, because he added, "Live well in the Lord, my Erasmus, and love Christ with public peace, as in fact you do." [7] The confusion that pervades Capito's letter is therefore genuine. He did believe Luther's party to be "the better," but, good Erasmian that he was, he could not believe that true reform or true religion would carry disorders and strife in their wake. Consequently, when he told Erasmus that only two religious alternatives lay before the world, he was looking desperately for the possibility that reform, along the lines of which Luther spoke, would occur without rancor.

It is not surprising, then, that at the same time he began more and more to dislike his post with the Archbishop of Mainz. He complained to Erasmus in August about rumors regarding Sickingen,

> The passion for fighting, for bloodshed, blaze up to be sure; all the conspiracies, all the leagues that have been declared, flame, and Christ, the author of peace, is used as a pretext everywhere. I long for the old security. I am, moreover, not out of the trap, caught, of course, with a prince to whom I am more pleasing than I would have wished.[8]

Although he remained in Albert's service until February 1523, he had made up his mind to leave by late January, when Hedio was forced to address a letter to him simply as the provost of St. Thomas, "wherever he may be." His immediate plans were in doubt. Hedio knew he intended to retire to his prebend, but there was some question whether he even had legitimate possession, in spite of having spent 120 ducats on a bribe. He was unaware that Aleander was then carrying a letter of papal provision, which stipulated that the Pope expected only continued zeal "in serving the peace, tranquillity, and order of the Catholic Church" in exchange for the provostship. But Aleander never sent the letter.[9] Still in Nuremberg in February,

---

[7] *EE*, V, 73-74. The letter will not bear the interpretation appropriated by Massaut, *Clichtove*, II, 377 n. 19, from Kalkoff, *Capito*, p. 112, that Capito was urging on Erasmus "a final commitment to the evangelical party." The difficulty comes in understanding the term, *imago Christi*, which Kalkoff has refer to Luther's evangelical religion.

[8] *EE*, V, 116.

[9] Herrmann, *Evangelische Bewegung, Beilage VII*, 221. Kalkoff, *Capito, Beilage VIII*, 145-146, for the letter of provision. Capito reported the bribe in *Antwurt*, sig. Piii.

Capito tried to secure provision through Johann Bader, a procurator of the Rota Romana, the highest papal court. For a time he planned to travel to Rome and press his case in person. But when he arrived in Strasbourg, he apparently discovered that the canons of St. Thomas would allow him to occupy his benefice without hindrance. He then decided, probably in late March, to sever his ties with Mainz, to settle in Strasbourg, and to continue to seek final legal possession through highly placed friends in Germany.[10]

The motives for Capito's move to Strasbourg at this time were entirely commonplace. He did not need to reside there in order to secure his benefice. By leaving Mainz he in fact gave up the influential position that persuaded Aleander to support him in the first place. Nor is there any evidence that Albert had suffered a change of heart that weakened Capito's position with him. Albert recalled him from Strasbourg three times, but he insisted upon being released. "I demanded it so urgently that he could not honestly and properly refuse," he reported to Erasmus in June 1523.[11] No high drama surrounded his move. At the end of his service to Albert he was caught, suspended over the seemingly unbridgeable gulf between the need to preserve public order and the obligation to follow the truth. He could not avoid being "Mr. Facing-Both-Ways" when he wrote Erasmus in August 1522 about Luther's response to Henry VIII's *Assertio*: "Luther slanderously replied to the Englishman with the harshest invectives," he announced. But, he added, "If we of the papal party were not more foolish and departing so much from the truth, the world would never tolerate so much impudent offense." [12]

Capito did not leave Mainz with the intention of declaring openly for the reform movement the moment he was safely in Strasbourg. He was simply sick of life at the court. "I have been shaken by more than half of my senses by all the troubles, all the plots, all the traps . . ." he wrote Erasmus in June 1523. A month later he declared, "Those

---

[10] Oecolampadius asked Capito to undertake a mission for him while he was in Rome. *BAO*, I, 218. For efforts within Germany, see Capito to Michael Sander, 24 April 1523, Th. B., II, 8-8(v). On his arrival in Strasbourg see Protocollum Wurmserianum. Archivum St. Thoman, 192, fol. 4(v), "Dominica Letare doctor Wolffgangus Capito incepit residentiam suam. . . ." From a transcript by M. Jean Rott.

[11] *EE*, V, 293. Kalkoff, *Capito*, pp. 124-125, and Herrmann, *Evangelische Bewegung*, pp. 102; 109, ignore this letter while arguing that Albert had suddenly decided to suppress Luther and that Capito consequently elected a prudent but precipitate withdrawl.

[12] *EE*, V, 116.

thoroughly annoying duties of the court . . . in these three years
exhausted the strength of a talent that was, as you know, already
less than modest and extremely meager." [13] He believed Luther's
evangelical message when he moved to Strasbourg, but he was not
yet a reformer. It was fitting that he again began to correspond with
Erasmus as he prepared to leave Albert's service. Faced with a dis-
maying and unpleasant situation, he was fleeing public responsibility
in order to return to the study of sacred letters that he once pursued
with Erasmus in Basel.

On the surface Strasbourg [14] seemed an ideal city for a scholar
who wished to retire to his studies, especially if his needs were
handsomely provided by the provostship of St. Thomas. It was a
prosperous city whose wealth was founded upon small manufactures
and trade on the Rhine, and it was a Free Imperial City whose obliga-
tions to Bishop and Emperor were minimal. But Capito was wrong if
he felt that he could in time avoid the religious controversy by
returning to private life. There was no escape even in Strasbourg,
he complained to Erasmus in June:

> And now truly there is yet a new tragedy. The Lutherans attack
> me with pictures and slanderous books. The papists on the other
> hand consider me . . . a complete Lutheran because of false testimonies,
> or, assuredly, the flatterers of Rome. And there are those who would
> freely give their ears to such sycophants, although I have never
> written a word about that affair and have never been interested enough
> to advise the cause of those who are zealous about changing things.

But these public attacks proved to be the least of his concerns. He
would have been better advised to worry about what was occurring
within the city, for Strasbourg was then approaching the first of a
series of crises that led finally to its enlisting with the evangelical
party. By the early 1520's the city's presses were widely distributing
Luther's tracts and sermons, and at least two preachers had already
lost their pulpits for preaching heretical notions.[15] Like Mainz,

---

[13] *Ibid.*, V, 293; 304.

[14] Among older works on the Reformation in Strasbourg, see Timotheus-
Wilhelm Röhrich, *Geschichte der Reformation im Elsass und besonders in Strassburg*
(Strassburg, 1830-1832), 3 vols.; Johannes Adam, *Evangelische Kirchengeschichte
der Stadt Strassburg bis zur Französischen Revolution* (Strassburg, 1922); Adolph
Baum, *Magistrat und Reformation in Strassburg bis 1529* (Strassburg, 1887). The most
recent and in many respects the best work is Miriam Usher Chrisman, *Strasbourg
and the Reform, A Study in the Process of Change* (New Haven, Conn., 1967).

[15] *EE*, V, 293. Chrisman, *Strasbourg*, pp. 98-100. Adam, *Evangelische Kirchengeschichte*, pp. 25-29.

Strasbourg gave Capito no opportunity to avoid the religious question.

The most important figure in these early disputes was Matthew Zell, preacher to the people in one of the cathedral's chapels. In a sermon in 1521 he denied that Luther was a heretic and announced that he would begin a series of sermons on the Letter to the Romans. Zell suddenly became such an immensely popular preacher that he tried to move to Geiler von Kaysersberg's pulpit in the nave, but the canons of the cathedral locked it. The Bishop of Strasbourg, William III of Hohenstein, warned Zell early in 1522, but the preacher, emboldened by his success, ignored him, and the eager crowds grew ever larger. Bishop William then urged the canons of the cathedral chapter to try Zell and to expel him, but they were intimidated by the crowds and refused. In August the Bishop announced to the city council that he intended to prosecute Zell on the basis of the Edict of Worms, and he ordered the preacher to appear before his vicar to answer twenty-four charges of heresy. In his defense, which he published a year later, Zell replied simply that he was bound to hold to the pure Word of God, even if Luther preached it. Now the city authorities took a hand. Zell's popular support frightened them, and so they advised the chapter to continue Zell in office so long as he preached only the Word of God. With that, the Bishop's efforts to remove Zell collapsed. On March 10 he protested the council's decision, but he declared that he would postpone the case for one year in view of the citizenry's threatening mood.[16]

Capito arrived in Strasbourg on the heels of the Bishop's capitulation. This was not the peace that he sought when he left Mainz. Feelings had risen to the point that Zell's case was being argued in the unhallowed confines of Strasbourg's beer halls. This was not the way that Capito felt the church should be reformed. Sometime between June 18 and July 6, he engaged Zell in conversation. According to his own later report, he told Zell that true preaching would "build a peace-making spirit with the words of Christ" but that the "bitterness, jealousy, and hate, as were evident at that time, are not a fruit of the Spirit but a shame to all respectability." He could not believe that Zell's sermons were the true Word of God, he said, because they

---

[16] On Zell, see William H. Klaustermeyer, "The Role of Matthew and Catherine Zell in the Strassburg Reformation" (Unpublished doctoral dissertation, Stanford University, 1965), esp. pp. 36-66 for early developments. See also Chrisman, *Strasbourg*, pp. 100-108.

caused "nothing but bitterness, rebellion, and perfidy among the people, under the shimmering facade of the Gospel . . ." whereas the mark of true preaching was that it "would also serve the same end as the Spirit of God, a Spirit of wisdom and understanding, a Spirit of council and strength, a Spirit of knowledge and of fear of the Lord, which also certainly leads us to the good order that Paul commended to the Colossians." Viewing the disorder about him, Capito told Zell that it would be better if he left Strasbourg for a time and preached somewhere else until peace was restored.[17]

Zell was of no mind to submit humbly to Capito when he had just stood up boldly to Bishop William's vicar. "Beloved Provost," he said, "you speak as one for whom the question was not very important, and who considers the Scriptures to be a work of art rather than a gift of God." Your understanding of the gospel "makes the Word of God insipid and powerless, and it becomes in your mouth a worldly wisdom, which is truly a darkness to God." On the contrary, added Zell, "we consider what we are obliged to do as servants of the Word and of Christian freedom; we do not look at what profit we might increase and maintain." Zell admitted that his preaching on the Letter to the Romans led to the charge that he "perhaps opened up the truth too quickly," but he demurred on the grounds that "the truth is never revealed too quickly." Zell was willing to grant Capito one point, that the gospel did not lead to tumult. The uproar that Capito saw about him was really the fault of those "hardened, impenitent, stiff-necked wolves who devour the worth of all preachers." He did not attack good order when he criticized the governors of the faith, Zell insisted. If bishops would "conduct themselves in all things as servants of God . . . then they would be truly honored from the heart as Apostles of Christ." Zell added that he knew it would be more pleasant to leave Strasbourg, but, he said, "how could I honorably desert the pious people . . .?"

Capito was astounded. "Master Matthew gave me such a measured answer that I could bring forth nothing more against him with honorable reasons. . . ." In essence, Zell's answer was the same that Capito received from Luther, but this time it succeeded. "I do not much care to struggle against God," he wrote five months later.[18]

<hr />

[17] *An den Hochwürdigen fürsten vnd herren Wilhelmen Bischoffen zu Strassburg . . . Entschuldigung D. Wolffgangs Fa. Capito* (Strassburg, 1523), sig. BBiii(v)-[BBiv(v)]. Wolfgang Köpfel, Capito's nephew, published this edition on November 11. For the dispute around Zell, see Chrisman, *Strasbourg*, pp. 103-105.

[18] *Entschuldigung*, sig. [BBiv(v)] -CCiii.

Capito's subsequent actions suggest that this confrontation occurred much as he described it. In brief, he began to behave more and more in the manner of a reformer. Urbanus Rhegius wrote him on June 24 from Augsburg that he was then being investigated by his bishop and might be cited any day. But he closed with the optimism of the true evangelical. "My excellent Wolfgang, how delighted I am to have been born in this age . . . . May Christ keep us strong and persevering up to the very end." By July 6, when he replied, Capito was equal to the implied challenge. "The people thirst for war, not so the women and children who surpass our madmen in Christian wisdom. . . ." Previously, such circumstances would have horrified Capito. Now he declared, "But, my dear Urbanus, let us practice the constant reading of the Scriptures in order to confirm our faith, since it appears that we must meet the foe hand-to-hand." [19] Capito was taking a public stand. And however much he still disliked it, he was ready even for a fight.

The confrontation with Zell altered even his relations with Erasmus. On June 18 he was still the master's unquestioning disciple. "They say that a book by Hutten has been published," he reported that day. "I do not know what could befall a man in his mind that he would have pitched an attack against you, the author not only of the rebirth of letters but also of the return of piety." [20] But he was unable to find a courier for Basel until July 6, and by then his letter no longer adequately expressed his views. So he wrote a second letter, in which he complained to Erasmus that "you were deriding me among your companions in revelry as a courtier and as one estranged from good studies." While he still sought the quiet to accomplish his studies, he again defended his engagement in the *vita activa*:

> No time was left from the work of the court to breathe freely, although from time to time as opportunity presented itself, I took care to follow the state of scholarship as it presented itself to the public, which was not very difficult for one involved in high places and public business, since it relates more to current feelings and public opinion than to the judgment of genuine scholars.

He seemed to be saying that public engagement was justified even for men of letters, if only because the religious question had in part become a public issue.

[19] Th. B., II, 16(v); 27. "At exerceamus, mi Urbane, assiduo usu scripturarum ad confirmandam fidem, siquidem cominus videtur congrediendum."
[20] *EE*, V, 293-294.

But he had more on his mind than defending his tenure at Mainz from Erasmus' slurs. For the first time he also criticized Erasmus for remaining aloof from the struggle: "Any good men, whose cause, because it is stronger, is beginning to prevail, meanwhile limit the freedom of a Christian to the breadth of the Scriptures. They begin to suspect that you have changed your mind, who, having to some extent taken the initiative in casting aspersions on the Lutherans, have more than once exalted the papal majesty with eloquent praises." How different such a remark was from his earlier confession that he was part of "the papal party." Having read the references to the freedom of a Christian and to the scriptures, Erasmus could hardly have been surprised when he read a little further, "You have been placed on the stage of the world whether you wish it or not; the times are such that one must be the manifest friend of the truth, and be regarded as that, or else be one who ignores it, and be known as that." [21] For the first time, Capito was urging Erasmus to declare publicly that he was with Luther. He was giving Erasmus the same treatment that Zell had given him.

An extraordinary, but as yet incomplete, change had overcome Capito. In March 1522 he first began to agree with Luther's evangelical message. During the remainder of that year he carried on with the task that he had assigned himself at Archbishop Albert's court, only to move to Strasbourg in spring 1523, filled with dismay and with the knowledge that what seemed true did not seem right because it was leading to religious war. He intended to resign from the public arena, only to be confronted by Zell. Zell's forthright defence of his preaching was able to win Capito over because Capito already agreed with the basic content of Zell's sermons. And by insisting that it was not he, but his opponents, who caused disorder, Zell was able to free Capito from the fears that led him to flee public responsibility. Yet, both personal concerns for his own position and an insistence that reform need not be schismatic retarded his final break with the Church of Rome. For a time he tried desperately to contain reform within the Old Church, but in the end the opposition's intransigence led him to condemn it irrevocably.[22]

---

[21] *Ibid.*, V, 304-305. The last line reads, "Es enim in theatro orbis velis nolis: amicum esse et haberi veritatis manifestum, aut huius dissimulatorem oportet, ut nunc sunt tempora."

[22] Compare this discussion and the argument following, with Baum, *Capito und Butzer*, p. 230, who treats the meeting with Zell as a total conversion.

The conversation with Zell in fact pushed Capito into exchanging a position he found untenable for one that proved to be even more untenable. In November he published an apology for his activities over the summer, in which he explicitly stated his intentions. On the one hand, he condemned those he called "bad Lutherans," like Sickingen, who "seek and endeavor only to acquire justification under the guise of the Gospel for foul undertakings, for they wish to seize clerical treasures for themselves. . . ." On the other hand, he attacked the "false Papists . . . whose god is their belly" and who hid behind the church in order to traffic with impunity in every sort of ecclesiastical position. "These false papists, even the Roman Chair and the regular priesthood, are a disgraceful burden and cancer" on the true church, he wrote. In his view, good men would disown both parties. "The latter hates the name of Christ and the Gospel as a disagreeable message for his life and being; the former, Pope, monk, and priests, as if they were all thought to be led away from Christ." Rather, he declared, "I have moved to the side of the pious Papists and Lutherans who seek only the soul's salvation and nothing temporal; and I admonish them to Christian unity, as much as God gives me grace. . . ." The aim of all his efforts, he proclaimed, was that "the pious Papists speak to the noble Lutherans with cool words" and, at all costs, "not encourage a destructive battle of words." According to his apology Capito had no intention of introducing schism. "I do not want to withdraw from the Church, from the old pious Fathers, from the devout, old practices. . . . I want to tell the common people of the Holy Spirit, the indweller of the inward Church, of the old, pious Prophets, Apostles, Martyrs, and Confessors, and of good practice as confirmed by the mouth of God." [23]

It was a noble task that Capito set himself after deciding to come to Zell's aid. But ignoble, as well as noble, reasons lay behind his intentions. He continued to try desperately to maintain possession of his prebend, which naturally came into question. In his letter to Erasmus on July 6, he remarked about an attack from the Lutherans, "A book of theirs, so I hear, has already been put up for sale here. If it is as they say, it is trivial and ridiculous because it condemns me with so much disgust. I think nevertheless that it will be a blessing for me with the Pope." [24] Four months later he was trying to use

---

[23] *Entschuldigung*, sig. [CCiv]-DD; EE; DDii.
[24] *EE*, V, 305. The attack was the *Iudicium de Erasmo*, to which Luther's letter

this book, which contained Luther's letter of January 1522, to bolster his position. On November 12 he complained to one Dietrich Spät, a Roman official, how "viciously the troops of the Lutherans have attacked me." He promised to send an example of these slanders, and he urged Spät to convey his sentiments to Aleander and Chieregati.[25]

The same concern was on Capito's mind when he composed the apology, which was addressed to Bishop William and which was published the day before he wrote Spät. This document, which is the most important source for Capito's life during 1523, has traditionally been treated as the symbol of his wholehearted commitment to the Reformation, but it was also part of the campaign to protect his benefice. In the preface he said he was defending himself from charges that he was preaching, that he had purchased citizenship, and that he had asked for a public disputation. According to Capito these harmless acts were being misconstrued by Jacob Abel, his old rival for the provostship, who "has at one time struggled for a hundred prebends" and claims he "has the right to all prebends even when there are no grounds for it. . . ." When the truth was known, Capito concluded, the Bishop of Strasbourg would render "not only a princely but a Christian opinion on the pending action." [26]

The conversion was still too shallow to cause a full-scale revolution in Capito's behavior. He knew Aleander still held the latch-key of confirmation to St. Thomas, and he was willing to indulge in duplicity in order to acquire it. His criticism of his rival's greed, too, had a hollow ring, because he was at the same time trying to obtain yet another prebend. He bitterly fought his old student Hedio over the post of Strasbourg's cathedral preacher, which was vacant because a number of reforming preachers had been expelled. Although Capito was actively seeking the position in late summer 1523, it was offered to Hedio, who accepted it under the canons' condition that he preach "inoffensively." Capito felt betrayed, and Hedio pleaded

---

to Capito of January 1522 was appended. On the book, see Otto Clemen, "Ein Strassburger Sammeldruck von 1523," *Zeitschrift für Kirchengeschichte*, XLIII (1924), 219-226.

[25] Th. B., II, 52-53(v).

[26] *Entschuldigung*, sig. AAij-AAij(v); AAiij-[AAiiij(v)], where, after briefly rebutting the complaints against him, Capito concluded, "Deszhalb glaub ich nit das mich E. G. nit mehr wölle für ein Probst zu. S. Thoman halten, alsdan etlich verhoffen vnd auszgeben." Consequently, it is impossible to see this document as proof of his final conversion, as do Baum, *Capito und Butzer*, pp. 220-230; 237-239, and Chrisman, *Strasbourg*, pp. 108-111.

with Oecolampadius to intervene with him. But in spite of Oeco-lampadius' scolding, he continued to pout, declaring that Hedio "acted so perfidiously with me, more so than anyone thus far in a lifetime." He declared that Hedio knew he wanted the post and that Hedio already held a position at Mainz that he should not have deserted. "I will not retaliate," Capito added self-righteously, "rather I pardon for Christ's sake, but it will not be at all easy to make myself encourage such familiarity with him a second time. . . ." [27]

In 1523 Capito still had a keen eye for his own security. His deci-sion on July 9 to purchase citizenship, which could be taken as defiance of his Bishop and a testimony to his evangelical connections, must also be understood at least partially in the light of his anxiety for personal position. [28] In the apology he defended his becoming a citizen with the declaration that "The mark of a Christian is to live within the community, not to seek a special way." He denied that he purchased citizenship in order to protect himself from the Bishop's court. On the other hand, he could hardly have been una-ware of Bucer's case, which was settled less than three weeks earlier. Bucer was a married priest, and on June 16 Bishop William requested the city council to expel him. The council refused for the reason that Bucer was the son of a citizen and the city was obliged to protect him. Capito did not refer explicitly to Bucer in the apology, but he did remind the Bishop that "there have been other individuals, prelates, and members of the regular clergy . . . who have become citizens or have come under the civil protection up to this point." He added menacingly that the city had no love for those who sought to disturb its order, especially since no one could easily demonstrate a higher right to the provostship than he. [29] Capito had narrow personal motives, as well as noble justifications, for having purchased citizenship.

Aleander was nevertheless wrong in 1521 when he thought that ecclesiastical preferment would keep Capito from openly becoming a reformer. The insecurity of his hold on St. Thomas did encourage his natural desire to avoid schism. It was one of the motives that lay behind the mediating posture he assumed in his apology, but it was not the most important if only because the Bishop of Strasbourg

---

[27] *BAO,* I, 255-256.

[28] Charles Wittmer and J. Charles Meyer, eds., *Le Livre de bourgeoisie de la ville de Strasbourg, 1440-1530* (Strasbourg, 1954), II, 685. Eell

[29] *Entschuldigung,* sig. BB; BBij. On Bucer, see Eells, *Bucer,* p. 27.

could hardly have read the *Entschuldigung* with approval. Capito's agreement with the main lines of Luther's theology showed through the careful evasions and protestations. Even his "pious Papists" reflected more his own stance at Mainz than the position of someone like Aleander or Eck. They were "true and upright Israelites . . . who wish no one any harm" and who sought "a renewal" without upheaval. On the other hand, Capito's "good Lutherans" were more recognizable. They were those who "day and night reflect the glory of God in the Image of Christ," and who "place all their righteousness upon the promise of God and the priceless acquisition of Christ Jesus." He praised them because they asserted that only the Scriptures determined the limits of Christian life and the content of Christian faith.[30] Capito's "pious Papists" were in fact tepid Papists while his "good Lutherans" were the very best Lutherans. However much he proclaimed that he was holding the select middle ground between the two parties, he clearly leaned toward Luther's side.

If his picture of "pious Papists" and "good Lutherans" was not enough to reveal his true position, Capito proceeded to argue for the evangelical faith. "Christ says, 'He who believes in the Son shall have eternal life; he however who does not believe in the Son shall not see life, but the judgment of God remains on him.' " From this Capito concluded that "God has freed us and does not want us to become the slaves of men. . . . Therefore the body is under the sword and the temporal authority; the soul, however, under God alone and the eternal Scriptures of His Spirit." This was the substance of the gospel, Capito proclaimed, "that Christ Jesus came into the world to make sinners blessed. . . . This understanding is the same among the faithful everywhere, in all languages, throughout the world." Because his sermons contained this truth, he declared, the enemies of the faith charged that he was preaching seditiously. He had not, he protested, called the Virgin Mary a dog. That would be untrue, for she was "the most blessed person." He said only that she should be no more the object of prayer than a dog. Capito did not use the phrase "justification by faith alone," but his insistence that salvation came from Christ alone amounted to Luther's famous doctrine, as any reader could have told.[31]

---

[30] *Entschuldigung*, sig. DD-DD(v).

[31] *Ibid.*, sig. FFiij(v)-[FFiiij]; EEiij-EEiij(v), and [CCiiij(v)], where in regard to indulgences, he wrote, ". . . Papisten . . . die vns bereden, jnen vnser sund mit gelt genugzuthun . . . alsz ob Christus nit gnug than vnd Bezalet, sonder alsz ob er

Any suspicions Bishop William may have felt would have been confirmed by Capito's treatment of religious authority. When he and Zell requested a disputation before the senate, Capito pledged that they would prove that they preached "only the Scriptures and the Spirit of God." [32] In the apology he defended this petition by arguing that a disputation would accord with the Biblical injunction that "we should test the spirits, whether they be from God." And the best source with which to judge their preaching was the Bible, for only it was certain. He noted that "in human affairs advocates act against the law because the law is from men and often contradictory. But this is not possible in the Scriptures, where the Spirit is simple and where the important understanding of the Gospel is simple (einfach). . . ." He thus denied his earlier belief, expressed to Melanchthon, that the Scriptures were obscure. In fact, he declared, "The higher the skill, the less there is of necessity to salvation." He joined Luther in maintaining that the Scriptures explained themselves. "For that reason we so justly push on to the unchanging Scriptures which hold forth the divine will to us surely, which may have no more than one simple and bare understanding, and from which we cannot believe this today and that tomorrow out of frivolous hearts." The Scriptures were "no wax nose," Capito declared, quoting Luther.[33]

Adopting Luther's views on the Scriptures had immediate consequences for Capito's understanding of papal and conciliar authority. To be sure, he never was a defender of high papal authority. Even in defending the papacy to Melanchthon in 1521, he did so only on the grounds of expediency.[34] Now he did retain the papacy, but in terms that would have been even more unacceptable to the curia. He wrote that, in settling disputes among themselves, the five patriarchs "elevated the Archbishop of Rome as their head in the meetings and no farther, even as before those from Alexandria and Constantinople had been such in practice." He did grant some scriptural sanction

---

etliche schuld vnd sünde der kirchen so man jnen gelt gebe zuuernugen vberig gelassen hette. . . ."

[32] Th. B., II, 36-38, for the petition.

[33] *Entschuldigung*, sig. HHij(v)-HHiij(v), "Das evangelium ist kein wechsene nasen. . . ." Luther used this expression in his *Auslegung Deutsch des Vaterunsers für die einfältigen Laien*, which went through two editions in 1519 from Adam Petri's press in Basel. *WA*, II, 116; 77. The work was well known to the Basel group. See Beatus Rhenanus to Zwingli, 2 July 1519, Horawitz and Hartfelder, *Briefwechsel des Beatus Rhenanus*, p. 163.

[34] See *CR*, I, 464-465, and the discussion in Chapter III, above.

for papal authority, but he thought that "the help of partisan bishops" led to the use of the power of the keys for this purpose. On the other hand, he wrote that he did not wish "to strike down such a citation and use of the Scriptures." Then too, he added, "the necessities of the world demand good order, even as the temporal magistracy has arisen among Christians, and of necessity." [35]

He thus repeated the argument from expediency, but Capito was not much of a papalist, especially when he argued that if papal authority could be derived from the Scriptures then it must be exercised in accordance with the Scriptures. He applied the same principle to a church council, which, he said, rendered a decision after having read the books that occasioned a dispute and having consulted the universities. "Order is good, and it is the authorities' prerogative to create, to change, and to improve, to be sure within limits, like all the free Christian councils in the time of the Fathers." But where the Scriptures have clearly instructed Christians, he declared that ecclesiastical authority dare not "vary a hair's breadth." He was, thus, willing to maintain some sort of papal and conciliar authority whose absolute digression he limited to indifferent questions, much as he implied in the letter to Agrippa. But on matters of faith the Scriptures remained for Capito the final norm. God "gave us the Scriptures ... through the Prophets, Apostles, and Christ Himself, confirmed by the Holy Spirit, demonstrated by the many thousand martyrs who died," he wrote, "so that we might be certain of the divine will." [36]

Such a willingness clearly to proclaim and to defend Luther's proscribed teachings, although he did not mention Luther by name, suggests that Capito's apology was a more candid portrayal of his thought and intentions than the circumstances of its publication might suggest. He could, to be sure, continue to act in mean and selfish ways that diverged sharply from his professed faith. On the other hand he had sufficient courage to include in his apology ideas that were obviously heretical. And he concluded it with the warning that "whoever wishes to turn us from God we will resist as our archfoe with the shield of the Word of God, and we will bring to the light of day that whatever is against our belief and trust in God the Lord is from the devil." That promised resistance finally forced him into schism, but in late 1523 he honestly intended to take the side

---

[35] *Entschuldigung*, sig. [FFiiij(v)]-GG.
[36] *Ibid.*, sig. HH(v)-HHij; FFiiij-[FFiiij].

of the "pious Papists" and "good Lutherans" whom he termed "a coverlet . . . for the bad Lutherans and false Papists." [37] His public life had changed since his conversation with Luther and his letter to Agrippa in 1522, but his understanding of the way in which reform should be conducted had not. He was still a religious elitist who desired to remain within the Church of Rome, to avoid schism, and to maintain the peace. Such a position was consistent with his every utterance on the subject of reform since 1516. And his desire to maintain his prebend was consistent with his declared stance. If he intended to contain reform within the Old Church, why then should he not also retain his benefice? Moreover, if all that opposed his preaching was "from the devil," was he not the rightful possessor of his benefice? Honorable and self-serving motives joined to create the mediating posture Capito adopted in 1523. In reading his apology one can scarcely avoid the sense that he had changed much more than he knew. He was already outside the Church of Rome, and events finally forced him to recognize it.

Every public deed from mid-1523 through early 1524 drove Capito farther from the mediating work he intended. One example was his preaching, in which he probably emulated the sermons of Luther that so moved him in 1522. Beginning sometime before July 6, 1523, he commonly preached at noon so he could reach the largest possible audience. In his *Entschuldigung*, he maintained that he had no intention of inciting people against the temporal and ecclesiastical authorities. "In such a public uproar and danger," he wrote, "it has seemed fitting to me to want, by God and for the sake of his glory, to offer all my powers . . . that peace, unity, reconciliation, oneness of under-standing, and the progress of the Word of God might be furthered among us." Given his long-standing desire to maintain the peace, his sermons were probably as conciliatory as he described them. In June he gave Anton Firn, the parish priest at St. Thomas, precisely the advice that he claimed to have been following between July and November. He reprimanded Firn for his tendency to slander, but urged him to "preach the Gospel and the truth to the people, from which none of us wish to hinder him." [38]

Capito's sermons nevertheless caused controversy both in Stras-bourg and elsewhere. The canons of St. Thomas did not like his

---

[37] *Ibid.*, sig. II(v); OOij(v).
[38] *Ibid.*, sig. [DDiv(v)]-EE; CCiij-CCiij(v). Protocolls of the St. Thomas Chapter, cited by Baum, *Capito und Butzer*, pp. 210-211.

preaching, perhaps partially because he was provost and had assumed a task that such higher clerics usually found uncongenial. On September 6 his old teacher Wimpheling wrote that he had heard from Augsburg that Capito was insubordinate to his Bishop and had called Augustine, Albertus Magnus, Gerson, and William of Paris "insipid" in his sermons. Wimpheling exhorted him not to desert Biel, Summenhart, and "your old teacher Gregorius Northoffer" for "the foul-speaking Wycliffites." [39] The report that reached Wimpheling was probably exaggerated; Capito was not the sort to lash out at the opposition. But his sermons were destined to be controversial so long as he preached "the Gospel and the truth."

Preaching was the most common means by which the reformers spread their new teachings. It was only natural that Capito's sermons would raise the ire of the defenders of Rome no matter how conciliatory their tone. He therefore came under attack not only from such far away places as Augsburg but also from the environs of Strasbourg. As he told the story in his apology, in September a priest from one of the nearby villages came into Strasbourg and so slandered him and Zell that the senate called Capito before it on September 14 to answer charges of disturbing the peace. He left the hearing with the premonition that he and Zell were about to be gagged. They met the following Thursday evening and composed a "Supplication" in which they asked the council to authorize a disputation between them and their attackers. They hoped, Capito wrote, that in debate the councilmen would understand that this priest, rather than they, was disturbing the city. All he and Zell were doing, Capito wrote, was preaching the Gospel.[40]

The two reformers presented their petition to the senate on September 21. It was exactly as Capito pictured it in the *Entschuldigung*. They asked only to be heard before the Council acted. Capito complained that the "*Messpfaffen*" were slanderously calling him a "schismatic" and a "rogue." He requested an opportunity to defend him-

---

[39] Th. B., II, 33. On the reaction of the canons, see Chrisman, *Strasbourg*, pp. 111-112, who cites a chronicle that falsely reports that Capito was dismissed from St. Thomas. Rather, he voluntarily laid down the provostship, only to reclaim it in 1538. See Th. B., II, 285-285(v), and Gustav Knod, *Die Stiftsherren von St. Thomas zu Strassburg (1515-1548). Ein Beitrag zur Strassburger Kirchengeschichte* (Strassburg, 1892), pp. 27-29.

[40] *Entschuldigung*, sig. EEiij(v)-FFij, and AAiij(v), where he reported that it was said, "Ich habe das volck wider die priesterschafft hefftig angereitzt ... vnd fürter gesagt auff stund greifft an, lieben Brüder, es ist yetzund zeit, schlagt todt, schlagt todt, alle pfaffen vnd müniche mit einander."

self on the basis of the Scriptures. These attacks, he maintained, were part of a plot to deprive him of the provostship. The priest charged that they were trying to stir up the citizenry against the authorities. On the contrary, said Capito, he and Zell proclaimed only "the Scriptures and the Spirit of God." Moreover, they had not counter-attacked in spite of severe provocation. Justice demanded that they be heard, and the best test would be a disputation with their opponents, with final appeal to the Bible. At the end of the petition, almost as an afterthought, Capito did declare that the city could be returned to peace only on the basis of "the truth and honor of God," but his request was not an attempt to reform the city by means of a disputation.[41] It was rather a defensive reaction for which his fear of losing his benefice was once again an important motive. Capito was not seeking a definitive clash with the opposition.

When he arrived in Strasbourg, Capito was an evangelical who wished to remain uninvolved. In the latter half of 1523 he was a reformer who wished to remain within the Church of Rome. But he was no more able to control events in fall 1523 than he was in the spring. His position became increasingly awkward as the movement for reform, which began in Strasbourg with evangelical preaching, turned quickly into a direct assault on the Old Church. Anton Firn, the parish priest of St. Thomas whom Capito reprimanded in June, had been retaining a housekeeper as his mistress for years. On October 18 he shook Strasbourg's ecclesiastical order by announcing to his parishioners that he would marry her and bring her to church the following Sunday. Three days later Bishop William reminded the city authorities of the Diet of Nuremberg's mandate against clerical marriage and requested them to stand aside while he did his duty. He ordered the canons of St. Thomas to depose Firn. On November 9 Firn and his housekeeper were married in the cathedral by Zell.

As the provost of Firn's chapter, Capito was the local official most responsible for carrying out the Bishop's instructions. At the chapter's request he did reportedly remonstrate with an episcopal representative about the danger of deposing Firn in the face of popular opposition. But he probably did not welcome provocations at that time. Just as Firn was marrying, he was composing his apology in an attempt to rebut attacks upon his prebend. He did not even refer

---

[41] Th. B., III, 36-38, for the petition, where it is clear that one of his fears was being cited to the Bishop's court.

to the issue of clerical celibacy in the *Entschuldigung*, although it was published four weeks after Firn's announcement and two days after the marriage. He apparently decided to avoid further problems for himself by allowing Firn's case to run its course. In spite of his official position he was conspicuous by his lack of involvement in the events that led to the final crisis.

Faced with an order from the Bishop, the canons of St. Thomas requested the city authorities' support while they deposed Firn. The senate granted the canons' request, but Firn would not allow himself to be removed. On Sunday, November 15, he ejected the priest who had been appointed to his position from the chancel and proceeded to conduct the service. The canons turned to the city council, which promised Firn's living if only he would step down. Firn stubbornly insisted that the position was his, and that he was acting in accord with the Word of God. The city authorities hesitated, and on November 22 they meekly suggested that the canons leave Firn in his post. The canons formally deposed Firn again on November 29 and for the third time on December 7. Their resolve finally collapsed when the parishioners came to the church armed, ready to fight to retain their priest. On December 12 the Chapter informed the city authorities that it would allow Firn to remain, but it washed its hands of any responsibility for the ultimate consequences.

True to the dire prophecies of the noble canons of St. Thomas, the city council's hesitancy to act forthrightly threw the gate wide open. Zell married on December 3, and at least three more clerics followed suit by the end of January 1524. The authorities were in a desperate position. They could not easily resist the Bishop's demand for action. In early December they pledged to support him. They requested him to enforce the Nuremberg Mandate, and also to discipline clerics who violated the rule of celibacy in other ways. Bishop William responded on December 14 only that he intended to prosecute the married priests.

The blow fell in late January 1524. Firn, Zell, and the other married priests were ordered to appear before the Bishop at his residence in Saverne within five days. Bishop William allowed them two delays of five days each but he suspended them from their posts for the interim. The city authorities were put in the middle again. The cited priests appealed to them for protection and for the opportunity to defend their actions on the basis of the Scriptures. The councilmen vacillated. Two representatives went to the Bishop to request a continuation of the case until after the second Diet of Nuremberg, at which a general policy for the cities might be formulated. Bishop William agreed to postpone action, and he fulfilled the city's earlier request by ordering all clerics to exclude women from their residences on pain of losing their privileges. But nothing was accomplished at Nuremberg. On April 3, rejecting an appeal from the city council for further delay, Bishop William ordered that letters of excommunication be nailed to Strasbourg's church doors.[42]

Through all this Capito did nothing of record, except to suggest to Bishop William's representative the advisability of delay. In his apology he did quote the Biblical description of a bishop as "once married," but beyond that his own thoughts at this time about clerical marriage are unrecorded.[43] Although he could hardly have welcomed Firn's initiative, he probably approved a married clergy in principle. After the crisis had passed, he related the events in a letter to Ambrosius Blaurer, the reformer of Constance. He wrote that before the issue arose, he thought the Bishop of Strasbourg would react reasonably to legitimate reforms. The pronouncement of the ban came as a shock. If the Bishop should be successful here, what might he attempt next? "We fashioned together an appeal in the name of the brethren the same night that the Bishop posted the bull of excommunication," he reported. Bucer wrote Otellie von Utenheim, a niece of the Bishop of Basel, that Capito not only was present that night but in fact drafted the appeal himself. It was quickly published in German and Latin.[44]

Capito's principles finally won out, but only in a limited fashion. He loyally supported the married priests with his pen and with his advice, but he carefully guarded his anonymity. The German edition closed simply with the words, "In the name of the Lord, Amen." With it Capito intended, as he wrote Blaurer, to reassure the populace in the face of its priests' excommunication.[45] The Latin edition,

---

[42] A. Baum, *Magistrat und Reformation*, pp. 33-36. Chrisman, *Strasbourg*, pp. 134-137.

[43] *Entschuldigung*, sig. EE(v). But Baum, *Capito und Butzer*, p. 235, suggests that Capito may have been the author of the parishoners' complaint in *Supplication des pfarrhers unnd der pfarkinder zu san Thoman eim ersamen Rath zu Strassburg* (Basel [*sic*! Strassburg], 1524).

[44] *BB*, I, 104-105. Köpfel published the apologies in April. *Appellatio sacerdotum maritorum, Urbis Argentinae, adversus excommunicationem Episcopi* (Argentinae, 1524), and *Appellatio der Eelichen Priester von der vermeinten Excommunication des hochwirdigen fürsten herrn Wilhelmen Bischoffen zu Strassburg* ([Strassburg, 1524]).

[45] *Ibid.*, sig. [Biiii(v)]. *BB*, I, 105.

although similar in content, was a different sort of document. It was a formal judicial defence, as well as an appeal to the Scriptures. It concluded with a lengthy formula that included date, appellees, witnesses, testates, and notary. Although he wrote it, Capito was not one of the co-signers.[46] As provost of St. Thomas and past adviser to the primate of Germany, he was one of Strasbourg's most important clerics. His name could have lent weight to the married priests' appeal, and it would have been especially valuable in bolstering the citizens' confidence in their clergy. But he held back from openly associating with obvious violators of canon law. He could not bear the thought of endangering the fingernail grip he had on his benefice. Aleander was very nearly right when he said that Capito would not dare to become a reformer openly if he were granted a prebend. He did become a reformer, but a very timid one for a time.

He reacted almost identically to a far more serious challenge in spring 1524. Conrad Treger, the provincial of the Alsatian Augustinians, mounted a campaign to undermine the reformers' moral authority with the people. And he was a formidable opponent. He had already secured the imprisonment of Stuttgart's first evangelical preacher, and had driven those sympathetic to Luther out of Strasbourg's Augustinian cloister. In March he advertised that he sought a disputation with Capito, Bucer, and Zell. In such a confrontation, he declared, he would prove that the institutional church rather than the Scriptures was authoritative in matters of faith. He composed and published 100 theses for the projected debate. Capito and the others were delighted, but when they accepted the challenge, Treger said he could not debate without the Bishop's approval, which William obligingly declined to give.[47] On March 22 Capito, Bucer, and Zell asked the city council "to order him to dispute in his cloister or anywhere that seems for the best...." A disputation finally occurred, but in private. According to Capito, Treger defended the proposition that "the writings of the Evangelists and Apostles are uncertain and erring human writings, which have no governance over the faith if they are not supported by the Church, which alone sets forth the single and impeccable rule for the faith, which alone points out the secrets of our faith...." [48]

---

[46] *Appellatio sacerdotum maritorum*, sig. [B-B(v)].

[47] Treger's theses were published by Johann Grieninger on March 12 under the title, *Ad Reverendum ... Lausarensum Episcopum paradoxa Centum fratris Conradi Tregorii ... de ecclesiae conciliorumque auctoritate* (Argentinae, 1524). On the affair, see Röhrich, *Geschichte*, I, 217-225, and Adam, *Kirchengeschichte*, pp. 78-81.

[48] *Verwarnung der diener des worts und der Brüder zu Strassburg* (Strassburg, 1524),

Treger's agitation was successful. Wolfgang Köpfel, Capito's nephew and the publisher of his first treatise against Treger, noted in its preface that the gospel had made great strides in Strasbourg with the publication of Zell's *Christliche Verantwortung*, Capito's *Entschuldigung*, and the daily preaching of the Word. But Treger's attacks undercut these gains, Köpfel reported, and it was now necessary to respond. Capito himself tacitly admitted the gravity of Treger's allegations. In the *Verwarnung* he urged the citizenry to steadfastness. "The tyranny of the Antichrist," he wrote, "stands securely on dissension among the people, which is greatly furthered by attacks on the truth. For there can be no greater division in the whole earth than when people oppose one another in belief." He exhorted the burghers to reject "the devil's rule . . . which finds great consolation in dissension, uproar, rebellion, and misunderstanding. . . ." [49]

There was good reason for Treger's initial success. He had struck boldly at the heart of the reformers' position. In his theses he defended the absolute authority of the church in pope and councils against the reformers' claims for the normative value of the Scriptures. To Treger the Church of Rome was always "*sacrosancta ecclesia.*" For Treger, all should believe Augustine literally when he wrote, "I would not believe the Gospel unless the authority of the Catholic Church compelled me." [50] Capito's published response was equally direct. "You know that the Word of God, made physical in the Scriptures, gave birth to the Church and not the other way around. You know that all the Councils, all the Popes, all the Fathers may not give the smallest article to be believed. . . . [T]he command of God as revealed through the Scriptures is opposed to your slavish ecclesiastical righteousness." He dismissed the notion that "the Church must be right and the Scriptures false whenever Church and Scriptures are conflicting" as a "seductive, heretical, blasphemous article." [51] He was adamant. "We know nothing else to proclaim except that those doctrines of Popes and Councils that oppose and

---

sig. Biij(v)-Cij; [Ciiij(v)], not an entirely fair rendering of Treger's position, which was sufficiently extreme. "Quo plane constaret omnibusque palam fieret sacrosanctam ecclesiam sicuti omnibus supereminere, ita apud omnium doctrinarum etiam Apostolicarum iudicium fore, vt quod ipsa non approbasset nullius robaris vel momenti esset." *Paradoxa Centum*, sig., B.

[49] *Verwarnung*, sig. Aij-Aij(v); B.

[50] *Paradoxa Centum*, sig. B(v), "Hinc Divus Augustinus contra epistolam fundamenti. Capite. V. inquit, Evangelio non crederem nisi me catholice ecclesyae auctoritas commoneret."

[51] *Verwarnung*, sig. Dij-Diij; [Ciiij(v)] -D.

destroy the Scriptures are outrages, godless vanities, and insufferable mischievousness." The Church must rather "confess the truth of the Gospel and of the Scriptures." For Capito this truth was derived in faith only "from the invisible grace thus promised in writing through Christ Jesus, to whom all the Scriptures point." Nothing could be put ahead of this central faith. "For through faith in Christ Jesus, the name and glory of the Father are revealed; through faith in the Church and the Fathers, they are obscured and disintegrated, just like too many cooks in a kitchen." [52] For once Capito did not mince words. He even indulged in character assassination. "Even as the almighty God has called and elected some from among all people," he began, "he has therefore hardened some rejected haters of grace .... The one among these who concerns us is brother Conrad of the Augustinian Order at Freiburg. . . ." [53]

These were powerful words, but once again Capito lacked the personal strength of his convictions. In October, in his second polemic against Treger, he revealed that he wrote the *Verwarnung* "in about two days." [54] Those two days fell in April, the same month that the married priests were excommunicated, but as with their appeal, Capito did not sign the *Verwarnung*. He rather let it be published under the ambiguous authorship of "the ministers of the Word and the Brethren at Strasbourg." This time even more than before, his great personal standing could have contributed to ending the dissension that Treger's attack caused. "You would not believe how much Capito's authority accomplishes among the people," wrote Nicholas Gerbellius, Strasbourg's eminent lawyer and supporter of Luther, on December 28, 1523.[55] Yet Capito hid himself. He was too anxious for his position to risk an open attack on Rome.

There was nevertheless as much method as fear in Capito's careful guarding of his prebend. At the same time that he was anonymously

---

[52] *Ibid.*, sig. D(v); Dij-Diij. The identity Capito saw between Christ and the Scriptures is very like Luther. "Vnd Joannes s. vnuerdunckelt gesagt das die wort so im sein almechtiger vatter geben habe er seinen Aposteln geben zureden, vnd die selb rede sey die warheit vnd folgends, im gebett Bittet er nit allein für die apostel sunder für alle die in seim namen durch ir wort dasz da gottes wort ist in jn glauben werden. Dann durch den glauben in Christum Jesum wurdt der name vnd die eer des vatters geoffenbart, durch der kirchen vnd vätter glauben so nach der kuchen zu vil reucht wirt sy verdunckelt vnd auszgelöscht."

[53] *Ibid.*, sig Aiij(v)-[Aiiij].

[54] *Antwurt*, sig. Bij-Biij(v).

[55] Henricus Schwebellius, ed., *Centuria Epistolarum Theologicarum ad Johannem Schwebellium* (Biponti, 1597), fol. 63.

defending reform in Strasbourg, he was carefully preparing for a definitive break with the Old Church. On March 2 the parishioners of New St. Peter's asked him to become their preacher. Such a request had already led the city authorities to install Bucer temporarily as priest at St. Aurelia, but they tried to delay Capito's move. They had no legal authority to make such an appointment and they probably wished to avoid further difficulties with the Bishop while they were still embroiled in the controversy of the married priests. But the parishioners persisted, and by May 4 Capito was preaching at New St. Peter's.[56] He thereby broke with the Hildebrandine tradition of hierarchical authority in favor of the Reformation principle of the called ministry. More important for his own future, he now had a position that no longer depended upon the pleasure of the defenders of Rome. Even bolder acts followed.

Capito irrevocably cast his lot with the reform party when he married on August 1, 1524. His customary shrewdness showed through even in this act. He began looking for a wife in the critical month of April. Bucer recommended him to Ottelie von Utenheim, who, as an outsider and the recently widowed niece of the Bishop of Basel, would certainly have been above reproach. In spite of Bucer's suggestion that she regard his courtship on Capito's behalf as the call of God, Ottelie refused, and Capito was forced to look elsewhere. He finally settled upon an equally prestigious choice— Agnes Roettel, who was a daughter of a member of the Council of Fifteen.[57] By marrying her, Capito further strengthened his position in Strasbourg, but he also testified to his faith, as Bucer declared he intended to do. In 1537 Capito wrote, "A man does not so much accept a woman in his heart for the sake of passion, but God, who does not love those who are unalike but those who are joined by true religion, brings her to him according to his Word." God did not join a man and woman "like two stones," according to Capito, but his will cooperated in every true marriage. He came to cherish "Gnese," as he called her, and he deeply mourned her death in

---

[56] A. Baum, *Magistrat und Reformation*, pp. 81-82. *BB*, I, 105. The story is briefly recounted in the entries for 6-8 April of Diarium Gerbelli. Archivum St. Thoman, 38, fol. 10(v), from a transcript by M. Jean Rott.

[57] Bucer cited by Baum, *Capito und Butzer*, pp. 260-264, who follows Röhrich, *Geschichte*, I, 204, on date and person. The only extant contemporary evidence for the marriage itself is in a suit from the canons of the collegiate churches in February 1525. See A. Baum, *Magistrat und Reformation*, pp. 197-202, who prints their complaint.

November 1531. In spite of his careful preparations, he was forced to bear the opprobrium of being a married clergyman in that age. "Then foul rumors, devised and authored by the adversaries, were cropping up again and again," he wrote Oecolampadius in November 1527 when the Basel reformer was considering marriage. "Accordingly, there are those who approve and those who disapprove. But what is it to us, who depend upon the Lord?" He concluded that "marriage is an honest and holy thing, especially in a Christian and a bishop. Besides, celibacy has its vices and dangers." [58] Such was the hindsight of 1527; in 1524 his marriage was a public declaration of his new allegiance.

If any doubt remained about Capito's public commitment to the reform party, he quickly dispelled it in October when he published a second polemic against Treger. This time he signed a treatise in which he freely identified himself with Hus, whom he called "a learned, pious, eloquent man of unimpeachable life, whom God had graced with his truth and had given the comforting Spirit to teach the truth." Gone were the careful distinctions between "pious Papists" and "good Lutherans." In their place appeared the declaration, "I say also that Luther writes nothing new, that the truth is always the truth and has been known to some. And I confess that I have learned much from him, although I have not burdened his writings with the business of memorization, nor have I lately read as much as would be good and profitable for me." More important than such bravado was Capito's willingness to face the possibility that peace should not be purchased at the price of the Gospel: "It certainly was a fine peace for Pharaoh when the children of Israel, the servants of God, had not arisen. . . . But then Moses and Aaron came and said that God wanted his people to leave the burdens of the Egyptians and to serve him. . . . Yes, he undoubtedly brought destruction to the whole kingdom." By October 1524 Capito had taken the last step in his conversion. He was convinced that the Church of Rome was the Antichrist. The "ministers of the Word" have already borne their "several hundred year servitude" to the "Synagogue of Pharoah," he declared. "For what are the works, exercises, and commands demanded by the Papist church other than the work of the Egyptians who turned us from honoring the true God and kept

---

[58] *Responsio de Missa, Matrimonio et Iure Magistratus in Religionem* (Argentorati 1540), fol. 160(v); 132-133. Capito to preachers of Count Liechtenstein, *QGT*, VII, 363-364. *BAO*, II, 4-5.

us imprisoned in work without fruit?" Sentiments such as these could easily have cost Capito his benefice, but they did not. He rather resigned it voluntarily in 1526.[59]

Capito's conversion was complete. It went so deep that he even broke his friendship with Erasmus, the man who meant most to him personally. He saw and criticized an early draft of the *Diatribe on the Free Will*, and Erasmus did not like what Capito had to say. In June 1524 he wrote Hedio,

> For a long time I was silent while this monster was nourished. He admonished me at length on grave matters, of course, because I had mentioned something about free will before Luther had written on free will; and then too, because I may have written somewhere that the Law of Moses restrains the physical but the Gospel, the soul. 'On the contrary,' he says, 'the law is directed at the whole man.'

As was his custom, Erasmus began to suspect those who criticized his work of plotting against him personally. "Capito, the bishop of the new Gospel," he continued, "had no pleasures with which to entertain himself other than with the games of the most bankrupt. . . ." On September 2 he wrote his old friend Capito and flatly accused him of instigating the attacks of Brunfels and Eppendorf. "I labor for the Gospel much more sincerely than you believe," he complained.[60] But sincerity and good will were not enough for the Capito of late 1524. "Regarding Erasmus' 'free will,' " he wrote Nicholas Prugner, the reformer of Mulhouse, in September, "it quite frankly pleases the flesh and human strengths sufficiently, and it will be responded to superbly in this regard by M. Luther; some who are lesser talents, but surely sufficient to tear that kind of smoke of his to pieces, may also go against it." [61]

The wrath of Erasmus, who more than anyone represented his past, was a certain acknowledgment of Capito's great transformation. Conversions such as he underwent were common among the younger humanists throughout northern Europe. By becoming reformers they established the Reformation. Oecolampadius, Urbanus Rhegius,

---

[59] *Antwurt*, sig. [Ciiij]; M; G(v)-Gij. Knod, *Stifftsherren*, pp. 27-29.

[60] *EE*, V, 481-482; 532. Nicole Peremans, *Erasme et Bucer d'après leur correspondance*. CXCIV, *Bibliothèque de la Faculté de Philosophie et Lettres de l'Université de Liège* (Paris, 1970), pp. 51-54, suggests that Erasmus took Capito to be the person for whom Brunfels said he was writing, that is, someone who wanted to speak out in the confrontation between Erasmus and Hutten but who felt constrained for personal reasons (his prebend) to avoid public attention.

[61] Th. B., II, 124.

Ambrosius Blaurer, Bucer, Justus Jonas—their number was legion. Of them all, Capito's conversion is the most accessible. In his case, the transition from humanist to reformer was a lengthy process upon which personal and even self-seeking considerations continually impinged. But it is evident that Luther's evangelical message played the leading role throughout the process. Capito began his service at Mainz as a humanist who not only misunderstood but was in basic disagreement with Luther and who naturally deplored the virulence of Luther's attacks on Rome. In 1522 he appropriated Luther's teachings as his own beliefs, but even then he became a reformer slowly. First he was persuaded that he must act upon his view of religious truth, and then events forced him gradually to choose between his principles and the traditional order. Like Luther he finally chose principle. At the risk of great personal sacrifice, he condemned the Church of Rome as no true church at all.

CHAPTER FIVE

THE CAMPAIGN FOR REFORM

Capito differed sharply from the popular picture of the sixteenth-century reformer as a fiery man of God. He remained an astute politician as well. "I am taking pains . . . that with soothing words they may restrain the common people from an uproar," he wrote Blauer about the other preachers as the crisis of the married priests drew to a close; "it is up to me to see that the senate does not back away somewhat from the gospel. . . ." After discussing negotiations with the canons of New St. Peter's regarding his becoming a preacher there, he added, with special reference to his first book against Treger, "Now that the arguments of the adversaries have been weakened, I act with great freedom with the senate." [1] His conversion deeply altered his religious beliefs and party loyalties, but throughout his work for reform in Strasbourg, he remained a pacifist and a religious elitist with sure political instincts.

From the outset a willingness to work with the secular authorities was crucial to the reform party's success in Strasbourg.[2] Just as the movement for reform was gathering strength, the city was extending its authority over the clerics who resided within its walls. Relations between the city and its Bishop followed the common late medieval pattern in southwest Germany. Strasbourg had long been free of immediate episcopal authority, and had developed a compromise with its clergy. Priests were not required to swear loyalty to the constitution, as were citizens, nor did they pay the city's regular taxes. Rather, they purchased protection by paying a fixed sum as members of municipal corporations. The collegiate church of St. Thomas, for example, paid a *Schirmgeld* of thirty-six gulden and held a yearly mass for the city in accordance with an agreement that was reached in 1462. But the city authorities were never fully pleased with this arrangement. And when the treasurer of St. Thomas

---

[1] *BB*, I, 104-106. For a report on the disorders see Nicholas Gerbellius to Justus Jonas, 7 March 1524, Kawerau, *Briefwechsel Jonas*, I, 89-90, and the entry for 7 April 1524 in Diarium Gerbelli, Archivum S. Thoman, 38, fol. 10(v): "Varii ac insoliti tumultus in plebe; mirum odium adversus Wormszeros," one of Treger's supporters. From a transcript by M. Jean Rott.

[2] In general, see James M. Kittelson. "Wolfgang Capito, the Council, and Reform Strasbourg," *Archive for Reformation History* (1972), LXIII, 126-142.

arrived at the *Pfennigturm* on April 15, 1523, to pay the annual protection money, he was told that the city would no longer accept
Schirmgeld. On April 21 the same order was passed on to the officials
of the cathedral chapter and of the chapters of Old and New St.
Peter's.[3]

There is no evidence that religious considerations motivated the
senate's attack on clerical privilege at this time. It was rather part of
a movement toward increasing civil control over the church that
was common in the late Middle Ages. As Provost of St. Thomas
and not yet a reformer, Capito responded to the city's offensive in a
similarly traditional manner. At the chapter's request he went to the
city authorities on April 20 to ask their intentions. He learned that
the city no longer intended to treat the canons as members of chapters
but would require them to purchase citizenship as individuals. The
three chapters then conferred, and on April 26 they appealed to
Bishop William to defend them in their privileges. Then on June 13
the senate established procedures by which those clerics who chose
might become citizens. According to the new order, citizen-priests
would not have to carry out political missions for the city and they
would be allowed to buy off the obligation of standing watch. But
any priest who purchased citizenship would be required to swear
loyalty to the civil authorities, just like any other burgher.[4]

On July 9 Capito joined an ever increasing number of priests who
purchased citizenship under these terms. Generally, the canons of
the collegiate churches resisted the new order, and Capito was still
willing to perform his duty as provost when the senate, on August
19, 1523, ruled that the foundations must give their alms to the
common city chest for municipal administration of poor relief. The
canons of New and Old St. Peter's and St. Thomas rightly interpreted this decree as another attack on their traditional prerogatives.
In a long appeal to Bishop William in October they complained that
the city was menacing their religious duties and rights. They asked
him to intervene, to restrain the city authorities from legislating
"against God and against our privileges." Capito signed the appeal,
which also specifically mentioned the issue of protection.[5]

---

[3] A. Baum, *Magistrat und Reformation*, pp. 52-53. For backgrounds, Chrisman,
Strasbourg, pp. 32-44.

[4] A. Baum, *Magistrat und Reformation*, pp. 53-55. Röhrich, *Geschichte*, I, 187.

[5] A. Baum, *Magistrat und Reformation*, pp. 59-62. For the petition, Th. B.,
II, 49-50(v).

Capito's association with the canon's plea in October was somewhat inconsistent with his own purchase of citizenship the previous July. It can be understood only in the light of his continuing attempt to avoid a clash with ecclesiastical authority. Consequently, in the *Entschuldigung* he had difficulty explaining his behavior. He declared that "I openly and publicly pleaded with the priesthood . . . that they should not use their freedom so arrogantly against the common good, but should with others seek to bear civic and common duties." But, he wrote, he signed the petition because as provost he was required to carry out the chapter's wishes. On the other hand, he did not think it was right to occupy a special position in society. "We are enclosed, defended, and protected in the city with gates and nails; why then do we want to be exempt from and displeased by civic burdens? . . . As if the clerical estate alone were so highly esteemed that we might live all the more freely without temporal restrictions." [6] In November 1523 he wished to avoid any act that would encourage his rival for the provostship. So he side-stepped an open confrontation with the canons, while indicating that he favored the city's policy.

There was a brief pause in the city's campaign during winter and early spring 1523 and 1524. The authorities were already in conflict with Bishop William and the clergy over their vacillating policy toward the married priests, and they probably wished to avoid further disputes. But in spring, in response to pressure from the burghers, the senate gradually began to assume the right to provide preachers to the parish churches. Capito was one reformer who secured a position in this manner. At the same time rumors were spreading that many canons were fleeing the city and taking the ecclesiastical foundations' moveable wealth with them. On April 16 the senate appointed supervisors to investigate the matter. In the fall it suddenly issued a series of ordinances that formally settled the legal standing of the clerical estate in Strasbourg. In August the Senate drew into its hands legal authority to make all provisions to pulpits. A decree of September 3 established procedures for such appointments and provided that the city would support the preachers. Then on November 15 five members of the senate appeared in front of St. Thomas and demanded that all clerics, except those in the cathedral chapter, swear the oath to the city authorities. The

---

[6] *Entschuldigung*, sig. [AAiiij(v)].

chapters immediately appealed to the Bishop, whose representative arrived in Strasbourg on November 25. But the city authorities excused themselves from his inquiries by saying it was impossible to call a senate meeting at that time. They were determined to turn priests into citizens. What had been a trickle became a flood of noble canons fleeing the city.[7]

The canons had reason to fear the city's policy, if only because its most ardent defender was now Capito, whose attitude toward the Church of Rome was well known by late fall 1524. In December he published a pamphlet in which he demanded clerical obedience to the municipal authorities.

> Now it is, to be sure, a divine command that we clothe ourselves with brotherly love in regard to every man and not be self-seeking. The greater our position, the more obligated we are to serve everyone. The temporal princes rule, act with force, take and give freedom according to their pleasure. But the foremost among Christians is a servant to others. . . . What do you say, beloved Junkers? Are your consciences so narrowly circumscribed that everything which divine truth supports is against your conscience?

He thus maintained the position he adopted a year earlier when he defended in principle his own purchase of citizenship by invoking the law of love.[8] At the same time he now broadened the argument by detailing at much greater length the connection he saw between the law of love and the civil dictates of the common good. "For this [clerical] freedom exists at the expense of the community, against brotherly love and against obligatory servitude," he declared. Accordingly, a divine command had immediate civil consequences. "It is not difficult," he wrote, "to maintain that the priesthood should become citizens. . . . For God's command should take precedence over all human considerations."[9]

---

[7] A. Baum, *Magistrat und Reformation*, pp. 63-72.

[8] *Das die Pfafheit schuldig sey Burgerlichen Eyd zuthun On Verletzung irer Eren* (Strassburg, 1524), sig. [A(v)]-Aiiij. For a brief discussion that arrives at essentially the same conclusions, see Bernd Moeller, "Kleriker als Bürger," *Festschrift für Hermann Heimpel.* 36, *Veröffentlichungen des Max-Planck-Instituts für Geschichte*, II (Göttingen, 1972), 195-224, esp. 212-117. See also *Entschuldigung*, sig. [AAiiij(v)], "Sunst warlich dringt vns von possesz geistlicher Freyheit das göttliche gebott, brüderliche lieb, vnd natürliche erberkeit, welche nitt woll geprüfft wirdt in vnseren so gemachsamen müssigen freyheiten mit anderleüten so arbeitsamen vnd vnrüwigen dienstparkeiten," where the weight of his argument falls upon the law of love. Although it is essential to completing the argument, Luther's famous doctrine of the priesthood of all believers is only implied.

[9] *Pfafheit*, sig. aiij-aiij(v). "Dann dise freyung ist zu Beschwerde der gemein

Capito's open conversion to the reform party thus had immediate impact upon Strasbourg's policy of making priests into citizens. Much like Zwingli, he had a keen eye for the civil ramifications of the new religion. Consequently, he was able to become the principal public spokesman for the city's program, and in so doing he inevitably dragged the last phase of Strasbourg's traditional policy into the religious controversy. Put differently, he brought to the city's civil desires the powerful support of the reform movement. Loyalty to the municipal authorities and loyalty to Rome thus became incompatible on both religious and political grounds. To be sure, he was well within the Reformation tradition when he argued that the clergy deserved no special status in secular society. His insistence that priests become citizens was a natural corollary, which Luther himself drew, to the doctrine that all believers were priests. But, at least in tone, there is more to the matter in Capito's case. He explicitly emphasized the civil advantages that accrued to the common good from destroying the separate clerical estate in the name of brotherly love. His stand also had an immediate impact upon the balance of forces in Strasbourg in late 1524. By stoutly supporting the city's program, he earned for the reformers the mark of loyalty to the civil authorities. By comparison with Capito, who cooperated so readily, the most ardent defenders of the Old Church were traitors.

Whether reform could occur without disrupting established authority was the key question in Strasbourg in fall 1524. Capito was at one with Luther in demanding obedience to secular authority, but more than that, he was anxious to put to rest any thought Strasbourg's magistrates may have had that he and the other reformers caused popular unrest. Treger accused them of just that when he returned to Strasbourg on August 20, 1524, and published a response to Capito's *Verwarnung*. He called the reformers Hussites and declared that Strasbourg should expect the same upheavals that wracked Bohemia a century earlier. This was a politically damaging smear, and one with which men of position in Strasbourg might readily agree. The gardeners, a notoriously turbulent group, were particularly zealous for reform. And it was they who stormed the Augustinian

---

wider Brüderliche lieb vnnd wider schuldige dienstbarkeit." The existence of this argument in the *Entschuldigung* a year earlier suggests strongly that there was nothing original in Bucer's "religious view" of the common good, at least not as presented by Ernst-Wilhelm Kohls, *Die Schule bei Martin Bucer im Ihrem Verhältnis zu Kirche und Obrigkeit*. XXII, *Pädagogische Forschungen. Veröffentlichungen des Comenius-Instituts* (Heidelberg, 1962), pp. 50f.

cloister, dragged Treger to the senate chambers, and demanded a disputation on the spot. The mob soon became more interested in the cloister wine cellar than in Treger, and so his person was saved. The senate then exacted from him an oath never to write about Strasbourg again and expelled him from the city. But the damage had been done. Reform was associated with disorder. In late September, Bucer urged Capito to respond to Treger's charges.[10]

Capito worked quickly, and on October 24 he dedicated his *Antwurt* to the mayor and city council of Mulhouse in an attempt to strengthen the hand of Nicholas Prugner, the reformer of Mulhouse [11] who also had come under fire from Treger. His central concern in this treatise was to defend himself and his colleagues from the charge not only of being heretics but also of disturbing the peace. He did reiterate his argument that the Scriptures were the final authority in matters of faith, and he even suggested that peace should not be bought at the price of the gospel. But he was finally unwilling to allow to become common truth the notion that true religious renewal might cause violence: "Who then is the cause of disturbance?," he asked. "Answer: the peaceful Word of God is so unbearable because of the unfitness of the flesh, and it will be absolved of the charge. That is, all those who suffer because of the truth and substitute the temporal for the eternal—they complain that the Word brings discord. Thus only their stubborn character is disturbing." Capito was turning the tables on Treger, as he made clear at the end of his treatise. The city was perfectly calm, he addressed his opponent, "until you promoted the appearance of discord with your contrived essays, for truly there had been no discord." Treger went to Constance, libelled the pastors, the citizens, and even the city authorities, Capito reported. "Consider now, you pious reader, whether Treger's deeds serve the peace. . . ." He made his point well, and he included a clear warning to any senators who might think to end disorder by crushing the reform movement, when he queried, "Does dissension follow from the Gospel? It is true! But this comes from the princes of the world, who have thus far defended their desires in peace with the mailed fist, whom God kills with the sword of his mouth." [12]

---

[10] Röhrich, *Geschichte*, I, 217-225. For Bucer's urgings, see Th. B., 49-50(v).
[11] On Prugner, or Bruckner, see Phillippe Mieg, *La Réforme à Mulhouse, 1518-1538* (Strasbourg, 1948), esp. pp. 29-42, and Jules Lutz, "Les réformateurs de Mulhouse," *Bulletin de Musée historique de Mulhouse* XXVII (1904), 10-68.
[12] *Antwurt*, sig. Giij; Lij-Liij; [Kiiij(v)]; Cij.

By fall 1524 Capito succeeded in publicly identifying himself and the reform movement with the peace and good order of Strasbourg. And he used the equation of the gospel with order as a talking point in his effort to persuade the senate to initiate reform. The worship service began to be changed early in Strasbourg as a natural result of evangelical preaching. Worshippers received the eucharist in both kinds on February 16, 1524, and they heard the Mass celebrated in German on April 19. On August 23 the senate tried to settle the religious dispute by reaffirming its mandate of the previous December that all preaching should be from the Bible.[13] But this was not enough for the pastors. They were unwilling to tolerate anywhere in the city what they regarded as idolatrous practices. On August 31 they presented to the senate their first reform petition.

Capito's peculiar method of promoting reform showed through in this petition, which he probably composed. "In the past few days, we, the preachers and pastors," he began, "have pondered and considered among ourselves what might be the cause of the unrest among the common people. . . for it is certain that the Word of God furthers and establishes righteousness, peace, and joy in God the Holy Spirit, and complete loyalty toward temporal authority." In the pastors' view their opponents were the real source of the disorder that accompanied the disputes with Treger and the battle over clerical citizenship, "for we always diligently admonish [the people] to loyalty and forbearance. . . ." Capito and the others then urged the senate to abolish what they called "clear abuses" of the gospel, such as "the lighting of candles, the stations of the cross, masses, and other things." In their view, such reforms "would greatly hearten the entire citizenry and nearly pacify it. . . ." [14] Capito appealed for reform in terms that would make it congenial to the authorities. He carefully identified with their desire for order. He did maintain that the Scriptures enjoined such reforms, but a member of the Council of Fifteen could easily conclude from this petition that political stability, as well as true religion, demanded religious reforms.

The pastors may have been hoping to take advantage of the dispute

---

[13] A. Baum, *Magistrat und Reformation*, pp. 87-88.

[14] The petition is printed in *BDS*, I, 173-176. Although all the pastors commonly signed such petitions, the editors and Kohls, *Die Schule bei Bucer*, pp. 50-52, ascribe this one to Bucer. It is more likely Capito's work, if only because the appeal to peace, which is not to be found in Bucer's early writings, was by now Capito's stock in trade. See also n. 9 above.

with Treger and the burghers' growing opposition to the canons in presenting their petition at this time. But the request failed, and a crisis rapidly developed. On September 5 the senate ruled that it was illegal for the citizens to strip the churches on their own initiative. The authorities did not believe that the city required uniform religious practices.

About a month later a different sort of reformer stayed in Strasbourg for four days. He was Andreas Carlstadt, who had just been expelled from Saxony for repeatedly violating the sort of order that was issued in Strasbourg. He attacked not only Luther's view of the Lord's Supper but also his desire to reform worship in a slow and orderly manner. In Strasbourg, Carlstadt urged the citizens to take matters into their own hands and to carry out the reforms that the authorities proscribed. "Carlstadt did not honor my old accommodations with conversation, since he hid away this four-day period . . . and he unsettled our church, which we have calmed again with a little book," Capito wrote Zwingli the following February.[15]

Capito wrote this little book hastily, for it was published in the middle of October, while he was still working on his answer to Treger. Having just been disappointed by the senate, he could easily have remained silent, or he could have used the popular unrest to pressure the senate for the reforms that he and the other pastors vainly requested in August. But he never considered himself the leader of a popular movement against established authority. He therefore admonished the people to be calm.

> We still have the vestments, the chalice, posings at the altar, and similarly bad practices, which, God willing, should not remain long. Yet we do not wish to do harm to the timid in such things, nor to act against temporal authority, which is given to us by God and which also seeks God's glory through peace, without bringing harm to the common good.
> There is an Honorable Council [which] has courageously emptied the cathedral of some of its idols . . . and it will carry on with the same mildness and do away with all the idols as soon as God grants grace. Why then should men rush in and lay a hand on things rather than let the Word work on. . .? Let the images be a good creation of God.[16]

---

[15] A. Baum, *Magistrat und Reformation*, pp. 87-88. Hermann Barge, *Andreas Bodenstein von Karlstadt* (Leipzig, 1905), II, 207-211. *ZW*, VIII, 302.

[16] *Was man halten vnnd Antwürtten soll von der Spaltung zwischen Martin Luther vnnd Andres Carolstadt* ([Augsburg, 1524]), sig. Bii; Aiii. This edition, pirated by Philip Ulhart, is identical to the Strasbourg first edition by Wolfgang Köpfel.

Two years earlier Capito's colleague Bucer lost a position in Wissembourg because the authorities there thought that his presence was a threat to public order. In December he included in his *Grund und Ursach* a section in which he seconded Capito's admonition to keep the peace.[17] Carlstadt's visit provided a crucial test of Capito's sincerity in telling the Strasbourg authorities that the pastors always urged the citizens to be peaceful and loyal. And Capito passed it. Under his leadership the reformers eschewed spontaneous action from the masses as a method for securing reform.

Throughout his career as a reformer, Capito tried to accommodate reform to Strasbourg's political and legal order. But no one was able in the sixteenth century to control events with such care as he wished. The Great Peasants' War of 1524-1525 provided the reformers' opponents all over Germany an excellent opportunity to make good their charge that the reform movement threatened public order. Strasbourg was no exception. In April peasant mobs devestated the countryside in the vicinity of Obernai, to the west. On Easter Sunday some 3000 peasants occupied a cloister at Altdorf, not a day's ride from Strasbourg itself. Their program was a standard mixture of the gospel and social amelioration that was based upon the Twelve Articles of the Swabian peasants. Their social goals notwithstanding, they were very serious about religious reform. On Easter Monday they forced a priest to dispute in their presence with Andreas Prunulus, the Lutheran pastor of Dorlisheim. Capito, Bucer, and Zell were there, on commission from the local political authorities. Capito preached to the mob on the morning of April 17. He said he sympathized with the peasants' demands and with the dangers that they faced because he and the other preachers were also threatened for the sake of the gospel. He nevertheless urged the peasants to keep the peace and to go home. But they did not disperse until they were brutally put down in late May.[18]

Karl Schottenloher, "Philip Ulhart, Ein Augsburger Winckeldrucker und Helfershelfer der 'Schwärmer' und 'Widertäufer'," *Zentralblatt für Bibliothekswesen*, LII (1921), 104. A third edition appeared in 1525 without place of publication or author.

[17] *BDS*, I, 248-249; 277, although Bucer was more concerned here for unity among the reformers than with iconoclasm within Strasbourg.

[18] Günther Franz, *Der Deutsche Bauernkrieg* (Darmstadt, 1956), pp. 141-146. Hans Virck and Otto Winckelmann, *Politische Correspondenz der Stadt Strassburg im Zeitalter der Reformation* (Strassburg, 1887), I, 144-146. Günther Franz, ed., *Quellen zur Geschichte des Bauernkrieges* (München, 1963), pp. 261-262. They also preached against the peasants to the citizens. Diarium Gerbelli, Archivum

Capito's attempt to mediate and his efforts' meager results were common to other reformers' experiences in the Peasants' War. Luther too spent much of April 1525 rushing about the countryside trying vainly to cool the passions of revolt. Like Luther, Capito was suddenly faced with a two-front war:

> And even here in such a secure city we are not completely safe; some sort of betrayal was planned but failed, if the informers, or rather my own judgment, are correct. Now some of the chief leaders are face to face with the authorities; just now with torture they are inquiring about the truth of those rumors. And we, none the less comforted in the Lord, continue on in the freedom of the Word. . . .

He wrote this report to Blaurer on April 30. A month later he was depressed as he recalled the events in a letter to Oecolampadius, "We and our affairs will fail in our fleeting life. . . . For there is faith among the few and many pseudo-apostles seduce the simple from all sides. Nor does the Antichrist and his prince, the Lord of the World, cease while we are occupied elsewhere." [19] In the Peasants' War, the recurrent nightmare that reform would be associated with violence became a reality. He had already seen in Mulhouse how quickly the authorities turned against the reform movement if they thought it spawned public disorder. He feared the same would now happen in Strasbourg.

These fears proved to be unfounded. But within weeks of Capito's meeting with the peasants at Altdorf, the Bishop of Strasbourg was spreading the rumor that "We who preach peace and unity have now taught and advised them to subvert all order and polity with pillage, stealing, and murder, and to be subject to no authority." In the pamphlet that he published in response, Capito was more concerned to set straight the story of his involvement than he was to defend the gospel. He recounted how he and the other reformers in Strasbourg had become the objects of many slanders to which they did not trouble themselves to publish replies. His own books had been burned in Freiburg and yet he remained silent. But the charge that he and Zell had inflamed the peasants was too much, he wrote, "For what will people think of our preaching if we are considered the instigators of mass murder . . . ?" Far from encouraging the peasants, "We said then in every way uniformly what things they owed to

---

S. Thoman, 38, fol. 17. "Concionatores insectantur rusticos, maxime Mattheus et Hedio." From a transcript by M. Jean Rott.

[19] *BB*, I, 120; *BAO*, I, 368-369.

God and what to the world. Namely, life and goods to the authorities, forbearance to enemies, willing service to everyone; to God, however, all things concerning the soul. . . ." [20]

Capito's was a rather different response from Luther's. Ever the religious reformer, Luther finally exploded in May with his *Against the Murderous and Thieving Hordes of Peasants*, in which he exhorted the princes to stamp out the revolt. To him the peasants' mixture of social grievances and the gospel amounted to blasphemy. Capito in his pamphlet overlooked that problem. He was too much the pacifist to recommend violence, of course, but he was too much the tactician to forget the effect that adverse public opinion might have upon the chances for reform.

The reform movement in Strasbourg stumbled from crisis to crisis in 1524 and 1525. In each case Capito's actions demonstrated that his method of promoting reform was far more considered than that of most reformers. His talents were especially tested in the last round of the dispute over clerical citizenship. The noble canons of the collegiate churches refused to bow to the city's demand that they become citizens. Many fled the city even before the final decree of January 22, 1525. Their flight was within the terms of the senate mandates, but they also carried off much of the churches' moveable goods. Nicholas Wurmser, deacon of St. Thomas, took books, registers, statues, and ornaments across the Rhine to Offenburg in January. On February 1 he and canons from New and Old St. Peter's sought redress from the Imperial Court, which was then sitting at Esslingen. They begged that the court stop the city's persecution and return them to their positions.[21] This was a critical question, for the balance of clerical strength in Strasbourg was naturally shifting to the side of the reformers, as they complied with the city's orders.

As provost of Wurmser's chapter, Capito was the natural person to reply. Official notice of the suit arrived in Strasbourg on February 18. In response, Capito did argue that the canons' objections to the

---

[20] *Doctor Capito Mathis Zellen vnnd ander Predicanten zu Strassburg warhafftige verantwortung uff eins gerichten vergicht jüngest zu Zabern aussgangen* ([Strassburg, 1525]), sig. Aii-Av(v); [Aviii]. Baum, *Capito und Butzer*, p. 581, suggests Köpfel as the publisher. Capito's longtime devotion to order demonstrates the absurdity of the Marxist argument that he became a toady of the senate because he was frightened by the Peasants' War. Sigrid Loosz, "Butzer und Capito in ihrem Verhältnis zu Bauernkreig und Täufertum," *Weltwirkung der Reformation*, ed. by Max Steinmetz and Gerhard Brendler, (Berlin, 1969), I, 226-232.

[21] Chrisman, *Strasbourg*, pp. 235-241. A. Baum, *Magistrat und Reformation* pp. 198-199, prints the appeal.

reform of church life contravened the Scriptures. But his first and continuing impulse was to defend the city's policy with an ingenious countersuit. In late February he, five canons, fourteen vicars, and the organist of St. Thomas formally charged Wurmser with stealing the collegiate church's treasures. He petitioned the Imperial Court to order them not only to return the property but also to pay the chapter compensatory damages, "whatever by way of costs, burdens, labor, effort, risk, and loss in goods and reputation is incumbent, and is yet to be incumbent, upon us and our foundation from one and all in regard to this matter." [22] Capito put his time at Basel with "the lawyers" to good use. A veteran of court intrigue at Mainz, he proved that two could play the game of legal appeals. He called upon the law to protect him in activities that were patently illegal. And he was successful in doing so.

The status of the clergy in Strasbourg was the point at issue in the canons' suit at Esslingen, but behind it there lurked an equally important question. While seeking an injunction against the city's campaign to turn clerics into citizens, the canons also indicted the pastors for changing the form of worship in the city. Capito was their target, for he was then the leader of the reform party. The "Lutheran pastors," they charged, "and especially Dr. Wolfgang Capito, who was publically married at the front of the church, appointed themselves to preach publicly." According to the canons, therefore, Capito and the others held their positions contrary to the Nuremberg Mandate, which stipulated that there should be no further religious changes. Moreover, the canons complained, the reformers "preach that there is no true sacrament under the form of bread and wine, and that our singing and preaching are from the devil, and that praying and the holding of Mass are against Christ. . ."[23] The canons were right. The reforms that had been carried out in Strasbourg directly contravened the Nuremberg Mandate. If successful, the canons' suit could halt reform in Strasbourg.

In August 1525 Capito published a second response. He aimed this reply at the public at large and went beyond the issue of St. Thomas' treasures to defend the progress of reform from the canons' subsidiary

---

[22] *Der Stifft von Sanct Thoman zü Strassburg usschryben nvd protestation* (Strassburg, 1525), sig. Aii-[Aiiii]. That this was also intended as a propaganda piece is evident from sig. [A(v)], where Capito urged the citizens to read the entire pamphlet or have it read to them.

[23] A. Baum, *Magistrat und Reformation*, pp. 198-199, where Capito was mentioned by name twice and Bucer once, but then only in passing.

charges. On this occasion he freely appealed to the Scriptures. To the charge that he and the others preached Wyclif, Hus, and Luther, he retorted that they preached only the truth of the gospel. About the reform of worship he wrote, "Regarding their singing and preaching we have therefore brought forth from the Scriptures that it is not Christian, for it is not worship and reverence toward God. . . . God is Spirit; those who would worship him must worship him in spirit and truth. What does outward pagentry have to do with that?" [24]

This was a forthright defence of the reforms. In it Capito employed the standard methods of Reformation polemic. But he did not let the matter rest there. He also returned to the point of law. He began his treatise by narrating the affair and by reiterating his support for the city's policy. The only crime that was committed, according to him, was that the canons had stolen from St. Thomas treasures that were intended for the support of the collegiate church. The section in which he offered scriptural justifications for the reforms in Strasbourg began about halfway through the treatise. At that point he explicitly remarked that although the co-signers of the original countersuit agreed with his treatment of the legal issues, they did not necessarily share his theological opinions. [25] As a reformer Capito retained a lively and well-nigh peculiar awareness of the practical problems that the evangelical movement posed. He skillfully exploited the political and legal opportunities of the moment.

Treger's attack on the reformers and the city, the Peasants' War, and the fight over clerical citizenship were all instances in which Capito's desire to promote reform and the authorities' desire for order reinforced one another. His support for the city's policies was not only fortunate for the reform party but also natural. Political finesse alone, however, was not enough to establish the reform movement. There were several occasions in which his goal of promoting the gospel and the senate's insistence upon loyalty conflicted. He had sufficient opportunity to prove that he was a man of principle, as well as a capable politician.

Once he stumbled athwart the very civil authorities with whom he so much wished to work. He was too clever by half in an affair that grew out of the disputation on the Mass that was held at Baden im Aargau in May 1526. Oecolampadius debated Luther's famous

---

[24] *Von drey Strassburger Pfaffen vnd den geüsserten Kirchen güttern* (Strassburg, 1525), sig. Bii [sic! Aii]-B(v).

[25] *Ibid.*, sig. Ciii(v)-[Ciiii(v)].

opponent Johannes Eck before a panel that was stacked against the reformers. Although the coming confrontation was widely rumored, the Baden authorities ruled that no report of the actual debate was to be made public for one year. Minutes of the disputation somehow reached Strasbourg and Capito's nephew Wolfgang Köpfel rushed them into print with a preface that Capito probably wrote. Regardless of authorship, he was closely involved, for he sent a copy of the published report to Zwingli with a covering letter in which he deplored the Baden authorities' decision to retain the Mass. The letter never reached Zwingli. Johannes Faber, a participant in the disputation, a man whom Capito himself recommended for ecclesiastical preferment and the one who burned Capito's books in Freiburg, intercepted it. He was delighted with the victory at Baden, and he decided to take advantage of the windfall that the letter to Zwingli represented. He published it, after changing a word here and there and adding marginal notes that made it appear as if Capito were praying for Baden's speedy destruction.[26]

Suddenly Capito was accused of inciting to revolt. The officials of Baden met on June 25 and decided to prosecute him at the Diet of Speier. They were certain that he wrote the preface and they thought that he was responsible for the illegal publication of the disputation's proceedings. Moreover, according to Faber's edition of the letter to Zwingli, Capito had libelled the canton's authorities, and that was actionable, as Treger, one of Faber's associates, well knew from his own experiences in Strasbourg. On July 8 Sturm and Martin Herlin frantically wrote the Strasbourg senate from Speier that Faber had appeared at the Diet with the published account of the proceedings at Baden, and had read it to the delegates along with four letters from Capito, Farel, and Oecolampadius to Zwingli. Sturm and Herlin reported that they had delayed formal proceedings at the Diet, but they warned that "great evil" could come upon Strasbourg's budding political relations with the Swiss on account of Capito. They heard that Capito's letter was even being translated into Spanish so that the Emperor could read it.[27]

---

[26] *Warhaftige handlung der disputation in obern Baden* ([Strassburg, 1525]), Reprinted in *BAO*, I, 521-528. See Leonhard von Muralt, *Die Badener Disputation von 1526* (Leipzig, 1926), pp. 143-144, and Strasser, *Beziehungen*, pp. 9-13, for details. On the book, see François Ritter, *Histoire de l'imprimerie alsacienne aux XVe et XVIe siècles* (Strasbourg, 1955), pp. 242-245.

[27] Emil Dürr and Paul Roth, eds., *Aktensammlung zur Geschichte der Basler*

On the same day Capito was already writing letters of apology to Ludwig Ber, who was at the disputation, to the mayor and council of Basel, to the Baden authorities, and to the twelve cantons. He was in serious straits. At just that time Strasbourg was drawing closer and closer to the Swiss for purposes of mutual defence. That the authorities should find this affair unhelpful is understandable, but even his friend Oecolampadius, who wrote "severely and reproachfully enough" on July 5, was angry with him. On July 6 he received a formal letter of complaint from Baden.[28] His line of defence was two-fold, very like his response to the canons' suit at Esslingen a year earlier. In his dealings with Baden and the Swiss authorities he put the blame upon Faber and maintained that Baden erred by failing to follow Oecolampadius' advice to abolish the Mass. Secondly, he composed a careful rebuttal of Faber's charges, which he forwarded to Speier.

In each letter to the Swiss, Capito countered that Faber had changed the sense of his letter to Zwingli. But this was only one, albeit the more serious, of the charges against him. He more or less ignored the complaint that he was responsible for publishing the *Warhaftige handlung*. To Ber he expressed confidence that he would not fall into disfavor over "such a dull little book." To the mayor and city council of Basel he denied that he intended anything against the confederation. He noted that he received the book, passed it to a corrector, and instructed that anything offensive be deleted. He added that "we have better things to do with lecturing and daily preaching than to waste our time with a little pamphlet like that." [29] He came no nearer to telling the story of how the book was published.

On this occasion Capito's zeal for reform also led him to reply bluntly to the Baden authorities. He began his letter to them by observing that his love for Switzerland, as witnessed by his having lived there five years, would never have allowed him to do anything prejudicial to Swiss interests. Secondly, he pointed out that Faber had changed the sense of his letter to Zwingli. These were important points in his defence, but Capito devoted most of his letter to repeating his favorite charge that it was Faber and not he who "would like to

Reformation in den Jahren 1519 bis Anfang 1534 (Basel, 1933), II, 351. Virck and Winckelmann, *Politische Correspondenz*, I, 262-263.

[28] Th. B., II, 263-265(v); 269(v). Dürr and Roth, *Aktensammlung zur Basler Reformation*, II, 354-355.

[29] Th. B., II, 268-269(v). Dürr and Roth, *Aktensammlung zur Basler Reformation*, II, 354-355.

provoke the collapse of the truth through abominations, lies, and bloodshed." If Eck and Faber succeeded in their plans to stop reform, Baden and the whole Confederation would be destroyed. To his mind, the Baden authorities erred by failing to follow the reformers; they risked disaster because they placed "their trust on the old belief and not on the happy Word of God, which understands only God's glory and the trust from Christ. . . ." [30] This was his real message to the Baden city council. In the *Entschuldigung*, in the *Antwurt* to Treger, in the pamphlet on the Peasants' War, and now in the Baden affair, the same argument reappeared ever more forcefully. Peace could be reestablished only on the basis of the truth.

Although he was in serious danger of prosecution, Capito yet exhorted those whom he had wronged to change their ways. Perhaps his boldness was strengthened by his loathing for Faber, whom he called a "whoremonger" early in 1526.[31] In this instance he was willing to risk punishment for the sake of the gospel, but he was not one needlessly to jeopardize his position. He countered Faber's machinations at Speier with his own legal appeal, and he marshalled his many important friends in his defence. In his published defence, which appeared in German and Latin, he recounted again how Faber had altered the sense of his covering letter to Zwingli. He also made a bold, and apparently successful, attempt to impugn Faber's character and motives. For this purpose, he included in the appeal two letters from the preachers of Strasbourg in which they challenged Faber to a disputation. He then republished the original and Faber's version of his letter to Zwingli. In this last section he pointed out that his letter referred to the disputation itself as a catastrophe and did not call catastrophe down upon Baden. Capito concluded that Faber was untrustworthy personally, that he had a motive for altering the letter, and that certainly his word could not be taken over that of the maligned appellant.[32]

This appeal was published on August 2, and the Strasbourg authorities put it to immediate use. They sent it to the Basel city council with a note that they were now satisfied of Capito's innocence. Köpfel, the publisher of the *Wahrhaftige handlung*, was fined for his involvement.[33] But Capito was still uneasy. His position with the

---

[30] Th. B., II, 263-264.

[31] *BAO*, I, 455.

[32] *Epistola V. Fabritii Capitonis ad Huldrichum Zwinglium* (Argentinae, 1526), sig. [A(v)-D]. For the German edition, see Baum, *Capito und Butzer*, p. 581.

[33] Dürr and Roth, *Aktensammlung zur Basler Reformation*, II, 371-372.

Strasbourg senate was secure, but was his name cleared at Speier? So he counterattacked, much as he had two years earlier in response to the canons' suit at Esslingen. On August 13 he published another appeal in which he called the Imperial authorities' attention to the troubles that Faber had caused him. He reported that the Strasbourg senate would have imprisoned him if he had not kept a copy of his letter to Zwingli by which he could prove that he never called for Baden's destruction. He demonstrated once again that Faber altered his letter with marginal notes and by translating it incorrectly. He requested that the Imperial Court prosecute Faber for libel.[34] Capito was still not finished. Two days after the second appeal was published, he was writing Spalatin to ask him to intervene against Faber, whose duplicity Capito was sure Spalatin would appreciate when he read the enclosed account of the affair. Capito felt that he had received satisfaction by August 25. He wrote Blaurer that Philip of Hesse showed the second appeal to Archduke Ferdinand himself. "Ferdinand," Capito concluded, "is now at least aware of Faber's crimes." [35]

Capito's almost obsessive desire to clear his name of Faber's trumped-up charges revealed his characteristic anxiety to remain in the authorities' good graces. When he was put to the test he did cast caution aside and stoutly defended the gospel. That done, he rushed to shore up his position not only in Strasbourg but also in Speier. He could perhaps have responded with Luther that he would commit himself to God's care if he lost the protection of his prince, but he was far more likely to follow the example of Jesus' disciples in the storm on the Sea of Galilee. He would first do his humanly best to keep the ship from sinking. Throughout his career in Strasbourg he carefully cultivated his relations with the civil authorities in order to guarantee, insofar as possible, the success of his reform program.

Strasbourg differed from a few cities such as Nuremberg in that the authorities consistently failed to take the lead in carrying out reforms. [36] All over Germany, whenever a city or territory abolished the Mass, it testified that it adhered fully to the reform party. Abolition was a momentous political, as well as religious, act and it was

---

[34] *An gemeyne stend des heyligen Römischen Reichs . . . wider D. Hanns Fabri* (Strassburg, 1526), sig. Aii-Aiiii(v).

[35] Th. B., II, 227-227(v). *BB*, I, 137-138.

[36] On Nuremberg, see Gerald Strauss, "Protestant Dogma and City Government: The Case of Nuremberg," *Past and Present*, XXXVI (1967), 28-58, and for Strasbourg, the judgment of Chrisman, *Strasbourg*, pp. 175-176, as expanded upon by Kittelson, "Capito," *Archive for Reformation History*, LXIII, 126-142.

certain to bring the wrath of the Emperor down upon the city. There were some committed evangelicals, such as Sturm and Daniel Mieg, among Strasbourg's leading figures, but as a whole the senate was extremely unwilling to do the pastors' bidding. There was thus in Strasbourg first a popular demand for reform and then an official decision by the authorities to adopt the reformers' program. Through their preaching Capito, Bucer, Zell, Hedio, and others created the popular movement. Then, by convincing the authorities that they were responsible for the religious life of the city, Capito in particular persuaded them to abolish the Mass. He did so by arguing that the senate could gain domestic peace if it reformed the church.

Capito began to hold heterodox opinions about the Mass in 1512 when he substituted a spiritualist understanding of the elements for the doctrine of transubstantiation. And in 1516 in a letter to Erasmus he included "the sacraments" among current erroneous teachings. By the time he wrote his apology in 1523 he had advanced to an evangelical opposition to the doctrine that the Mass was a sacrifice.[37] And when he was writing in October 1524 about the dispute between Carlstadt and Luther, he noted that "we shun the term 'mass' and are resolved to call it 'the Lord's Supper,' for 'mass' means sacrifice in the Hebrew tongue. . . ." To his readers he declared, "We have admonished you daily from the Epistle to the Romans about what we should sacrifice. Namely our bodies, a living sacrifice, holy, pleasing to God, which is the proper service of God." [38] Like the other reformers, he maintained that there was no place where the Scriptures taught that the eucharist was a sacrifice.

This naive Biblicism was the less important of his objections to the Mass, and indeed to the Roman cultus generally. He was probably following Luther's view in *The Babylonian Captivity of the Church* when he further asserted that forms of worship must point to the thing worshipped. In his apology the "good Lutheran" said, "I allow good church customs that have not been ordained by God, but that carry a useful sign, to remain. . . ." In Capito's view, the Mass did not fulfill this criterion, because it led the worshipper to depend upon itself rather than upon God's mercy in Christ.[39] Why

---

[37] See *Entschuldigung*, sig. DDiiij(v), where he referred to the eucharist as "dise heilsame gedechtnüsz des einigen opffers."

[38] *Von der Spaltung*, sig. Bii. Bucer repeated Capito's argument from Hebrew in his *Grund und Ursach*. BDS, I, 209, and n. 47 where the editors incorrectly identify Carlstadt to be the source of the argument.

[39] *Entschuldigung*, sig. DDii(v), to which he added, "so ferr si mich nit weitters

did the Strasbourg reformers oppose the Roman service, Capito asked in the final essay against Treger? "To that I say, we do it because these things occur without faith and have no grounding in Scripture or the approval of God, but come from human inventions alone, through which God is little honored; and that the main sum of our salvation, which should be founded upon Christ alone, is through powerful error founded on such things. . . ." [40] Capito repeated this view in the 1525 apology against the canons. The Mass was against the Scriptures because it was considered a sacrifice; it opposed faith because it was preached as a good work; it was an improper ceremony because, through the notion of transubstantiation, it led the sinner to trust the Mass itself rather than Christ's life, death, and resurrection. Later in life he summarized his views. The Mass "denies Christ more atrociously than the Talmud," he wrote. "These things concerning the Mass in general," he concluded, "which, so I may say everything in a word, is against this commandment: you shall have no other gods." The Mass was not just superstitious on the grounds that transubstantiation was ridiculous. It was profoundly, perversely blasphemous; it was "*caput impietatis*." [41] With Luther, Capito moved beyond the humanist critique of empty formalism to the doctrinal position of an evangelical reformer.

Given his condemnation of the Mass and his insistence that only established authority should carry out specific reforms, it was natural for Capito to seek from the city council a mandate that would abolish the Mass in Strasbourg. On this issue he and the other Strasbourg reformers found themselves in the difficult position of acting as intermediaries between a popular movement and a senate that desired most to maintain the peace. Strasbourg had a restive populace. One group of citizens even joined in petitioning the city council for the suppression of the Mass. [42] Probably in April 1525 the pastors took advantage of more unrest to advise the council to undertake a thorough religious and moral reform of the entire city. In place of the Mass they urged a simplified service that would feature the singing of Psalms, the reading of regularly appointed passages from the Bible and their explanation in a sermon. They wanted the Lord's

---

binden weder mich gottgebunden hat vnnd mein glauben auffsich ziehen der auff gott allein steen solle."

[40] *Antwurt*, sig. Fii(v).

[41] *Von drey Strassburger Pfaffen*, sig. Dii-Diii(v). *Responsio*, fol. 72-73(v), 120-126 for a fuller discussion.

[42] Chrisman, *Strasbourg*, pp. 148-150.

Supper to be served under both forms, and they advised the senate to abolish private Masses because they divided the populace. In addition they suggested that the city dissolve the monasteries, close the taverns, eliminate begging by providing for the poor, and establish schools from the income of secularized monasteries. All this, the pastors assured the authorities, would accord with the Nuremberg Mandate to preach only the gospel because the Scriptures enjoined these changes.[43]

In this supplication the pastors essentially repeated their petition of August 1524. They presented the same requests, and, especially in regard to abolishing the Mass, they argued their position in the same manner. This time, however, they followed their formal petition with what must be described as an attempt to influence the senate through one of its members. On an evening before April 10 they met with Klaus Kniebis, who was then *Ammeister* and a committed evangelical. The next day they sent him a written summary in which they emphasized one part of their earlier petition. This was their desire to see the Mass abolished. They told Kniebis that the entire citizenry was awaiting the council's decision, "full of hope that the Honorable Council will at the earliest time do away with the remaining Masses and erect in their place a different Christian service." The previous October, Capito argued to the citizens that delay was necessary out of regard for "the timid." That night in April he and the others maintained that those who still attended Mass were no longer to be considered "weak, but stubborn and perverse." The Word had been preached long enough, the pastors insisted. The time had come to abolish the Mass in the entire city.[44]

The pastors were attempting to move the senate to do their bidding by bringing popular pressure to bear upon it. But they failed again. In a mandate of July 1, 1525, the authorities did command the canons of each collegiate church to speak with their preacher about the order of service. They also decreed that there was henceforth to be a Lord's Supper at 7:00 A.M. with Bible reading in German and a short sermon on the text. Consistent with earlier mandates, nothing contrary to the Scriptures could be said at any point in the service. Nevertheless, the senate allowed the canons to retain a Latin Mass at 5:00 A.M. and forbade anyone to disturb them. The main issue

---

[43] Th. B., II, 208-210.
[44] *BDS*, II, 462-465.

was accordingly decided against the reformers.[45] The senate merely made official what already existed in practice. They thereby reaffirmed the continued existence of just those private masses that drew the reformers' fire in the first place.

Popular pressure thus proved insufficient to persuade the senate to abolish the Mass, as well it might. The authorities rendered their decision in the aftermath of the Peasants' War with the armies of those loyal to Rome in control of the countryside. As Capito remarked to Blaurer on April 30, "There is a strange fear of the papists, nor does less terror grip the legacy hunters of this world; the rich are extremely worried about their fortunes." [46]

Once these momentary dangers passed, the pastors returned to the offensive. On August 10 they appeared as a group before the senate and reiterated their requests of the previous August and April. According to the minutes of the meeting, again they were most concerned about the masses that were still being celebrated. They reiterated their contention that the Mass was against the Scriptures and they recommended that the senate begin by abolishing it in the three lesser foundations. Capito was probably responsible for one curious aspect of this interview. In a manner that was typical of him, the pastors also addressed themselves to the authorities' worries about the political consequences of suppressing the Mass in Strasbourg.

> And in this regard consider that we are Christians, and that Christ will acknowledge before his heavenly father whoever confesses him here. And do not calculate whether it is against this person or that person, for among our ancestors there has always and everywhere been covert conflict between the princes and the cities, even before the gospel was so clearly purified and preached. If one should revert to the Pope's party, then such bitterness will still not be quieted but become more pronounced so that tumults and calamity will spring up.[47]

Capito thus broached what he knew to be the senate's chief concern. Against the city's poor strategic position, surrounded by Catholic princes, and against its dependence upon short-haul trade, which these princes could disrupt, he counterbalanced the threat of internal disorder. This was an artful ploy, but for the moment it failed; the

---

[45] *BDS*, II, 466-467. Chrisman, *Strasbourg*, p. 150, considers this decree a gain for the reformers, when it merely reaffirmed the *status quo*.

[46] *BB*, I, 120.

[47] *BDS*, II, 468-469.

authorities were unwilling to proceed farther with reform in 1525.

Perhaps because they were frightened by such opposition, the pastors seem to have ignored the question of the Mass during winter 1525-1526. Capito may have been too much involved in the dispute of the canons to direct energy to agitating against the Mass, and the city fathers probably did not desire to give the canons any more arguments to use against them at Esslingen. During these months the senate was proceeding on its own initiative, according to earlier decrees, with the orderly removal of statues, crosses, relics, and other symbols of the Roman cultus from the churches in Strasbourg. The statuary in the cathedral itself was pulled down on the day after Christmas in spite of the chapter's opposition. The populace was still restive, however. As spring again approached, disorders again grew more frequent. On April 10 an unruly mob broke into Capito's home.[48]

The tumult shocked the pastors into action. Capito led them in a new offensive against the Mass. On April 16 he wrote Zwingli, "We will negotiate with the senate today concerning the abolition of the remaining masses (for five of them are carried on daily), and I am writing about it in a few words." On May 6 the senate received from Bucer a lengthy denunciation of the Mass in theological terms and a proposal of how services "may be erected and carried on at Strasbourg according to the Word of God." [49] Ten days later Capito wrote Zwingli again, "Negotiations are going on concerning the abolition of the remaining masses." On May 18 the reformers presented their most uncompromising attack on the Mass to date. It was probably the "few words" of which Capito wrote Zwingli a month earlier, but with corrections by Bucer. "The Mass is no service," they charged, "but a hateful thing and the greatest blasphemy against God, and should be abolished by a Christian authority." Their petition accordingly had two parts. First they argued "that the Mass is not only an alternate service, which is unfaithful to the true one, but is also absolutely opposed to it. . . ." Secondly they maintained that "no one can deny that a temporal authority is responsible for abolishing such a Mass, which is against God in so many ways. . . ." In a manner that was typical of Capito, the pastors charged that "the command of the authorities is not only to satisfy the common good, but also as a

---

[48] A. Baum, *Magistrat und Reformation*, p. 155. L. Dacheux, ed., *Fragments des anciennes chroniques d'Alsace* (Strasbourg, 1892), III, 258.

[49] *ZW*, VIII, 566. *BDS*, II, 470-482.

Christian Authority to defend with the sword and to magnify the glory of God." Here they employed examples of the Old Testament prophets and of the kings of Israel who were struck down because they strayed from the paths of righteousness.[50]

The pastors spoke bluntly in this petition. They had long argued that only the senate had the authority to abolish the Mass, but now they maintained that it was obliged to do so. These strong words nevertheless fell on deaf ears. The city was then enmeshed in delicate negotiations at Speier, and Capito's hands were more than filled during the summer with trying to extricate himself from the Baden affair, a dispute that severely strained his relations with the senate. But these diversions were scarcely past when the reformers returned to the offensive. "We are again directing every trick against the Mass," he reported to Zwingli on October 11.[51] The pastors did in fact present another petition in late October which reiterated their demands. Capito was becoming increasingly single-minded on the issue. He included in his catechism of 1527 a request that the catechumen pray for abolition.[52] But the authorities steadfastly opposed more changes, and in spring 1527 they even corresponded with Bishop William about the pastors' behavior. They asked him to intervene, and especially to supervise the pastors' sermons, which, they suggested, were so filled with attacks on the Mass that they were beginning to disrupt the body politic.[53]

Capito and his colleagues were being frustrated at every turn in their efforts to reform the church in Strasbourg. They could not even accomplish the reform of morals on which the senate might have been less stubborn. As Capito wrote Blaurer on August 1526,

---

[50] *ZW*, VIII, 597. *BDS*, II, 483-496. When seen in the context of Capito's letter to Zwingli, Bucer's marginalia on the first half of this petition suggest Capito's authorship of at least the first draft of the whole piece. Moreover, the theological arguments against the Mass here do not follow Bucer's petition of April.

[51] *ZW*, VIII, 751.

[52] *Kinderbericht und fragstuck von gemeynen puncten Christlichs glaubens* ([Strassburg], 1527), sig. Bii(v). (Hereafter cited as *Kinderbericht-1527*). Another slightly revised edition appeared in 1529 with Capito designated as the author. *Kinderbericht und fragstück von glauben* (Strassburg, 1529), also published by Köpfel. (Hereafter cited as *Kinderbericht-1529*.) F. Hubert, "Strassburger Katechismen aus den Tagen der Reformation," *Zeitschrift für Kirchengeschichte*, XX (1900), 395-413, notes a Latin version of the 1527 catechism that I have not located.

[53] Chrisman, *Strasbourg*, pp. 158-161, rightly corrects the judgment of A. Baum, *Magistrat und Reformation*, p. 97, that the reform party was victorious by 1524.

We have accomplished nothing as yet concerning brothels. Our public affairs were the most corrupt, adultery the most widespread; no street was free from whores. We so often spoke out against this abomination; but the Lord diverted our attentions elsewhere to new labors from somewhere else amongst the disturbances. There is as yet no firm ordinance against adulterers, although the public disgrace is beginning to be felt. The prestige of fornicators, which once used to be their sacred privilege, has become cheapened in the public eye, and I have good hope that we shall someday have the appearance of a righteous church.[54]

In 1526 and 1527 the Strasbourg authorities began to balk at the reformers' repeated demands for changes in the life of their city. Some of the senators may have been wishing that Capito and Bucer had never come to Strasbourg.

The authorities' intransigence, and their complaint to Bishop William, brought to life once again the fear that motivated Capito in his dealings with the senate three years earlier. In two petitions in September and October 1527 he and the others once more carefully acknowledged the authorities' desire to maintain order. They assured the senate that they did not act "so that we might compel Your Graces or seek after ourselves in any way or fashion, or, moreover, stir up, wish, or hide behind disorder, God forbid!" They excused themselves by declaring that they acted "only as loyal, obedient citizens who therefore acknowledged and testified to your zeal for the glory of God and love for the common civil peace and unity, as our Gracious Lords and divinely ordained authorities." A month later the pastors prefaced a lengthy petition with a disclaimer of any desire to disturb the rule of the city and the declaration that they were only fulfilling their own duties in urging the senate to abolish the Mass. But they concluded their remarks by charging that "the city will either be led by you to God and therefore to all prosperity and well being, or to the Antichrist and therefore into irretrievable ruin." At the end of the petition they put the issue bluntly: "You are the vicars of God," they declared.[55]

Capito, Bucer, and Zell were nothing if not persistent. When it appeared momentarily in mid-1527 that the authorities were about to turn against reform, Capito briefly retreated to his earlier assurances that only the senate had the right to abolish the Mass. But by the end of the year he was insisting again that they must reform the church or

---

[54] *BB*, I, 138.
[55] *BDS*, II, 498-499; 500-501; 517-518.

face God's wrath. He was in an awkward position. He had rejected the authority of the bishop and pope to regulate the affairs of the church, but he equally deplored mass action. Like Zwingli in Zurich, he was therefore compelled to depend upon the civil magistracy. But unlike the Zurich authorities, the Strasbourg senate was unwilling to accept the new responsibilities that Capito and Bucer thrust upon it. Capito, however, would not counsel disobedience even if the secular authority commanded wrongly in religious questions. When the Basel city council, too, refused in September 1527 to abolish the Mass, he wrote the Basel pastors a letter in which he probably described his own reaction to repeated failure. He declared that it was an honor to be persecuted by "tyrants" and he urged the pastors to submit. "Drink deeply now of the quiet Spirit in private sermons, from whom those who. . . are becoming hardened in the leisure of the inane and in foul tranquillity abstain," he wrote.[56] Apart from revolution, there was little else he could suggest.

In January 1528 Capito and Bucer saw an example of the way in which they thought reform should occur. They were among the last to be invited to the Disputation of Bern, probably because suspicion still lingered in the minds of Swiss councilmen about Capito's involvement in the Baden disputation two years earlier. Zwingli and Oecolampadius, of the better known reformers, were the main performers, and it was at their suggestion that polite invitations were extended to the Strasbourgers, but only as observers. One of their motives for attending was the opportunity that the disputation offered for a definitive encounter with their old foe Conrad Treger, and his associate in that dispute, the Franciscan, Thomas Murner. The Bern council invited these two at Capito's and Bucer's request. Capito broke his silence only once. On January 9 he rose to contradict Treger's assertion that the Word depended upon the Church of Rome. This was the substance of their exchanges four years earlier, and neither carried the argument forward. Capito was not persuasive, for with Bucer's support his position received but four votes to Treger's six. Capito and Bucer left for home on January 23.[57]

But the reform party was victorious in Bern. The Mass was abol-

---

[56] *BAO*, II, 97-98.

[57] Strasser, *Beziehungen*, pp. 15-33, details Capito's participation. R. Steck and G. Tobler, eds., *Aktensammlung zur Geschichte der Berner Reformation* (Bern, 1923), p. 582, for the invitations. On Murner, see Theodore von Liebenau, *Der Franziskaner Dr. Thomas Murner* (Freiburg, 1913), an apologetic account.

ished, and that act was the turning point in the campaign against the Mass in Strasbourg. "We have marvelously excited our church with the success at Bern," Capito wrote Blaurer on February 8, "and now I hope that it can be built up accordingly." [58] On their return Capito and Bucer mounted one more all-out offensive. Capito's sermons made such an impression upon one chronicler that when he noted in 1528 that Capito and Bucer were preaching daily against the Mass, he repeated himself to remark especially about Capito, who aimed his barbs directly at the chapter churches.[59] On December 26 he became so violent and so roused his audience that the senate called him before it to apologize. These sermons, and those of the other pastors, encouraged groups of citizens to petition the authorities. They said they would await the magistrates' decision because the pastors instructed them not to act on their own initiative. But they insisted that the council was responsible for the religious life of the city and that it must abolish the Mass or risk the wrath of God.[60]

At the same time the pastors themselves pressured the senate with petitions for abolition. The senate began to waver. On February 3, 1528, it decreed that those masses that were said privately and "without scandal" might continue, and that anyone who interfered with them would be punished. But on March 21 several citizens petitioned that these masses be replaced by evangelical worship services. The pastors duly prepared an order of service that the senate then sent to the collegiate churches on May 16.[61] But it said nothing about its plans regarding the status of the Mass.

Capito's reaction was characteristic of his reforming style. He was no longer provost of St. Thomas but he retained great influence among the chapter's remaining canons, whom he had converted to the reform party. Under his guidance they composed an unexpected inquiry regarding the senate's suggestion that they follow the new order of worship. They were pleased with it, they remarked, but

---

[58] *BB*, I, 146.

[59] Dacheux, *Fragments*, II, 37. See also Diarium Gerbelli, for 27 December. Archivum S. Thoman, 38, fol. 59(v), "Dominica proxime sequenti Capito, Mattheus, Hedio, Bucerus rem missae magna vehementia agunt ita ut fere nemo fuerit quem res ista non commoverit," from a transcript by M. Jean Rott.

[60] For one petition, see Th. B., II, 117-120. Chrisman, *Strasbourg*, pp. 163-171, remarks that the pastors may have composed these petitions, a ruse Capito had already used in *Verwarnung*, sig. C-Cii.

[61] *BDS*, II, 519-527, for the order of service. A. Baum, *Magistrat und Reformation*, pp. 173-174.

they noted that it said nothing about the Mass. Was it possible that the authorities intended to suppress it? They fervently hoped so. In their view abolishing the Mass was the only way "to calm the various disputes between the two estates of citizens and priests." It was also, they charged, necessary for the proper honor of God. The canons added, in a pledge typical of Capito, that they would not act without the senate's command because they had no authority.

Capito engineered this inquiry. To it he added a postscript in which he went beyond the innocent, impeccably loyal approach of the canons. He took upon himself the role of a prophet. "Presently," he wrote, "I speak as a preacher and as one with authority from God. For God's sake, I beg you to act in accordance with the perceiving light . . . and to do away with the idols . . . so we may come to a consequent improvement of things and avoid God's wrath . . . ." [62] Before the campaign against the Mass became so heated, he argued only that the secular authority was the sole agency that was competent to carry out external reforms of the church. At the same time he maintained that civil peace would return if only the Mass were suppressed. But in 1528 he bluntly asserted that when he spoke in his office as a minister of the Word he had authority over the senate in matters of faith. He held to this position on December 27 when the senate demanded that he account for having preached so violently against the Mass the day before. Capito denied that he urged the citizens to take matters into their own hands. They had no authority in this matter, he said. Nevertheless, he added, everyone had had time to learn that the Mass was "blasphemy." And by now the authorities should have no doubts about their responsibilities. "In this affair we [pastors] surpass prince and lord, King and Emperor, as those with authority from God." [63]

The pastors' agitation put the civil government in a steadily worsening position. By the second half of 1528 they faced an aroused citizenry within Strasbourg and an increasingly unified Catholic

---

[62] Th. B., III, 88-91. "Lieben Herren, Ich rede jetzundt als ein predicant vnd befelchhaber gottes. Ich bitt euch umb gots wyllen, furderlich jesehen zuthun vnd wessen vnd götzen absuthun, das offentliche ergernussen vnd thuerer gegenwürff der gotslesterung sindt vff das wir zu nachgender besserung dester besz komen, vnd gotes zorn abwenden mögen. Dan jn gott allein angesehen wyl sin, vnd hasset alle so vff beiden achselen tragen vnd Im nit gantz vertrawen wöllen. Die welt vernunft musz wichen vnd sich vnder Im gehorsame Der glauben begeben."

[63] Th. B., III, 117-120(v). "In welchem wir fürsten vnd Herren, König vnd Kayser vergön als befelchhaber der almechtigen gott."

party outside the city. "We are not negligent," Capito protested to Zwingli on November 1, 1528, "But, since we have been warned of abundant dangers, we are more cautious." Capito reported that Strasbourg's wealthy citizens feared the reaction of the Emperor and the local princes, to whom their banking and trading enterprises were vulnerable. He told Zwingli that he and the other reformers were doing their utmost to see the Mass abolished, but their position was extremely delicate. In late June the Imperial Vice-chancellor visited Strasbourg. He urged the city fathers to do nothing until after the Diet that was to meet at Speier the following February. Although the councilmen did not commit themselves to honoring the emissary's request, they were disturbed by the prospect of Imperial intervention.[64] What Capito and the others desired was, after all, plainly illegal.

Capito aided the city in the only way he could. Sometime in late July he and Hedio composed a short defence of the religious changes in Strasbourg. They dedicated the summary to the imperial Vice-chancellor and began by pledging loyalty to the secular authority and to the Emperor in particular. They added, however, that they were obliged to hold to the truth, and that meant abolishing the Mass. On the other hand, they emphasized that theirs was a conservative program that envisaged no unnecessary changes. "All agreeable things that it is impossible to maintain and that are considered to be against God, we freely say are to be let go; whatever, however, may remain with God, should be zealously upheld." [65] This pamphlet was an attractive statement of the reform movement in Strasbourg. Capito's remarks revealed the depth of his understanding of the political problems of reform; his publishing them testified to his desire to aid Strasbourg's authorities whenever he could.

"Grace and peace, dearest brother," Capito wrote Blaurer on February 21, 1529. "Yesterday the Mass was abolished among us. . . . Thanks be to the Lord, who has given us at last to defy the vain threats of the tyrants." The reformers were finally victorious, and Capito's method of approaching the senate was an important factor in their victory. He conducted the campaign with the finesse of the politician, as well as the customary zeal of the religious re-

---

[64] *ZW*, IX, 593. Chrisman, *Strasbourg*, pp. 171-172.

[65] *Kurtze Summ aller Lere und Predig so zu Strassburg gelert und gepredigt würt* ([Strassburg, 1528]), sig. [A(v)]-Aiii. This was consistent with the position he took in the *Entschuldigung*, sig. DDij(v); see n. 39 and the discussion, below.

former. It was appropriate that he should, for political considerations ranked high in the minds of the magistrates right up to their final decision. In mid-January 1529 a figure no less inclined to reform than Sturm himself recommended postponing a decision until the Diet of Speier recessed. The vote in the Great Council was split, with 184 favoring abolition and 94 following Sturm's request for delay. In the decree that followed, the senate declared that it was suppressing the Mass in order to avoid the wrath of God.[66] This statement reflected in part Capito's repeated argument that peace could be reestablished if only the Mass was abolished.

Capito had finally persuaded the Strasbourg senate to assume the duties of a Christian magistrate. He did so by continually asserting that religious reform and public order went hand in hand. And his own impeccable loyalty to the authorities finally lent credibility to his argument. In 1526 he dedicated his commentary on Habakkuk to Sturm, with the observation that it was necessary for all the preachers in Strasbourg and its environs to preach the same doctrine, "For diversity disturbs the weak judgment of the masses. . . ." Accordingly Capito pledged that he and the others would therefore preach "not with insane ragings, but with zealous, flaming spirits." He was true to his word. He never indulged in the unbridled polemics that were so common in the Reformation. "We have seen Murner's utterly inept blasphemies," he wrote Oecolampadius in 1527, "and we are laughing at the unworthiness of the thing, to which we urge you not to respond in kind. Do not sling dung!" [67] Capito's zealous efforts to maintain order and his continued assurances of loyalty undoubtedly made the reform movement more palatable to the authorities of Strasbourg.

One factor in Capito's willingness—nay, desire—to depend upon the Strasbourg senate to reform the church was the high position that he personally occupied in the city. Socially, he was as much a part of Strasbourg's upper class as a pastor could be. He was acquainted with some of the city's leading figures even before his arrival. As adviser to Albert he treated with Strasbourg's delegates to the Diet of Nuremberg in November and December 1522. As provost of St. Thomas he was one of the city's most important clerics from the outset, rather than merely another refugee reformer.

---

[66] *BB*, I, 183. Chrisman, *Strasbourg*, pp. 172-174.

[67] *In Habakvk prophetam V. Fabritii Capitonis enarrationes* (Argentorati, 1526), fol. 2. *BAO*, II, 34.

His parish at New St. Peter's was the city's second largest, and when he purchased citizenship, the city secretary assigned him to one of the socially important merchants' guilds. His marriage to a daughter of a member of the Council of Fifteen attests to his status, and he had received a family coat of arms from no one less than Ferdinand himself.[68] It was natural for him to have confidence in Strasbourg's ruling oligarchy, for in some ways he was part of it.

He nevertheless was engaged in more than expedient posturing when he insisted that only established authority had the *ius reformandi*. It is true that he was forced to depend upon the senate to abolish the Mass, because he cast aside the coercive powers of the medieval church. "Thought and belief, it is said, are tax-free; no one judges them except God the Lord, who gives faith," he wrote in 1524. "But in outward worship, the authorities should let nothing against God continue. . . . With that, we end up in the soup." [69] The true measure of his sincerity was nevertheless that he always disapproved disloyalty to established authority, even during the darkest days of the campaign against the Mass. His theological views on government were in accord with those Luther propounded in *On Secular Authority* of 1519. "And even if it should act with wickedness and brute force," he wrote in 1524, "it is yet incumbent upon a Christian to bear the burden and to suffer. For we should not resist evil." [70] In the 1527 catechism in which he urged the student to pray for the suppression of the Mass, he also asserted, "the Christian accepts civil orders from his temporal authority to which he is obedient and loyal with his life and goods, and knows that he who resists authority resists the very order of God." [71] However convinced Capito was that continuation of the Mass amounted to public idolatry, his understanding that all authority came from God compelled him to work for reform within established political and legal norms.

There was, however, a peculiarity in Capito's anxiety to gain the favor of the Strasbourg senate for his reform program: he remained

---

[68] Virck and Winckelmann, *Politische Correspondenz,* I, 62; 65. Wittmer and Meyer, *Le livre de bourgeoisie,* II, 686. Ph. Mieg, "Capiton, le réformateur strasbourgeois. Quelques details biographiques à propos de ses armoiries," *Société de l'histoire de protestantisme français. Bulletin,* LXIV (1926), 177-187. That he was well connected is evident also from Sturm's having helped him acquire the provostship of St. Thomas as early as 1520. See Sturm to Capito, 28 June 1520. Collection Labouchère, 756. Bibliothèque de l'histoire du protestantisme français.

[69] *Antwurt,* sig. Miij-Miij(v).

[70] *Pfafheit,* sig. [A(v)]-Aii.

[71] *Kinderbericht-1527,* sig. [Avi(v)-Avii].

a religious elitist who distrusted the common man. "We have requested permission from the authority constituted by God ... to act for the masses against certain godless things," he replied to Treger in October 1524; "it would not be right for such things to occur without the knowledge and desires of the authorities. For that might create much misfortune and unrest among the common people." [72] Capito's urgent desire to cooperate with the authorities was deeply rooted in his own past, from his years as a reforming humanist in Basel, when he called for reform from above, through his service to the Archbishop of Mainz, when he begged Luther to be moderate, to his mature years in Strasbourg, when he skillfully conducted a campaign to suppress the Mass. "Give peace to our time, oh Lord. The night is gone, the day begun," were the words with which he began a hymn that he composed in 1524.[73] With them he expressed the abiding pacifism and elitism that lay behind his peculiar style as a reformer. In this respect he remained a humanist even while he was a reformer.

[72] *Antwurt*, sig. Fiij.
[73] The hymn is noted by the chronicler in Dacheux, *Fragments*, III, 33. It was first published in Augsburg in 1533. G. H. A. Rittelmeyer, "Die evangelische Liederdichter des Elsasses," *Beiträge zu den Theologische Wissenschaften*, VI (1855), 157-161.

CHAPTER SIX

THE MAN OF UNITY AND THE SACRAMENTARIAN CONTROVERSY

Two abstract values inhibited Capito's conversion to the Reformation between 1522 and 1524, and they continued to play a role in his career as a reformer. One was his conviction that any true religious reform was necessarily peaceful. The other was his corollary attachment to the unity of the church. On the first count, with the help of Zell, he gradually came to the convenient and, for him, necessary conclusion that it was the opponents of the gospel, rather than the reformers, who caused disorder. The true evidence of his commitment to peaceful proceedings is that he then conducted his own reforming activities with an eye to minimizing the possibility of public unrest while purifying the church in Strasbourg. His love of religious harmony also continued to shape his activities. For his allegiance to the universality of the medieval church, which he decided was no true church, he substituted a passion for unity among the reformers, with whom he now identified the true church.

But in the 1520's and early 1530's the reform movement was subject to ever greater disunity. Andreas Carlstadt's visit to Strasbourg in October 1524 provided Capito's introduction to doctrinal division within the reform party. When he arrived, Carlstadt was convinced that Luther perfidiously engineered his eviction from Saxony after inviting him to a literary duel over their differences. In Strasbourg he not only urged the populace to strip the churches on their own initiative but also spread his own teachings on the eucharist and the story of his supposed mistreatment at Luther's hands.[1] Earlier Carlstadt had found himself in agreement with a letter from the Dutch spiritualist Cornelius Hoen, who maintained that the bread and wine were symbols of Christ's body and blood and that Christ was not physically present in the elements. For Carlstadt, the efficacy of the Lord's Supper thus depended upon the faith of the communicant who received spiritual nourishment by participating in a memorial of Christ's crucifixion. Luther believed that Carlstadt's teaching contravened the clear intent of the

---

[1] On Carlstadt's break with Luther and stay in Strasbourg, see *WA*, XV, 326-329; 334-341, and Barge, *Karlstadt*, II, 206-207.

Scriptures, that Christ was physically present in the Lord's Supper regardless of the status of the communicant's soul. And so the lines were drawn in a controversy that raged throughout the Reformation and that irretrievably split the reform movement.

Carlstadt's sojourn compounded the difficulties of the Strasbourg reformers, who already were embroiled in the battle over clerical citizenship and were defending themselves from Treger's charges that they were disturbing the peace. Thirteen of Carlstadt's essays preceded him to Strasbourg and they were shortly joined by five more that he published in Basel. Capito's response to this situation exemplified a man's doing as he preached. He personally detested Carlstadt, who was a constant source of irritation while Capito was adviser to the Archbishop of Mainz. The quarrel with Luther and the visit to Strasbourg confirmed his opinion. "Carlstadt yielded our church up to disorders with his virulent books," he wrote Blaurer on December 10, 1524. "How cowardly he snatches at Luther! Oh, wickedness! Oh, shameful deed!" Capito's disgust was unabated ten months later. To Oecolampadius he wrote, "That man has always seemed to me to be the following—a seeker after fame." [2]

These were Capito's private sentiments, reserved for himself and his closest colleagues. He did publish a treatise on the dispute between Carlstadt and Luther in the middle of October 1524, but in print he described Carlstadt as one "whom we have esteemed and still want to esteem as a learned helper in the Word." He avoided taking sides openly by suggesting that the quarrel arose "because of the slanderers" on both sides. Much as at Mainz, he put doctrinal division down to human perversity. "One should consider all men to be men," he wrote, "and hope for more from no one; our faith depends everywhere only on God."

Capito tried to smother the doctrinal dispute, too. He granted that the observances of Rome were blasphemous, but, he cautioned, "Here, however, is a small difference; we desire first to bring all abuses and improper services of God out of the hearts of men through the Word, and then to abolish them outwardly also." He urged his readers to remember that "At the Lord's command, we should concern ourselves entirely with that which is the main thing: love from a pure heart and a good conscience, and from an unstained

---

[2] *BB*, I, 115. *BAO*, I, 405.

faith. Whatever does not concern these things leads only to useless babble." In regard to the Lord's Supper itself he argued, "We should nourish our faith only with the Lord's bread and wine through the memory of his body and blood and let everything else go. Should anything further be necessary, then let God reveal it to you.[3] The true test of his belief that the exact nature of the elements was not worth quarreling about came in his second book against Treger, which he also published in October and where he praised Hus and Wyclif. "Although to be sure Wyclif and Hus taught differently from us about the Sacrament of the Mass, it does not concern us; no main point was changed, for it is an outward thing. The main sum remains, that Christ Jesus came to make sinners blessed." [4] Capito would not use disagreement on the eucharist even to save himself from the damaging charge of being a Hussite.

Nicholas Gerbellius, an ardent follower of Luther in Strasbourg, thought he saw only confusion in Capito's treatise. In a letter to Luther on November 22 he reported, "Meanwhile, truly, those who would begin to grow in Christ cling to both sides; they waver and wander about between them. . . ." [5] Gerbellius misunderstood. Capito's treatise was for public consumption, and his refusal to take sides was premeditated. As a young man he was deeply shaken by doubts about the elements, and as a mature man he held strong opinions about them. But he honestly believed that the unity of the true church took precedence over a precise understanding of the eucharist, and he therefore insofar as possible avoided taking sides publicly.

Capito taught that the Lord's Supper was a spiritualistic memorial even before it became a controverted question. In conversation with Pellican in October 1512 he substituted a spiritual view of the elements for the doctrine of transubstantiation. In the *Entschuldigung* of November 1523 he declared that "the Mass is a daily remembrance (*gedechtnüsz*) of the one sacrifice," while maintaining that the Fathers considered "no one to be so thick as to understand that the birth of Christ were occurring at this time and not several hundred years

---

[3] *Von der Spaltung*, sig. [A(v)]; B(v); Aii(v). The view of Strasser, *Beziehungen*, p. 35, that Capito actually favored Carlstadt is obviously unfounded.

[4] *Antwurt*, sig. H-H(v).

[5] *WABr*, III, 379. On Gerbellius, see Jean Rott, "Le Humaniste Strasbourgeois Nicolas Gerbel et son Diaire (1522-1529)," *Bulletin philologique et historique* (Reprint: Paris, 1950).

ago." [6] In the second treatise against Treger, which he composed while Carlstadt was in Strasbourg, Capito wrote,

> At the same time we say however that no outward thing makes us justified from sin, gives grace, or promotes the gift of salvation; we are justified in the recollection (*gedächtnüsz*) of the death of Christ for our sakes. We refresh ourselves through such recollection and openly revere it while accepting the Lord's bread and wine, and we know that the foremost point is that faith in the promise of God is exercised through Christ Jesus whose last will and testament is that we become blessed through his body and blood alone. [7]

There can be no question of Carlstadt's or Zwingli's influencing him to a spiritual view of the sacrament. His youthful encounter with Wyclif was the point of departure for his own development of what came to be called the "Zwinglian" teaching on the Lord's Supper. The stages of his progress are not clearly marked, but a refusal to allow temporal things in and of themselves to carry grace could be expected of someone who as a young man was such a devoted follower of Erasmus.

Although Capito had a clear understanding of the elements before October 1524, others among the Strasbourg reformers did not. Before Carlstadt's visit, Bucer in particular scarely gave the matter much thought. [8] But he did agree with Capito that they should seek the advice of their counterparts in Zurich and Wittenberg. Capito probably wrote the letters to Zwingli and Luther in November because they contained both his memorial view of the Supper and his desire to avoid controversy. After outlining Carlstadt's opinion, he reported to Luther what was taught in Strasbourg:

> The bread and the cup are external things, and however much the bread may be the body of Christ and the cup his blood, it nevertheless contributes nothing to our salvation, seeing that the flesh, in short, is useful for nothing. But on the other hand, to remember the Lord's death—in this matter that is the only thing that brings salvation; in that very use alone is the bread to be eaten and the cup drunk. . . . [9]

---

[6] *Entschuldigung*, sig. DDiii.

[7] *Antwurt*, sig. H(v).

[8] On Bucer, see Hastings Eells, "The Genesis of Martin Bucer's Doctrine of the Lord's Supper," *Princeton Theological Review*, XXIV (1926), 225-229, and Robert Stupperich, "Strassburgs Stellung im Beginn des Sakramentstreits," *Archiv für Reformationsgeschichte*, XXXVIII (1941), 249-262. The most recent work is James M. Kittelson, "Martin Bucer and the Sacramentarian Controversy: The Origins of his Policy of Concord," *Archive for Reformation History*, LXIV (1973), 166-183.

[9] *WABr*, III, 383.

The central portion of Capito's letter to Zwingli was almost identical:

> That that bread and cup are an external thing, whatever it may be, and that by itself it accomplishes nothing for salvation; on the other hand, that the memory of the Lord's death is both beneficial and necessary (*et salutarem et necessariam*); therefore we admonish ours to eat the Lord's bread and to drink the cup for this purpose (*in hunc usum*) while passing over other things.[10]

Under Capito's direction, the Strasbourg reformers were in Zwingli's camp before there was such a thing.

In a letter that he devoted largely to other matters, Zwingli quickly replied to the Strasbourg theologians that he did not wish to require any particular attitude toward the elements, but that he personally was convinced that the bread and wine were symbols of Christ's body and blood. The Christian, Zwingli wrote, referring to John 6:63, was bound not to the letter but to the spirit. Christ sat at the right hand of the Father. Although his return was expected, he should be worshipped in the spirit for the present.[11] Luther, on the other hand, replied tardily, in great heat, and in a published attack on Carlstadt rather than in a confidential letter. Carlstadt, he declared, was "a devil" and his teaching was "so much smoke and steam." Referring to the Words of Institution, Luther wrote, "I can not get out; the text is too powerful there and will not allow itself to be wrenched out of sense with words." [12] Luther not only broke the Strasbourg pastors' confidence; he also contravened their desire for concord, even with Carlstadt, while he taught a view of the Lord's Supper that differed sharply from their own. They sided with Zwingli in the controversy that followed.

One reason the Strasbourg reformers joined Zwingli as a group was that Capito converted Bucer to a spiritual understanding. On December 31, 1524, he replied to Zwingli that now "Bucer agrees wholeheartedly with your view; he was long ago more favorable to Luther's opinion, which I convinced the diligent and acute man always declared more of the temporal than of the truth." [13] Before

---

[10] *ZW*, VIII, 248. Note the similarity of both letters to Capito's views as quoted above, and, for a clear statement of the symbolic view of the elements, to *Entschuldigung*, sig. DDii(v), "Von sacramenten halten wir, wie sie Christus gesetzt, vnd sein Aposteln gehalten, das es gewisse warzeichen seind der verheissenen gnaden, deszhalben heilsam, das sie vnsern glauben beuesten."

[11] *ZW*, VIII, 275-276.

[12] *WA*, XV, 393-394.

[13] *ZW*, VIII, 279-280. Eells, "Bucer's Doctrine," *Princeton Theological Review*,

Carlstadt raised the issue, Bucer's chief concern regarding the eucharist was to attack the sale of masses as simony. That was in an apology for his preaching at Wissembourg that he wrote in July 1523, but in the *Grund und Ursach*, a defense of reform in Strasbourg that he wrote in December 1524, Bucer adopted Capito's desire for concord and his understanding of the Lord's Supper. To Carlstadt he addressed the question, "You certainly hear that Christ says, 'The flesh is of no profit;' for what reason then are you raising questions about the flesh?" [14]

Capito's and Bucer's fond wish that everyone hold his own opinion in peace, while maintaining the unity of the reform party, nevertheless went unfulfilled. In summer 1525 Luther's colleague Bugenhagen published a letter he wrote to Johann Hess in which he attacked Zwingli, who had also published his views. The Strasbourg pastors countered by dispatching one of their number, George Casel, to Wittenberg in November on a mission of concord. He carried a short letter of accreditation from Capito, a longer letter in which Capito refuted Bugenhagen's views point by point, and a long appeal to brotherly love from Bucer.[15] In his letter Capito forthrightly maintained that the bread "is the external symbol by which we confess ourselves to be members of the external body" of Christ. He would not abide the real, physical presence as Bugenhagen taught it. But even while denying Bugenhagen's teachings, Capito was first concerned to dampen the growing dispute. "The sum of our position, accordingly, is that we admonish you, my Pomeranus, to exert yourself in every way for the continuance of concord among the leading ministers of the Word, by which we have thus far proved the unity and power of the Spirit, and almost to the enemies too." Capito seemed oddly unable to believe that anyone would be willing to quarrel over the exact nature of the elements in the Lord's Supper. He recounted his own youthful struggles over the issue and asserted

---

XXIV, 228, quotes this letter while omitting Capito's claim to have converted Bucer. Stupperich, "Strassburgs Stellung," *Archiv für Reformationsgeschichte*, XXXVIII, 254, declares that Capito could not yet have known Bucer's position because Bucer had not yet published it. But surely the two conversed with one another!

[14] *BDS*, I, 119-125; 252. Eells, "Bucer's Doctrine," *Princeton Theological Review*, XXIV, 228, falsely asserts that Bucer adopted Carlstadt's argument, according to which Christ was pointing to himself when he said, "This is my body."

[15] On the mission, see Jean Rott, "Bucer et les débuts de la querelle sacramentaire," *Revue d'histoire et de philosophie religieuses*, XXXIV (1954), 236-242.

that the present controversy was all Carlstadt's fault. He judged two of Luther's recent attacks on Zwingli and Carlstadt with the observation that "The danger lies in our minute examination of what we have thus far affirmed more than is expedient for edification." Capito composed his letter carefully to demonstrate first that the elements were nonessential and then to appeal for unity, but his initiative failed. Bugenhagen thanked Capito for his letter, but he also attacked him in a letter to Gerbellius, who soon refused even to speak with Capito or Bucer.[16]

The failure of this early attempt at concord embittered Capito. Before Casel's mission he did refer privately to the Wittenbergers as the *"Impanati Dei,"* and he declared to Oecolampadius that "We who defend the liberty of the faith, who refuse to grant that through a new tyranny they may create a doctrine out of their sleep, are the safest." But after it became apparent that Luther would not budge, his feelings were such that he felt compelled to confess to Oecolampadius, "Now the Spirit deplores the stubbornness in me of refusing to concede the sincerity of his thought and corrupt faith." On the other hand, he declared, "There is no place for abuse among Christian brothers." [17]

Capito therefore still admonished Zwingli and Oecolampadius to practice brotherly love. In January 1526 he wrote Oecolampadius again, "Concerning the book that Zwingli is now considering, I very much fear that it may exacerbate the matter further; it would appear to be ended by silence in dissent, not by a battle of wits." His plan, Capito wrote, was that "we would expound concord." Later in the year Bucer translated Bugenhagen's commentary on the Psalms and altered his statements on the Lord's Supper to make them accord with Zwingli's. Capito advised Bucer against it, for he feared that such perfidy would worsen the situation as indeed it did. Even in September, he could not forgive Bucer's inept tampering. He could pardon Luther's bombast less, but while condemning it, he insisted to Zwingli that Luther and Melanchthon were true, if erring, brethern.[18] As a reformer Capito's attitude toward the *Sakramentstreit* paralleled his policy as adviser to the Archbishop of Mainz. He implored both sides to remember the law of love.

---

[16] Vogt, *Bugenhagens Briefwechsel*, pp. 32; 35-37; 45. Rott, "Gerbel," *Bulletin philologique et historique*, pp. 5-6.

[17] *BAO*, I, 405; 421.

[18] *BAO*, I, 454. *ZW*, VIII, 724.

Capito's mediating policy at Mainz had theological underpinnings in his Erasmian belief that the gospel was fundamentally the law of love and that precise doctrines were undemonstrable in any event. His search for unity among the reformers during the sacramentarian controversy also grew naturally from a theological position, this time from his understanding of the Lord's Supper itself. In an important sense his spiritualism was so thorough that he could judge the elements unworthy of controversy. In January 1526 he wrote Oecolampadius that the Lord's Supper "is an external thing. . . . Therefore it is not necessary for salvation. . . ." Before 1530 Capito often explicitly denied that the bread and wine became Christ's body and blood in any physical sense. He devoted much of his 1525 letter to Bugenhagen to repeating Oecolampadius' and Zwingli's argument that *"est"* meant *"significat"* in the Words of Institution. "Nor do I see why we are so horrified at metaphor in this place," he wrote, "when we frequently accept others in nearby individual verses of the Scriptures." [19] In the catechism that he wrote in 1527 he included this exchange:

> *Question*: But what use do you have from the words [of institution?]
>
> *Answer*: My remembrance of the eternal salvation, as it occurred through the body and blood of Christ, is renewed, refreshed, and strengthened, and therefore I truly have Christ—not that he is therefore bread or that he comes either under or with the bread. For Christ attends to the spiritual matter with physical signs. . . . After he had breathed upon his disciples, he also said 'Receive the Holy Spirit.' This breath was not the Holy Spirit, nor was it either near or under the breath. But the believing disciples received it truly into the heart, even as we receive the body of Christ in faith, even though he is not physically in or near the bread.

Capito could then add, "To the unbelieving, it is void of significance." [20] As someone who believed the elements signified nothing in and of themselves, he had difficulty understanding how Luther and Bugenhagen could dispute so seriously about the matter. "Certainly the trouble of inquiring about the body become bread," he wrote Bugenhagen, "is of no importance to salvation. . . ." [21]

The poverty of the elements was a negative theological reason for seeking unity, but there was also a positive one. This Capito took over

---

[19] *BAO*, I, 454. Vogt, *Bugenhagens Briefwechsel*, pp. 42-43.

[20] *Kinderbericht-1527*, sig. C.

[21] Vogt, *Bugenhagens Briefwechsel*, p. 41.

from Bucer, who declared in the *Grund und Ursach* that the eucharist "is surely neither a good work nor a sacrifice . . . as the papists have lied, but as Paul calls it, communion." [22] Capito seized upon the understanding of the Lord's Supper as communion. Before 1524 he did not mention it, but he included this notion in all his writings on the subject thereafter. In the second edition of his catechism he wrote,

> *Instructor*: So the sacrament strengthens the conscience?
>
> *Youth*: Not in itself; but the remembrance, through the Holy Spirit, from its meaning strengthens, refreshes, and secures faith and love in us. For in the midst of eating, we confess ourselves to be members of all the faithful and give ourselves over to a common mass as one bread and body of all.[23]

In his commentary on Hosea of 1528 he taught that, "The eucharist is assuredly at one time a sign of this internal anointing, at another that we are members of the one body, of the one mass, of the one bread . . . of the one Father, and together partners of his inheritance." [24] After 1524 he was thus more concerned with the inward spiritual benefit of the sacrament than with the exact nature of the elements. "Accordingly that which is peculiar to the body of the Lord is to be well understood here," he wrote in 1532 in a confession for the Synod of Bern. "Namely, the body through which we are nourished, and that we have community." Such an understanding of the Lord's Supper naturally led Capito to fervent advocacy of concord, "For the sacraments should serve us to the end of perfection and not to bringing forth physical sensuality." [25]

The controversy raged in spite of Capito's admonitions. Bucer was one of the active pamphleteers. But in April 1528 he read Luther's

---

[22] *BDS*, I, 243. For the argument that this is the sum of Bucer's position, see Kittelson, "Bucer," *Archive for Reformation History*, LXIV, 166-183.

[23] *Kinderbericht-1529*, fol. 33. *Kinderbericht-1527*, sig. Dii(v)-Diii(v).

[24] *In Hoseam prophetam V. F. Capitonis commentarius* (Argentorati, 1528), fol. 155(v). "Eucharistia uero nota est tum huius internae unctionis, tum quod sumus unius corporis membra, unius massae . . . unius patris, eiusdemque haereditates una participes."

[25] *Berner Synodus, Ordnung wie sich pfarrer und prediger zu Statt und Land Bern in leer und leben halten sollen* ([Basel], 1532]), sig. eiii. For a somewhat different statement of the same understanding, *Kinderbericht-1529*, fol. 21(v)-22, "Christus ist eyn geystliche speisz im hertzen, vnd er würt nit mit mundt als ander leiblich speisz gessen." For Capito's authorship of the *Berner Synodus*, see Berchthold Haller to Capito, 16 March 1532, Th. B., V, 48. On the editions, in Latin, French, German, and Dutch, most recently in 1889, see Strasser, *Beziehungen*, p. 171 n. 1. Although Capito composed the work unaided, it became Bern's official confession.

Von Abendmal Christi, Bekendnis and became convinced that Luther really taught that Christ's body was joined with the elements in a sacramental rather than a physical sense. From then on Bucer, too, vigorously promoted concord. He died, convinced that if only the right formula could be found, a lasting agreement could be struck between the Swiss and the Saxons. At the same time the evangelical princes, led by Philip of Hesse, were becoming increasingly anxious about the political danger of disunion within their party. Frightened by the closing of Catholic ranks at the Diet of Speier in April 1529, Philip brought together Luther and Melanchthon, Zwingli and Oecolampadius, Bucer and Hedio at Marburg in October 1529. The purpose of the meeting was to see if enough agreement could be reached on the doctrinal question to provide an ideological basis for a political alliance. But the issue was decided before the colloquy began. Luther would not budge from the literal meaning of the text, "This is my body." He told Bucer that he belonged to the devil, and he refused the hand of brotherhood to Zwingli.[26]

As he went to the colloquy, Bucer thought that the dispute between Luther and Zwingli was merely a matter of words. Capito did not. He possessed an irenic spirit, but he was never willing to sacrifice his candid understanding of the eucharist for the sake of agreement. Illness prevented his attendance at Marburg,[27] but it is doubtful that he could have made a positive contribution to concord, although he was the first of the Strasbourg reformers to take it seriously. In 1529 he published a second edition of his catechism in which he declared,

> *Youth*: He has given his body and blood to the disciples to eat and to drink spiritually, that is, for faith. . . .
>
> *Instructor*: Therefore, you do not believe that he transformed his body and blood in the Lord's Supper in a fleshly way or has hidden them under the bread and wine.
>
> *Youth*: I do not believe it. . . .[28]

As though this blunt condemnation of Luther's teachings were not enough to make Capito unwelcome at Marburg, he also contributed

---

[26] Eells, "Bucer's Doctrine," *Princeton Theological Review*, XXIV, 242-245. On Marburg and the events leading up to it, see Walter Köhler, *Zwingli und Luther, Ihr Streit über das Abendmahl nach seinen politischen und religiösen Beziehungen* (Gütersloh, 1953), II, 1-164.

[27] Bucer to Blaurer, 18 October 1529, *BB*, II, 385, "Capito modo ex sudore laborat illo Anglico. . . ."

[28] *Kinderbericht-1529*, fol. 20(v)-21.

in June a laudatory preface to Caspar Schwenckfeld's apology for his teachings on the Lord's Supper. Schwenckfeld was a Silesian nobleman who was an early convert to the Reformation, but he broke with Luther over the Lord's Supper and arrived in Strasbourg in May 1529. Capito spent most of the preface defending Oecolampa-dius' argument in his *De genuina expositione* of 1526 that *"est"* meant *"significat"* and *"corpus," "figura corporis"* in the Words of Institution. Capito concluded that "the body of Christ is neither physically in the substance of the earthly bread nor physically under the form of the same, as the Papists claim, but that it is truly in the supper of the faithful through the Word in the Holy Spirit." He did not specifi-cally mention Luther, but the import of the preface was clear when he declared that Schwenckfeld "describes the matter of the Lord's Supper as it stands known before God and among the faithful . . . in so far as I presently understand it." [29] For Capito, whether healthy or ill, to go to Marburg would have been impolitic.

His behavior during 1529 was both peculiar and revealing. He knew that delicate negotiations were underway in preparation for the meeting at Marburg. Yet he published views that implicitly denied Luther's teachings. His personal efforts to establish concord amounted to little more than earnest admonitions to the reformers to love one another. The tolerance that he advocated was, thus, of a distinctly modern sort, consisting largely of a willingness to agree to disagree. He never appreciated that Luther and Zwingli considered one another blasphemous in their views of the eucharist. His campaign for concord was thus more than merely foolish. Because the entire question of the eucharist was genuinely an outward matter for him, once the doctrine of transubstantiation was rejected, he felt there could be no harm in declaring his candid understanding, as long as he coupled it with a warning against contentiousness. He was there-fore helpless in the face of the rising controversy, for outward har-mony without confessional uniformity was an impossibility here, just as it was during his service to the Archbishop of Mainz.

For the Strasbourg reformers the turning point in the *Sakrament-streit* came at the Diet of Augsburg in 1530. The city was in a danger-ous political situation. It abolished the Mass the year before and thereby incurred the wrath of Emperor Charles. Yet it had no alli-ances with German principalities while it sat like an island in the

---

[29] *Apologia vnd erclerung der Schlesier das sy den leyb und blut Christi* ([Strassburg], 1529), sig. Aii; Aiii-Aiii(v).

then Catholic sea of southwestern Germany. Strasbourg was asso-
ciatively allied with the reformed Swiss cantons, but they could not
be expected to provide much aid in the event of war in the Empire.
Everyone of position knew that Charles V intended to make one
last effort to settle the religious dispute, and some deluded themselves with the hope that a free church council might be called on
German soil for that purpose. In any event Strasbourg would be
called upon to account for its having suppressed the Mass, and the
city's politicians were concerned about the outcome.

Strasbourg's pastors and civil authorities made extensive preparations for the coming Diet at Augsburg. On the one hand Sturm and
Mathis Pfarrer, the representatives to the Diet, desired to supplement the city's strong tie with the Swiss by association with the
German Protestants. This objective required some understanding
with the Saxons in regard to the Lord's Supper. Bucer drafted a
memorandum for the city's delegates in which he outlined a formula
that would encompass the positions of both Zwingli and Luther.
On the other hand the city would have to justify abolishing the
Mass, and three other documents were written for this purpose. In
one Capito gave Sturm and Pfarrer arguments to use in urging that
a free Christian council be called. In another the jurist Jacob Kirscher
considered the points of law that touched upon the reform of the
church in Strasbourg. In the third Capito and Sturm argued that the
need to keep order compelled the city to suppress the Mass.[30] These
latter three documents in particular did not necessarily represent the
true thinking of their authors. They were rather alternative lines of
argument for the city's delegates to use as they saw fit in defending
and improving Strasbourg's position at the Diet.

With the exception of Bucer's draft of an all-encompassing article
on the Lord's Supper, Strasbourg's preparations for the Diet were
worthless. The talk of a free church council on German soil proved
to be an unfounded rumor, and Charles V was in no mood to listen
to elaborate justifications for illegal, albeit official, repressions of the
Roman cultus. By the time Sturm and Pfarrer arrived in Augsburg,
it was apparent that the Emperor wished only to receive formal
confessions of faith from the Protestants with the intent of refuting
them. Sturm and Pfarrer were alarmed. On June 2 they anxiously
reported to the Council of Thirteen, Strasbourg's committee for

---

[30] Wilhelm Gussmann, *Quellen und Forschungen zur Geschichte des Augsburgischen Glaubensbekenntnisses* (Leipzig, 1911), I¹, 33-39.

foreign affairs, that other delegations were at the Diet with an entourage of theologians. "It would accordingly not be unprofitable if Martin Bucer or Dr. Capito were here with us . . .," they requested. By June 8 Sturm and Pfarrer apparently decided to push for some agreement with the Saxons, for they repeated their call to send Bucer, who was inclined to compromise on doctrinal matters, but asked for Capito only in a postscript to their dispatch. On June 16 they wrote again, insisting that the Council of Thirteen send Bucer; they added that the Thirteen should send Capito too if they thought he would be helpful. Sturm and Pfarrer recommended that the pastors travel and arrive in Augsburg secretly, but they also reported that other reformers were at the Diet without guarantees of safe conduct and were not being molested.[31]

On June 25 the Thirteen replied that Capito and Bucer had left Strasbourg separately to find their own discreet ways to Augsburg. They urged Sturm and Pfarrer to use Capito's "short memorandum," [32] which was his recommendation for the calling of a free church council. The Thirteen were poorly informed about the situation in Augsburg, or they would not have made such a recommendation nor would they have allowed Capito to leave Strasbourg. The phantasy of a church council with or without the pope, in Germany or elsewhere, was dead when Capito crept into Augsburg late on the evening of June 26. Melanchthon's Augsburg Confession had already been read to the Emperor. Capito and Bucer borrowed a copy from Philip of Hesse and set to work on a statement of faith for Strasbourg.

The confession that Capito and Bucer wrote, which became known as the *Confessio Tetrapolitana*, derived its basic outline from Melanchthon's Augsburg Confession. The only exception was the article on the Lord's Supper, which Capito composed. His authorship is evident not only because the entire piece is in his hand but also because it varied so much from Bucer's professed intention to seek a broad formula that would accommodate the teachings of both Zwingli and Luther. In its draft form Capito's article covered six folio leaves and excluded Luther's doctrine of the bodily presence. In the crucial section he declared "that Christ the Lord is truly in the Supper and gives his true body truly to eat and his blood truly to

---

[31] Virck and Winckelmann, *Politische Correspondenz*, I, 453; 455.
[32] *Ibid.*, I, 561-563.

drink. But especially to the spirit, through faith." [33] Capito put his denial of the physical presence in positive rather than negative terms. He did not specifically deny that Christ's body was physically in the elements, as was his custom. The import of his final statement was nevertheless clear; he was speaking of spiritual eating and drinking. By implication he therefore excluded Luther's teaching.

Capito may have felt that he worded his article sufficiently broadly to promote concord. His statement nevertheless scarcely fulfilled Bucer's wish for a formula that would be the basis for concord between the Swiss and the Saxons. At the end of the statement, possibly after he returned to Strasbourg, Capito wrote,

> In responding to this view, Jacob Sturm and Matthis Pfarrer were concerned that it should not appear as if we damned the light, also that thereby destructive contradiction might be all the more clearly avoided. And then, in order to please other cities, it was considered proper to shorten its content, as conceived in the book. Our scrupulous understanding was brought forth in that [revised version] but in the shortest possible manner. May God give further grace.[34]

Capito was pressured into changing this article and he evidently did not like it. But political exigencies forced his hand. At the insistence of Sturm and Pfarrer, and of the cities of Constance, Memmingen, and Lindau, Capito revised the article on the Lord's Supper to read, "In this sacrament he gives of the true body and of the true blood truly to eat and drink for the nourishment of your souls and eternal life, that you may remain in him and he in you." [35]

On balance little was changed in the new article on the eucharist, as Capito wrote in his postscript to the original version. In reporting the negotiations to the brethren at Strasbourg, he declared that

---

[33] Archives municipales de Strasbourg. Varia Ecclesiastica, IX, 103(v). ". . . das Christus der Herr im Abentmal worlich zugegen ist, und seyn woren leib warlich zuessen und sein blut warlich sutrinken gibt. Aber furnemlich demgeist durch den glauben." The entire piece is in Capito's hand. A later copy, also deposited in the Archives municipales, carries the title, "Anno 1530. Begriff vomm Sacrament des Lybs und Blutts Christi, Welcher an der Vier Stätte Bekandnüss nit Ingelegt ist, aber sonst ettlichen fürsten übergebn. Cap. 18." Archivum S. Thoman, 45, 1. Pollet, *Bucer*, I, 45-54, prints the text and maintains, without evidence, that Bucer was its author.

[34] Archives municipales de Strasbourg, Varia Ecclesiastica, IX, 106. The reference "wie *im libel* begriffen" is obscure.

[35] Archives municipales de Strasbourg, AA 420, 117(v)-118. "In diesen Sakrament vom woren leib und wors blut worlich zuessen gibt. zur speysz Irs selen und ewigen leben. das sy in Im und er in Inen plibe." To which Capito added the notation, "ist zur Augspurg Ingelegt werden. ano 1530."

"The article concerning the eucharist was essentially unchanged; although by that metonymy we accommodated those friends all the more rather than the opponents, we in fact distinctly affirm that only the spiritual eating is useful. . . ." [36] Capito was reporting the truth. Although in the revised version he did not go out of his way to limit Christ's presence to a spiritual mode, he did positively state that the Lord's Supper had a spiritual benefit and a spiritual purpose. The representatives of Constance, Memmingen, and Lindau signed the confession unhappily even with the changes. In spite of being under great pressure to produce an irenic statement of his teachings, Capito was unwilling to make many concessions. He carefully guarded his understanding of the Lord's Supper in revising his statement; he altered only its form in order to please Sturm and Pfarrer.

With their business accomplished, Capito and Bucer yet remained in Augsburg several more weeks, for talk of concord was again in the air. Sturm and Pfarrer in particular wished them to strike some agreement with Luther and Melanchthon, because they rightly felt that alliance with the small towns of Constance, Memmingen, and Lindau was a poor alternative to the protection of Hesse and Saxony. At first Melanchthon was cool to the new approaches, but about the middle of August, Philip of Hesse persuaded him to see Bucer, who maintained that he had misunderstood Luther's teaching and contended that a true basis for accord existed. There was, he claimed, little difference between the notion of Christ's spiritual presence and Luther's doctrine that Christ was really but not locally present in the sacrament. By August 26 these preliminary discussions led to Melanchthon's suggestion that Bucer compose a statement and send it to Luther. At the same time Bucer had to consider the feelings of the third member of the triangle. Zwingli, whose *Confessio Fidei* the Wittenbergers bluntly declared heretical, became suspicious of every effort for concord after the Marburg Colloquy. And so Capito was sent to Switzerland with Bucer's new formula, while Bucer continued negotiations with the Saxons.[37]

---

[36] Th. B., III, 302. "Articulus de Eucharistia immutatus est etsi ea immutatione magis ipsis imposuerimus sociis quam hostibus, expresse enim affirmamus spiritualem manducationem solam prodesse," to which he added, "exclusa est corporalis manducatio."

[37] Köhler, *Zwingli und Luther*, II, 220-228. See also Hastings Eells, "Sacramental Negotiations at the Diet of Augsburg, 1530," *Princeton Theological Review*, XXIII (1925), 213-233, now updated by Thomas A. Brady, Jr., "Jacob Sturm of Strasbourg and the Lutherans at the Diet of Augsburg, 1530," *Church History*, XLII (1973), 183-202.

Capito loyally carried out his mission to Switzerland. To all intents and purposes he was won over momentarily to Bucer's plan to achieve concord through broad formulae that would embrace the teachings of both Luther and Zwingli. He reached Basel on Monday, August 29, and spoke at length with his old friend Oecolampadius. The two men spent some time trying to draw up alternative wordings to Bucer's proposal, and the Basel authorities decided that the matter was sufficiently serious to merit sending Oecolampadius on to Zurich with Capito. Messengers were also sent to Bern to invite their representatives. Capito and Oecolampadius arrived in Zurich on August 31, but serious discussions did not begin until Friday, September 2, after the arrival of Caspar Megander, the reformer of Bern.

The meeting was a failure. When Capito began serious consideration of the matter by reading Bucer's new formula, Zwingli countered by reading letters from Johannes Brenz and Melanchthon in which they bitterly attacked every reformer in the room. It took Capito four hours to persuade Zwingli and his colleague Leo Jud to redirect their attention to Bucer's memorandum. In an attempt to cool personal feelings, he declared that he personally approved Bucer's articles, and he suggested that each individual state his opinions about them in writing the next day. On Saturday, Oecolampadius, Megander, Jud, and Zwingli had their reactions ready; Capito held to Bucer's formula. There was no hope for success. Six years of controversy had left too many scars. On September 11 Capito reported to Strasbourg's Council of Thirteen that Zwingli's response was "too sharply expressed and much too heated" to allow agreement with Luther and Melanchthon. All the group could agree upon was to entrust Capito to report the meeting to Bucer and to share the cost of a messenger. They met again briefly on September 5 to discuss various matters and then went their separate ways on September 6.[38]

There could be no questioning the earnestness of Capito's desire for concord among all the reformers. In the preface to his 1529 catechism he pleaded, "And if others should have a different understanding, or suppose themselves to have . . . I beg that the foregoing may start no quarrels. On the contrary, what God entrusts to them, they should pass on in due calm for the improvement of the churches." When he mediated a dispute among the pastors at Bern in 1532, he literally elevated his desire for unity into an article of faith. He

---

[38] Virck and Winckelmann, *Politische Correspondenz*, I, 493-495.

began article nineteen of the confessional instrument that he wrote for the Bernese with the declaration, "Concerning the Sacraments, we have considered in such manner that we wish all to have recalled and admonished one another very diligently that we all may remain in love toward everyone, as much as is in us. And that we would not allow ourselves to fall into any quarrel, especially concerning the Holy Sacrament. . . ." [39] After he became a reformer, the unity of the church remained for him a value that competed for his loyalty on equal terms with doctrinal purity.

Capito nevertheless remained an ineffective proponent of concord. His mission to Switzerland in 1530 inaugurated nearly a decade of such attempts to bring about unity within the reform party. All failed for many reasons, the most important of which was that a disagreement on principle divided the Swiss and the Saxons. At the very most Bucer's attempt to find a sufficiently general formula upon which to unify the two parties could have papered over the contradictions. But there was another subsidiary reason for Capito's and Bucer's failure to accomplish even that. Fundamentally Capito either did not understand or did not agree with Bucer's strategy, and this divergence was a critical flaw in their campaign. Bucer, after all, succeeded in his relations with Luther and Melanchthon. The failure occurred with the Swiss, who were Capito's responsibility. He had a fine opportunity to draw them into an agreement when both Zwingli and Oecolampadius died in fall 1531, for before the appearance of Bullinger, Capito was the dominant figure in Swiss reformed circles. In 1532 he helped both Basel and Bern put their churches in order after the Battle of Kappel. He might then have imposed upon them one of Bucer's broad formulae. Instead he encouraged them to retain a distinctly spiritualist view of the Lord's Supper.

In the confession that he composed for the canton of Bern in January 1532 he wrote that "The body of Christ Jesus and his true blood are therefore in the Supper, but it does not consist of the physical body in bread nor of the physical blood in wine, as the old error maintained." This statement was far more radical than the first draft of the *Confessio Tetrapolitana*. Nor was it a committee effort in which he was forced, as at Zurich a year earlier, to take account of views of others at the Synod. He wrote the confession himself after he travelled on to Basel.[40] He may have intended only to deny

---

[39] *Kinderbericht-1529*, fol. [1(v)]. *Berner Synodus*, sig. [Diii(v)].
[40] *Ibid.*, sig. eiiii. For authorship, see n. 25, above.

the doctrine of transubstantiation with his reference to "the old error," but his sweeping statement excluded Luther too.

At the Diet of Augsburg, Sturm and Pfarrer and the representatives of Constance, Memmingen, and Lindau considered Capito's initial characterization of Christ's spiritual presence too contentious. Even the revised version of his article was insufficiently board for Bucer, who composed yet another formula for discussion with Luther and the Swiss. Capito might well have learned a lesson from these events, but he did not.

He promoted the same viewpoint at Basel. At the end of 1532 he wrote Jacob Meyer, the mayor of Basel, a long letter that he intended for publication.

> Therefore the Scriptures say, 'The Lord took bread, broke it, etc.' Here bread is meant; that we all know. This he broke and gave to his disciples, and then he said, 'This is my body,' namely that which he broke. Therefore the Lord gave two things, the bread and his body, and he commanded to eat them both, the bread as body.

Such a statement might have been acceptable to Luther. But, just as in the first version of the *Tetrapolitana*, Capito added something else: "But his body as food for souls." Faith remained the prerequisite for Christ's presence in the sacrament. Believers, he wrote, "eat the bread with the mouth ... the body of Christ, however, with faith in a renewed soul." [41] Three times Capito went out of his way to clarify that he was speaking of a spiritual eating and drinking of Christ's body and blood. Such clarity muddied the waters for Bucer's attempt to secure concord on the basis of formulae that were deliberately vague.

Capito may never have understood the exact nature of what Bucer was trying to accomplish. In subsequent dealings with the Swiss, he desired only to prove that Zwingli and Oecolampadius did not intend to reduce the elements to "empty signs." As he wrote in the Bern confession, "our Sacraments are great secrets of God and not mere ceremonies. . . ." [42] He insisted to Meyer that Oecolampadius'

---

[41] Th. B., V, 178-178(v). "Die geschrifft saget also. Der Herr nam das brot, brachs, etc. Hie ist brodt gemeldet, das wissen wir all. Das bricht und gibt er synen Jüngern; zum andern sagt er: dis ist myn lib, nemlich das, das er bricht. Also gibt der Herr zwen ding, das brot zum lib. Aber sÿnen lib zum spis der selen." Then, picking up Bucer's theme, he added another symbolism, that the sacrament was instituted, "zur besserung der gemain an Gott durch Christum. Dwil wir aber blut und fleisch sÿn, beschicht es durch lipliche wort und lipliche Zeichen. . . ."

[42] *Berner Synodus*, sig. f(v).

picture of the bread as "a sign or figure of the body of Christ" meant it really conveyed Christ to believers. "I know that Zwingli never denied the presence of Christ, because he destroyed all the machinations of the Papists with this battering ram," Capito declared to Bullinger in January 1533. But the Swiss knew that Oecolampadius and Zwingli never taught that the elements were meaningless. In July 1532, when Bucer tried to persuade Bullinger and Jud to subscribe to the statement that he composed after the Diet of Augsburg, Bullinger responded, "We deny that bread is the body of Christ. . . . We clearly confess the sacred bread to be a symbol, a mystery, and a sacrament." Jud's reply was more wordy, but just as clear. "It is possible," he wrote in conclusion, "for the concord of the church to exist along with disagreement and a variety of words and symbols." [43] Capito could scarcely have objected, for Bullinger confessed Capito's own understanding of the Lord's Supper, and Jud his own prior inclination on the best means to achieve concord. Capito's dealings with the Swiss led to confusion and, ultimately, to bad feelings.

Moreover, he ironically led the Swiss to their first formal confessions of faith. His own *Berner Synodus* of 1532, with its explicit denial of the bodily presence, was the first statement of official Swiss doctrine. In 1532 the Baslers drew up the so-called First Confession of Basel. Positively they stated "that Christ is in his Holy Supper for all those who truly believe," but they began the article on the eucharist with the declaration that "the natural, true, physical body of Christ which was born of Mary, the pure virgin, was crucified for us and resurrected into heaven, is not in the Lord's bread or drink." Together the confessions of Basel and Bern made doctrinal accord between the Swiss and the Saxons impossible, unless the Baslers and Bernese were willing to repudiate their own statements of faith. [44]

Capito's work for concord with the Swiss was confused and ineffective. He could not consistently disapprove the Confession of Basel. Although the proscription of the physical presence was more sharply expressed than he might have preferred, it accorded with the *Berner Synodus* and his own letters to Meyer, which may well have served as models for the Baslers. Yet he was frightened by the Basel Confession. In November 1524 he wrote Meyer, "I have

---

[43] Th. B., V, 179-180; VI, 8-8(v); VI, 103-110, for an exchange of several letters.

[44] Dürr and Roth, *Aktensammlung zur Basler Reformation*, VI, 407. See the judgment of Köhler, *Zwingli und Luther*, II, 308-310; 319-320.

very much wanted to come up, my beloved brother, so we might talk through this dangerous passage of events and the Lutheran quarrel, for I have been apprehensive for the gravest disturbance." [45] Later in the year, or early in 1535, he did travel to Basel and pressed the pastors on just the point that he earlier urged on Meyer. The bread and the body were not mixed together in any physical sense, he said, but in a "sacramental union." On this basis, he maintained, one could confess that the communicant ate and drank Christ's body and blood.[46] This was precisely what the Baslers said in their confession; they merely added a definite proscription of the physical, localized presence. And Capito had done the same, time and time again.

While Capito was repeatedly blundering in his dealings with the Swiss, Bucer was coming ever closer to Luther and Melanchthon. These lengthy negotiations finally bore fruit in the Wittenberg Concord of 1536. When Capito and Bucer went to Wittenberg in late May the issue quickly came to the problem of what the unfaithful ate and drank—bread and wine, or Christ's body and blood? To Bucer, and to Capito in particular, it was unthinkable that unbelievers received the body and blood of Christ, for faith was the means by which he was transmitted to the communicants. To Luther and Melanchthon the Words of Institution established that Christ was present in the eucharist regardless of its recipient's status. In the Concord the two sides avoided the issue by employing the word "unworthy," and by asserting that, worthy or unworthy, the communicant received the body and blood of Christ. Luther understood the "unfaithful" to be among the "unworthy," and hence to receive Christ's body and blood to damnation. Capito and Bucer were allowed to believe that the "unfaithful" did not receive Christ, because for them to be unfaithful differed from being unworthy. This distinction was perhaps unclear to some who signed the Wittenberg Concord and who also agreed to abide by the Augsburg Confession. But concord of a sort was achieved at Wittenberg. When they heard that

---

[45] Th. B., VII, 287.

[46] Myconius to Bullinger, 4 February 1535, Th. B., VIII, 50. "Fuit praeter haec apud nos Capito rebus non paucis. . . . In primis de negotio Eucaristiae cujus summa fere in hoc est: Corpus, etc. Ich wills tütsch schriben wie es an uns kumme: Das der Lib Christi wehrelich vnd wehrhaftlicklich empfangen werde vnd das Brot und win Zeichen sind, signa exhibitiva . . . vnd halten also das der Lib vnd das Brot also bey ein ander sÿn. . . . Dan die weÿl man vff beden theilen halt, das Brot vnd win blibt, halten sÿ solche sacramentalem conjunctionem."

Luther would accept their views, Capito and Bucer wept for joy.[47]

The Wittenberg Concord was at best a fragile truce between two sides that had been observing an informal cease-fire for some time. It did not solve the paramount problem, the enmity between the Swiss and the Saxons. All parties to the Concord understood that Capito and Bucer would seek now to bring the reformers of Zurich, Basel, and Bern into the agreement. After signing the Wittenberg Concord, Capito was impeccably loyal to it. In this way he was won over finally to Bucer's method of securing unity. He was an old man now, and he was willing to go to any lengths to accomplish what he began to call "*sanctissima concordia.*" [48]

And yet he either still failed to understand fully Bucer's tactics, or he was woefully inept at implementing them. Bucer's conviction that the Lord's Supper was fundamentally a communal celebration led him to compose ever broader formulae about the elements in the hope of striking some one formula that would encompass all doctrines except transubstantiation.[49] Bucer's efforts thus had a basic consistency to them. But Capito's campaign commonly consisted of trickery at one moment and exhortations to brotherly love at another. On March 28, 1536, he wrote a long letter to Bullinger about the negotiations for concord that followed the Diet of Augsburg. There he tried to dupe Bullinger into believing that all disagreement on the Lord's Supper after 1531 was a horrible mistake, that in fact he and the other contemporary Swiss theologians were being unfaithful to the intentions of Zwingli and Oecolampadius just before their deaths. Regarding the *Confessio Tetrapolitana*, he declared, "Zwingli saw our confession before it was offered to the Emperor by us, and he approved it. . . . It pleased Oecolampadius to whom it was similarly shown for reading. . . ." Moreover, he added, the Saxons "saw that our confession did not clash with theirs." According to him the only reason that an agreement was not signed then and there was that it would appear to be trickery and give Eck a chance to attack them.[50] Consequently, Bullinger was being merely obstinate in refusing to agree to what Zwingli and Oecolampadius accepted in principle.

Capito was falsifying the facts as he, the author of the article on the

---

[47] Köhler, *Zwingli und Luther*, II, 448-449. See the text in Ernst Bizer, *Studien zur Geschichte des Abendmahlsstreits im 16. Jahrhundert* (Gütersloh, 1940), pp. 117-119.

[48] Capito to Jodocus Neobolus, Th. B., X, 122.

[49] Kittelson, "Bucer," *Archive for Reformation History*, LXIV, 166-183.

[50] Th. B., IX, 54-56.

Lord's Supper in the *Tetrapolitana* and the emissary to Switzerland after the Diet, well knew them. Only an advanced case of senility could have made him forget that Zwingli and Oecolampadius had no chance to see the Strasbourg confession before it went to the Emperor because it was composed too hastily. And the suggestion that Melanchthon approved the *Tetrapolitana* was a lie. Perhaps Capito confused it with the broad formula that Bucer composed after the Diet. In that case he well knew that Zwingli was unimpressed with Bucer's position, and that he himself concluded that there was no hope for concord. Bullinger was not fooled by this reconstructed history of sacramental negotiations after the Diet of Augsburg.

The slightest opportunity was enough for Capito in his declining years. Shortly after returning from Wittenberg he tried another tactic in a letter to Meyer. He sent him a copy of the Wittenberg Concord and urged him to compare it with the First Basel Confession. The two documents, he declared, were basically the same. He urged Meyer to make certain that Satan put no blocks in the path of unification. Perhaps he meant that the mayor should force agreement on Basel's pastors. He was not above such a suggestion, for he was ready to try anything. In September 1536 Bullinger agreed that he never taught that the bread and wine were "empty signs." Capito replied as if a great breakthrough had occurred. "Good hopes still hold us," he wrote Bullinger in November; "we will do our best so that the Wittenbergers and the Princes will know how fully you have acknowledged the truth. . . ." But later in the year the Swiss theologians decided at two meetings in Basel to discuss the matter further. By the following spring Capito began to despair, and in 1538 he hoped that just a kind word from Wittenberg might begin the movement toward concord. In January he set down his new plan in a letter to Jodocus Neobolus, one of Luther's persistent dinner guests. "I think Justus Jonas can be induced to write lovingly to Bullinger without discussing the matter . . ." he suggested.[51]

Luther and Bullinger did exchange correct letters in spring 1538, but there was never any hope for agreement on the Lord's Supper. Without mentioning the dispute, Bullinger suggested in March that they might cooperate at least to the extent of their common opposition to Rome. Luther replied in May in much the same manner, but he raised the question of differences with reference to Zwingli. He

---

[51] Th. B., IX, 142-143; 282; XI, 13-14. On this phase of the controversy, see Bizer, *Studien*, pp. 146-147.

said he respected Zwingli and learned of his death with sorrow. "You strongly believed that we err," he concluded; "I commend it to the judgment of God." [52] Earlier Capito tried to prepare the ground by writing, "My Bullinger, you see how opportunely you are situated and how many of the responsibilities of the questions you, unique among your group, could sustain. . . . When Luther responds pleasantly, then act . . . so that concord will not only be established but also so that the church will be reunified." [53] But Luther's letter infuriated Bullinger, and Capito's last attempt at concord failed. He could never understand what happened. On August 26, 1538, he wrote Joachim Vadian, the humanist mayor of St. Gall, "The Zurichers are thrown into an uproar on account of Luther's letter, which we feel was written in the most friendly way. . . . What is it that advances so much suspicion of a deranged soul?" he asked.[54] Capito never appreciated that even in the Sacramentarian Controversy there were questions of principle that appeals to brotherly love could not override.

There was a continuity in Capito's zeal for religious harmony. As a humanist one of his most telling criticisms of the scholastic theologians was that through disputations and the use of Aristotelian logic they introduced unnecessary doctrinal division. For the sake of Christian renewal he urged his mentor Erasmus to stop belittling superstitious practices, because he thereby created bad feelings. As adviser to the Archbishop of Mainz he urged Luther to be moderate for the sake of peace and unity. And the *Sakramentstreit* was only one of several instances in which, even after he became a reformer, he chose concord over absolute agreement on doctrine. In 1533 he broke with Schwenckfeld not over doctrine but because he was convinced Schwenckfeld was a troublemaker. "I do not want to burden you with how much he has damaged," Capito wrote Jacob Truchsess, an adviser to Duke Ulrich of Württemberg. "He considers that no one else is a Christian. . . and that he alone has the truth. . . ." [55] As Capito used it, such criticism applied equally

---

[52] *WABr*, VIII, 207-208; 224.

[53] Th. B., XI, 17. Nor was he above suggesting Bullinger use his influence, "Nam in te merito tua Ecclesia respicit, cujus ducatum sequax cometatur."

[54] Emil Arbenz, ed., *Die Vadianische Briefsammlung der Stadtbibliothek St. Gallen* (St. Gallen, 1894), V, 504-507.

[55] Th. B., VII, 109e(v). Literally, "Er acht niemand fur Christen dann die so Im sein furnemen gefallen lassen. . . ." For the same sentiments expressed to Blaurer, *BB*, I, 423; 495-496.

to Luther and Bullinger. Later in 1534 he advised the young reformer, John Calvin, not to publish his treatise against the notion that the soul slept between death and judgment. He said he agreed with Calvin, but,

> Concerning publication, if you would listen to us, you should certainly publish the judgment at a more appropriate time. Now everything causes an uproar among the sects, and the Germans have learned from experience that fighting against errors makes them more well-known, to the great disadvantage of religion; to preach Christ with the utmost precision to a distressed church is truly the surest way of taking measures against them.

For Capito unity and brotherly love were important characteristics of Christian faith. He could never bear the thought that true religion would lead to hate and discord. "Certainly time will teach a more heart-felt appreciation of all the Scriptures," he concluded his letter to Calvin.[56]

There were nevertheless important limits to Capito's desire for unity. Through all his pleas not to quarrel he never changed his own teachings on the Lord's Supper, and he never included the Church of Rome in his plans for concord. In the early 1540's Charles V, who was frustrated in his desire for a church council but still wished to end religious strife in the Empire, began to sponsor a series of colloquies to which he invited prominent Catholic and Protestant theologians. In 1540 Capito attended one of these, the Colloquy of Worms, but he was an unenthusiastic participant. "The Papists never commit themselves to disputations. . ." he complained. "Let the Lord look after his church. . . ." And in 1530, just as he was gathering arguments with which Sturm and Pfarrer could press at the Diet of Augsburg for a church council, he published a book on the reforming Council of Basel, with which he intended to quash talk among the reformers about reunion with Rome through a council. The history of the Council of Basel was a damning story as he read it. The Council met to allow the pope and the Emperor to strike an agreement regarding the disposition of prebends in Germany, and the papacy never observed the division of spoils. No matter, he declared; cardinals, bishops, and all prelates were too rich whether they were Germans or Italians. It would be better to secularize all prebends and divide their income among the poor.

---

[56] A. L. Herminjard, *Correspondance des Reformateurs dans les Pays de Langue française* (Paris, 1870), III, 243-244.

Capito began the book by stating flatly, "pope and council may err and have often erred, and conciliar and papal law does not bind us any further than God binds us through his Holy Word." [57] There was thus a degree of error to which his desire for unity did not apply.

Yet, his attachment to the unity of the church was deeply grounded in his own past. Tactical considerations were, to be sure, one of his motivations, especially after 1530. On March 28, 1536, he wrote Bullinger, "I beg you, consider the matter after having called upon the Lord. Our side knows what plans they are preparing against the free cities." The one time he outwardly altered his teaching on the Lord's Supper was at the Diet of Augsburg, when Sturm and Pfarrer pressed him to it for the sake of Strasbourg's security. Capito also appreciated the problems that division created for the credibility of the reformers' claim that they were the true church. In the same letter he complained to Bullinger that "it is possible for Eck to say 'Just as many churches as men' . . . for we are divided into three troops—Lutherans, Zwinglians, and we mediators who have refused the name of a sect in any way." [58] As a reformer Capito retained the blessing—or curse—of everyday sagacity that he developed as adviser to the Archbishop of Mainz. Tactical considerations dictated to him that, no matter how much they disagreed, the reformers must not quarrel among themselves.

Yet his humanist background was the critical element in his search for concord. His refusal to grant ceremonies any intrinsic merit reflected in part an Erasmian emphasis upon inward piety that he carried with him into the Reformation. In his commentary on Hosea of 1528 he wrote,

> Now because the Kingdom of Christ is brought forth inside us where it purges clean the souls of the servants of God . . . it follows that the Kingdom of God . . . is nothing other than justice, peace, and delight in the Holy Spirit, to which external purifications, sabbaths, circumcisions, and the remaining ceremonies do not properly pertain.

Such an Erasmian spiritualism encouraged Capito's natural proclivity to considering the Lord's Supper unworthy of a quarrel. After all, if the value of the sacraments depended upon the faith of their recipient, why argue about them? Moreover, the basic inclination to peace and harmony that characterized his career as a reformer may also be traced to the deep draughts of Erasmus' message of brotherly

---

[57] Th. B., XIII, 12-12(v). *Concilium zu Basel*, sig. Aiii(v); Lii-Lii(v).
[58] Th. B., IX, 54(v)-55.

love that he drank in Basel. His central recommendation to Truchsess on the construction of an evangelical church in Württemberg was that "The only thing to be brought forth is that the rule of Christian love not fail at the outset and that thereby some quarrelsome and heated dispute-provoking babble be brought forth and the poor commoners be talked into accepting that instead of the Gospel." [59] Erasmus himself would have approved such counsel. In a sense Erasmus' religious attitudes lived on in Capito's labors for concord.

There was nevertheless an important difference in Capito's search for unity as a reformer from his motives as a humanist. In and of themselves tactical advantage and Erasmus' message of brotherly love and inward piety could have led him to favor negotiations with the Catholics or to unity with anyone who opposed Rome, regardless of his teachings. But Capito was irenic rather than opportunistic or unprincipled. He finally determined what was indifferent according to the central evangelical doctrine that salvation came through Christ alone. In 1535, after settling a dispute between the Zwinglian and Lutheran factions in Frankfurt, he recommended that the city council adopt the *Tetrapolitana* as a middle position between the two parties, for

> The Lord strikes the earth with fire and sword . . . and sets daughter against mother. This is said concerning the cross of the godly, but it is . . . dreadful that pious Christians should be at odds with one another. . . . Yes, all ceremonies are not useful in themselves, but as a guide to Christ; the hearing of preaching is necessary, but other ceremonies are undertaken for well-being.[60]

He took much the same line on December 9, 1535, when he defended his activities in a letter to Blaurer:

> In the first place, it is abundantly clear from the record of previous times that it is not a question of reinstating abolished ceremonies nor of our betraying Christian freedom by struggling for peace with our adversaries, but of our being united in the Lord so that some do not impede the course of others. . . . Regarding the eucharist and doctrine in general I do not see any notable differences, for we all preach Christ, the complete justifier.

The preaching of the Word was so all-important to Capito that he could write Johann Schwebel, the reformer of Zweibrücken, that,

---

[59] *In Hoseam prophetam*, fol. 274-274(v). Th. B., VII, 109b.

[60] Printed by Johann Balthazar Ritter, *Evangelisches Denkmahl der Stadt Frankfurth am Mayn* (Franckfurth am Mayn, 1726), pp. 332-334.

although he and the other Strasbourg pastors did not know what Schwebel taught about the sacraments, he was certain they had no quarrel with him, "because we all preach Christ more, as much in words as symbols, whose divine grace alone cleanses souls." [61] Those who preached Christ alone could overlook everything else.

The peace and unity of the church were always dear to Capito, both before and after he became a reformer. Nevertheless, the key to his pursuit of concord as a reformer was not Erasmus' skeptical spiritualism but Capito's distinction between the indifferent and the essential on the ground that only Christ saved men. "Judgment in the church is two-fold," he wrote in the commentary on Hosea, "the one public, the other private." Public judgment was the province of the church as a whole and was exercised in accord with Paul's declaration at I Corinthians 12:7, "To each is given the manifestation of the Spirit for the common good." The test in these public matters was Christ the redeemer, for as Capito reminded his readers "the Apostle to the Corinthians knew nothing except Christ crucified...."[62] The ultimate value that Capito placed upon Christ the savior was his guiding principle in seeking concord. It was also the basis upon which he wrote Bullinger in 1535,

> Nevertheless, truth (which, once received by Christ's blessing, we shall maintain to our last breath) requires its constancy of proclamation. But what truth? For not just any truth has to be attested by one's life and blood, but precisely that truth which avails for attaining salvation; otherwise one would have to encounter death in support of the true doctrines of the philosophers, because all truth is from God.[63]

These remarks do, to be sure, assume that many abstract truths cannot be known with full assurance. Yet the difference between Capito's Reformation irenicism and Erasmus' Renaissance skepticism was that there was a central religious truth for which Capito declared he was willing to die. "In final summary, beloved, pious citizens," he wrote in his book on the dispute between Carlstadt and Luther, "stand steadfast upon Christ whom God the Lord has shown us

---

[61] *BB*, I, 765. Schwebel, *Centuria Epistolarum*, pp. 176-177.

[62] *In Hoseam Prophetam*, fol. 136-137.

[63] Th. B., VII, 252. "Nihilosecius constantiam profitendi suam veritas requirit, quam olim susceptam, fovente Christo, ad ultimum habitum nos continuabimus. Sed quae veritas? Nec enim quaelibet veritas vita et sanguine attestanda, sed ea demum, quae saluti consequendae, alioqui pro veris philosophorum dogmatis mors appetanda foret, quia omnis veritas ex Deo est.

alone through the clear Scriptures, and ignore whatever else agitates the learned spirits and seekers after fame. . . . Our salvation does not consist of words but of the power of God." [64] Capito remained something of the humanist in refusing to fight over words, but he became very much the reformer in holding to Christ alone.

---

[64] *Von der Spaltung*, sig. Biii(v).

CHAPTER SEVEN

ORDER AND RADICALISM

Capito's twin commitments—to the unity of the true church and to public tranquillity—reinforced one another in most aspects of his career. Because he was not overwhelmed by every detail of his view of religious truth, he was able to be a skillful campaigner for reform in Strasbourg and a persistent proponent of concord in the international movement. But when it came to constructing a new church to replace the one that was torn down, his attachment to public order clashed with his willingness to abide disagreement on nonessentials for the sake of unity. A new church required articles of faith and administrative procedures. Its confession, if stated broadly, could accommodate followers of both Luther and Zwingli, neither of whom was inclined to object on organizational matters. But the new church that Capito, Bucer, and the others built was incapable of including the sects that began to spring up in the reform movement's wake. Luther and Zwingli, moreover, were far away, but the sects were within the walls of Strasbourg. In the end they forced Capito to choose between his passion for order and his desire for unity.

The most important group of sectarians were the Anabaptists, and separatism was the great threat that they posed. The leading reformers commonly used the term "Anabaptism" as an epithet to denote a wide range of nonconformist opinions that they found repugnant, seditious, or heretical. As a group the Anabaptists were not, however, social visionaries or revolutionaries. They were rather a true religious type, alongside Protestants and Roman Catholics. Their objections to infant baptism and their practice of rebaptizing were signs of a desire to create a believers' church modeled on Apostolic Christianity. They taught that the true, regenerated Christian should have no dealings with the sinful world. Consequently they desired to separate themselves from the established churches, whether Catholic or Protestant. The separatists were not necessarily revolutionaries, but they did refuse to swear loyalty to the secular authority, to bear the sword, or to be part of a church that cooperated with or was supported by the secular authority. For the Anabaptist, the magistracy was both in and of the world and hence pernicious to the regenerate Christian.[1]

---

[1] Franklin Hamlin Littell, *The Anabaptist View of the Church. A Study in the*

Most sixteenth-century rulers and churchmen considered such teachings seditious, as well as heretical. The Anabaptists were thus persecuted and driven from place to place throughout central Europe. By such standards Strasbourg was tolerant. No Anabaptist was put to death in Strasbourg for his religious views. But because it attracted ever more religious radicals, the city's original mildness gradually gave way to greater repression. The first few separatists arrived in 1526, and the senate issued its first decree against them in 1527. When Augsburg expelled its radicals in 1528, many moved to Strasbourg, where another decree was issued against them in 1530. During this period the pastors and the municipal authorities were hard-pressed to formulate and enforce a consistent policy toward this large and varied group of religious dissidents. They pursued instead an *ad hoc* procedure of examining individual leaders, and then frequently imprisoning or exiling them. This policy failed to keep pace with the swelling number of radicals who entered the city, so the pastors and the senate held a synod in 1533 to define doctrinal and organizational norms. Under pressure from the pastors, the senate issued final decrees against separatism in 1534 and 1535. Although these mandates, like most in Strasbourg, were not enforced to the letter, they ended toleration for all practical purposes.[2]

Capito, with the support of Matthew and Catherine Zell, was most responsible for Strasbourg's relatively tolerant treatment of religious dissenters. He revealed his basic sentiments in 1527 when he wrote a long letter to protest the execution of Michael Sattler in Rottenburg in one of the Reformation's most pathetic incidents. "It is utterly unspeakable," he charged, "to hear that less mildness should be shown the flock of Christ by a Christian authority than there has

---

Origins of Sectarian Protestantism (Boston, 1958), pp. 86-94; 101-108. See the use of the term "radical Reformation" by George Huntston Williams, *The Radical Reformation* (Philadelphia, 1962), pp. xxiii-xxxi. For the attitude of the Lutheran reformers, see John S. Oyer, *Lutheran Reformers against Anabaptists, Luther, Melanchthon, and Menius and the Anabaptists of Central Germany* (The Hague, 1964), esp. pp. 6-40; 114-139. Because most "radicals" in Strasbourg were in fact Anabaptists, this latter term will be used interchangeably with "radical," "separatist," and sometimes even "religious dissident" or "dissenter" with no value judgment intended.

[2] For a superficial survey, see Robert Kreider, "The Anabaptists and the Civil Authority in Strasbourg, 1525-1555," *Church History*, XXIV (1955), 99-118. See also Williams, *Radical Reformation*, for capsule biographies of individuals. The standard work is Gerbert, *Sectenbewegung*, although a suggestive appraisal is in Chrisman, *Strasbourg*, pp. 177-200. The most important sources are published in *QGT*, VII; VIII.

been among the Pharisees." [3] Bucer, too, originally opposed harsh treatment of the Anabaptists, and he joined Capito in condemning Sattler's executioners. But he began to consider the radical movement a serious threat to the church in Strasbourg sooner than Capito did. He never favored persecution on the scale of that at Zurich, where Zwingli approved putting Balthasar Hubmaier on the rack, but he wanted a firmer policy for Strasbourg as early as 1527. By then he had no good words for the Anabaptists.[4] But Capito's mildness persisted. Only in 1532 when he finally agreed did the city begin to embark upon a more repressive course.[5]

Capito's relative toleration of religious dissent fell far short of a willingness to accept religious pluralism. From the beginning he joined Strasbourg's other reformers in examining individual separatists. Hans Wolff, a weaver from Benfeld, was the first Anabaptist leader to arrive in Strasbourg. In a letter to Zwingli on June 11, 1526, Capito reported that Wolff taught that "No magistrate is Christian. Infants are not to be baptized. No pious person may bear arms at the command of the magistrate. The devil and all the impious will be saved at the last day." During the middle of one of Zell's sermons, Wolff leaped out of his pew and demanded that Zell yield the pulpit to him because only he had the true spirit. The city authorities imprisoned Wolff with Capito's approval,[6] but he was only the beginning. Ludwig Hetzer, a Hebraist of note who was evicted from Augsburg and Zurich, arrived in Strasbourg in late October or early November. He was followed shortly by Hans Denck, who was one of the most important figures in the spiritualist wing of Anabaptism. Hetzer turned quietly to his Hebrew studies in Capito's house, but Denck contacted a separatist group in the city and tried to undermine Capito's attempt to convert Hetzer. "Hans Denck, a crafty and fickle man who makes a parade of all ministers of the Word with great faith and authority everywhere," Capito wrote Zwingli on December 10, "is giving us disturbances here." On December 22

---

[3] *Ibid.*, VII, 85.

[4] For Bucer's attitude, see Johann Martin Usteri, "Die Stellung der Strassburger Reformatoren Bucer und Capito zur Tauffrage," *Theologische Studien und Kritiken*, LVII (1884), 546-563, and Gerbert, *Sectenbewegung*, pp. 73-78. The most recent study is Charles Buell Mitchell, "Martin Bucer and Sectarian Dissent: A Confrontation of the Magisterial Reformation with Anabaptists and Spiritualists," (unpub. doctoral diss., Yale University, 1960), esp. pp. 110-122.

[5] For the literature on Capito, see the forward, above, and the works cited there.

[6] *ZW*, VIII, 623-624.

and 23 Capito and Bucer examined Denck in the presence of one
senator, and the authorities finally ordered Denck to leave the city.
In the letter in which he told Zwingli about Denck, Capito also
reported that he had interviewed two more dissidents in the city
prison. But he was unable to accomplish anything, "for they do not
negotiate in good faith." [7] Capito had no intention of abiding heter-
odoxy for the sake of toleration pure and simple.

In dealing with the Anabaptists, Capito desired more to convert
them than to repress them. His usual practice was to insist upon the
essentials and to let the rest go. Throughout Denck's examination
in 1526 he maintained that justification by faith alone was the sole
issue on which Denck should be questioned, and he took the same
line in questioning two more "baptizers" in fall 1528. In January
1529 he joined Bucer in requesting a disputation with Jacob Kautz
and Wilhelm Reublein. In October, Kautz was released to Capito's
custody for four weeks, and Capito volunteered to report his progress in converting Kautz two weeks later. With its jails filled with
religious prisoners, the senate used Capito for this purpose more
than once. In February 1530 it ordered one Venturinus, who declared
he was a prophet, to reside with Capito, and the city compensated
him for expenses that he incurred in boarding the man. [8] Capito
favored a policy of individual examination and conversion over
indiscriminate persecution.

This policy was well-founded. While most reformers viewed the
Anabaptists in the same light as Thomas Müntzer or the insurgents
at Münster, Capito insisted upon differentiating among them. In
September 1528 he wrote Blaurer,

> I have encountered excellent hearts, composed to true piety, among the
> Anabaptists. . . . On the other hand, many are not only overwhelmed
> with errors, but also by malevolence; they are anxiously zealous that
> things be changed by establishing the law of Moses; conspicuous
> vigilance and intense prayers are necessary to move against them.

In 1530 he composed a special memorandum on the radical problem,
which he may have intended for publication. He was defending his
policy of treating each individual separately.

> I consider that the Anabaptists, who are enslaved more by the letter
> than by the Spirit, err gravely, and they rashly offend whoever publicly

---

[7] *Ibid.*, VIII, 623-624. On the examination of Denk, see Gerbert, *Sectenbewegung*,
pp. 21-27; 32-47.
[8] *QGT*, VII, 60-61; 180-182; 185; 249; 254-256.

disapproves of their sayings; and nevertheless I acknowledge that for the most part they exhibit signs of fear of the Lord and true submission, as well as, to be sure, an ignorant zeal for pretence. . . . Hence, I consider that their heart should be examined and the gift of God by which they were strengthened against the flesh and Satan should be acknowledged, in so far as it concerns the maintenance of their lives.[9]

A willingness to distinguish among individuals and to base policy upon such distinctions was virtually unique among sixteenth-century reformers.

There were nevertheless always grounds upon which Capito favored imprisoning or banishing individual radicals. In May 1527 he wrote Michael Keller, one of the preachers in Augsburg, "Your book, published in the name of all against the Anabaptists, pleases us immensely, as much as is permitted from a little taste." Then he cautioned that the Anabaptists "have intolerable teachings, I of course know, but they are even more strengthened by external persecution." He accordingly advised the Augsburgers to be tolerant and charitable, "unless they sin against the laws of the republic. Separation from the Church and vituperation of our Word, I say for instance, are outrageous, an injury that we will vindicate with the sword of the Word." By referring to the "sword of the Word," he presumably meant to exclude handing an offender over to the executioner, but he was willing to take some sort of action against those who fit the criteria he mentioned. Four years later he wrote Wolfgang Musculus, another Augsburg preacher, that when it came to examining religious dissidents,

> I usually say, 'It is too much for me to judge concerning faith.' . . . But for all that, these three things are usually taken into consideration: 1) they must not make a public spectacle of the Word; 2) they must not assemble among themselves into a secret church, 3) they must not shirk proper political oathtaking (*iusjurandum politicum*), but submit, according to civil custom, to the commands of the magistracy.[10]

---

[9] *BB*, I, 167. *QGT*, VII, 186, and 81, where he employed just this distinction in the May 1527 letter to the authorities at Horb. "Disser Michael ist vns hie zu Strassburg bekant vnd hat wol etwas irrung jm wort gehabt, die wir jm getrulich haben durch schrifften angezaigt. Aber dwil er neben vnser vnd ander prediger worhafftigen leer vilicht etwas mangels vnd im volck, die christen syn wollen, ergerlich leben befunden, hatt jn, myner achtung nach, so vil weniger bertzigt, was wir zum beriecht der worheit grüntlich fürbrochten."

[10] *QGT*, VII, 589; 333.

In two statements separated by four years, Capito was consistent in describing the sorts of activities against which he was willing to act. These were very likely the real reasons for which radicals were banished or imprisoned in Strasbourg.

Throughout the period before the Strasbourg Synod of 1533 Capito did cooperate with Bucer and the city authorities in examining and punishing individual radicals. There was nevertheless a basic difference of opinion between the two men on the general policy that should be followed toward religious dissidents. Bucer preferred to outlaw Anabaptism, while Capito wished only to punish those individuals who committed the public acts that he mentioned in his letters to Keller and Musculus. Two subsidiary considerations lay at the base of Capito's disagreement with Bucer. One was the careful distinction among kinds of "Anabaptists" that he described to Blaurer and in his special memorandum of 1530. The other was his persistent unwillingness, as implied in his letters to Keller and Musculus, to persecute people for their religious beliefs as such. Capito was willing to allow the radicals to believe what they wished. Only when they acted on those beliefs did he think they should be prosecuted.

From 1528 to 1531 he and Bucer fought a running battle over the larger question of general policy toward the Anabaptists. Their latent disagreement first burst into the open in April 1528 when Capito published his commentary on Hosea. He publicized his argument that not all the radicals were dangerous, seditious heretics.

> There are nevertheless good people among those whom the power of the fear of the Lord has driven into that error, who are more to be pitied than they are evil; as long as they fail to have regard for the true glory of God, they run wide of the mark, superstitiously caught up by the small points, until they begin to turn more contentedly to the true measure of the glory of God, as in fact they are beginning to do here and there.

Alone among the major reformers, he did not consider rebaptism *per se* a seditious or heretical act,

> For those who, under the most grinding tyranny, affirm anabaptism with the confession of Christ sin without malice, if they sin, because that sign is not used as an argument for the separation of the churches, but they would have it in place of a password in order that they might identify themselves to be those who, having heard the Word of the Kingdom, trust and are prepared to lay down life for the sake of him who liberated us into true life by his death.

Capito began this work by taking notice of the recent persecutions at Zurich, by remarking that "the Church of Zurich, which is easily an example of long suffering, did not experience more dangerous enemies." Even so, he was willing to defend the Anabaptists and, at least by implication, to criticize Zwingli's handling of them. Then, while discussing persecutions in France, he warned that "A new ecclesiastical tyranny creeps along these underground passages." Here, at the height of the Sacramentarian Controversy too, Capito was coming to fear what he regarded as a mania for ever sharper and ever more exclusive confessional definition. "I repeat, unity and concord are lamed by our vice. Sometimes we discomfort those who are inexperienced in spiritual things; sometimes we learned ones are tied up in fraud because of too many things at the same time." He would not abide persecuting people for their religious beliefs, because he feared that much that was good might be lost. "Public tranquillity is to be provided," he wrote, "but not so that we would thereby prohibit prophets or extinguish the Spirit or slander the gifts of God that were provided for the common good." [11]

Later in life Capito recalled his commentary on Hosea as the one occasion on which he stepped into a public controversy. Bucer was appalled. On April 15 he wrote Zwingli, "I expostulated with the man because he did this unknown to me, because we have always before told one another everything. He responded that he held to his faith, nor could he see how the prophets might be explained differently." But Bucer was not concerned with Capito's explication of Hosea. What he disliked were Capito's independent attitude toward the Anabaptists and the implied criticism of himself and Zwingli for their intolerance. He was convinced that the source of Capito's permissiveness was his guest Martin Cellarius, who was in Bucer's judgement "a man truly seized by the Anabaptist spirit." He begged Zwingli and Oecolampadius to urge Capito to rid himself of the man. Then, Bucer suggested, Capito's love for the unity of the church would reassert itself and he would shun Anabaptists like Cellarius.[12] And, Bucer might have added, join him in pressing for a firmer policy against them.

---

[11] *In Hoseam prophetam*, fol. 177(v); [1(v)]; [7(v)-8], to which he added at fol. [8(v)], "Nam ingenio industriaeque nostrae tribuimus, quae propria Dei sunt."

[12] Capito to Calvin, 1534, Herminjard, *Correspondance*, III, 243-244. *ZW*, IX, 427-429.

Bucer's objections to Capito's commentary may have reflected the substance of their disagreement on how to treat the radicals. But the vehemence of his reaction derived more from the peculiar circumstances surrounding Cellarius, who arrived in Strasbourg in November 1526.[13] The Strasbourg pastors originally distrusted him because of unsavory stories about his previous activities. He was closely associated with Luther's enemy Eck until 1521, when he moved to Wittenberg and was well received by Melanchthon. But he disliked Luther's handling of Carlstadt and the Zwickau Prophets, and so he left Wittenberg in April 1522 and spent some time wandering about eastern Europe. In 1525 and 1526 he was in Königsberg where he wrote his major treatise, *De operibus Dei*. There is no evidence that Cellarius practiced rebaptism or was himself rebaptized. According to Capito he taught that "it would be better for infant baptism to have been eliminated, but that, according to the precept of charity, which regulates all externals, it should have been maintained for the moment." This was the view that Cellarius presented in the *De operibus Dei* when it was published in Strasbourg on July 12, 1527. And Capito wrote an enthusiastic preface to the work.[14] But at the end of the month Zwingli published his *Elenchus in catabaptistarum strophas* and went out of his way to attack Cellarius with the remark, "If they consider charity to be a kindness or indulgence . . . then I judge that those who say infants should be baptized for the sake of charity err perniciously." Bucer was then astounded to read Capito's recommending Cellarius work twice in his own commentary on Hosea. Moreover, Cellarius' had been a source of trouble between Capito and Bucer for some time. They exchanged criticism and defence of him in their lectures, and Bucer and Cellarius had angry words in the market place.[15] To Bucer the Hosea commentary proved

---

[13] Bernhard Riggenbach, "Martin Borrhaus (Cellarius), ein Sonderling aus der Reformationszeit," *Basler Jahrbuch* (Basel, 1906), pp. 47-70.

[14] *ZW*, VIII, 774-775. *De Operibus Dei, Martino Cellario authore* (Argentorati, 1527), esp. fol. 66 (v)-67 "Tamen, quia charitas semper meliora speret, et de domesticis praesertim; quo maior puerorum instituendorum cura habeatur: non esse, neque contra gloriam Dei, necque charitatem, praesertim cum Infantium baptisatio non sit palam prohibita. et aedificandi propensio ad benefaciendum omnibus sit exposita si ad tempus donec Dominus per misericordiam suam maiorem lucem orbi reddat. . . ." Thanks to Dr. Abraham Friesen of the University of California, Santa Barbara, for sending a copy of this treatise.

[15] *ZW*, VI, 181-183; IX, 428, where Bucer wrote, "Read, I beg, what he wrote at the end of his book and on about folio 50. . . ." The recommendations of Cellarius appear at *In Hoseam prophetam*, fol. 53(v); 284.

that Cellarius influenced Capito to be critical of himself and Zwingli.

Panic at the recommendation of Cellarius' *De operibus Dei*, rather than a careful reading of Capito's work, was the basis of Bucer's judgment. The commentary on Hosea was published "in the middle of April 1528," and Bucer wrote his letter on April 15. He had not time to digest Capito's book. Had he read carefully he would have discovered that his colleague was not applauding Cellarius' view of infant baptism by commending Cellarius' work. Upon receiving a copy of Zwingli's *Elenchus* in August 1527, Capito wrote, "Unless I err, there is the strictest agreement among us concerning the baptism of infants." He pledged that he would read Zwingli's work carefully and added, "But if it were to happen that we disagreed somewhat concerning this matter, we must dissent humbly and charitably." Perhaps Capito anticipated disagreement, but on September 24 he reported that there were only small points to which he objected, and he did not even trouble himself to enumerate them. "With what delight I read through the *Elenchus*," he wrote, "a book that is absolutely necessary in this tempest!" Capito could hardly have approved more. "The use of the Scriptures is free and honest, the power of the eternal covenant is accurately treated, and the nature of the glory of God and of the analogy of faith perfectly certain." [16] In his own commentary on Hosea, Capito was not rebutting Zwingli's rejection of Cellarius' teaching on infant baptism. He was criticizing Zwingli's repression of the Anabaptists in Zurich.

Bucer was right, however, in declaring that Cellarius influenced Capito. What struck Capito so forcefully was not Cellarius' backhanded defense of infant baptism, but his teaching on predestination, which Capito transplanted into his commentary on Hosea.

> Certainly it may be justly asked by whom and by what agreement the Word of God is carried forward. . . . I will indicate in brief, to be sure, what I think. Just as God elected us in Christ before the foundations of the world had been laid, so we would be holy and irreproachable in his presence, so too he determined before the composition of this world that there would be prophets, all of whom were manifest by his gift. This esteemed gift of God does not depend upon the energy and thought of man.

By the marginal note, "The calling of a people depends upon election," he declared, "Here the cause of summoning a people is learned, because the Lord declares himself to respect nothing except the plan

---

[16] *ZW*, IX, 193; 218.

of election," and, "Everything depends upon his utterly benign will." [17] For Capito the doctrine of predestination was the key to banishing the uncertainty that doctrinal controversy caused, especially when it centered on forms of worship.

> Certainly all external things are doubtful and, when argued by the evil, they are easily overtaken with hypocrisy. What, then, confirms the favor of God? The anointing, the down-payment of the Spirit, the promise of God, the certain, living, convincing of the heart of being predestined from the Father to inheritance. . . .

He identified *"fiducia ex fide praedestinationis"* as that "In which the strongest anchor of hope is fixed, the faith, I say, of God's predestination, and the undoubted persuasion of our salvation." [18] For Capito, the doctrine of predestination freed the Christian from anxiety.

A strict predestinarianism could undercut objections to Anabaptist teachings. If God's election was all that mattered, what consequence was it what ceremonies one practiced or to which church one belonged? But neither Capito nor Cellarius intended the doctrine to be used that way. In a letter to Oecolampadius, Cellarius defended his book by writing, "If they will take me for some sort of Anabaptist, I confess myself to write and think the contrary. . . . In fact, our book clashes with the entire teaching of the Anabaptists." [19] In its preface Capito used almost the same words to commend the *De operibus Dei* that he employed to congratulate Zwingli for his *Elenchus*: "We indeed consider the book to be not only useful but absolutely necessary in these days for healing contentions, annihilating the sects, checking the insolences that rage with peculiar ferocity against the chosen." [20] There was good reason for Capito to find the same merit in Cellarius' and Zwingli's books. In the *Elenchus*, Zwingli too taught the strictest double predestination. As Capito wrote Zwingli in September 1527 in defense of Cellarius, "I fully promoted his book, not because everything in it is new, but because it especially examined the rule of the glory of God. . . ." Zwingli may have sensed this basic agreement, for he virtually ignored Bucer's complaints when he responded to Bucer's appeal on June 17. He exhorted Bucer and Capito to let nothing come between them,

---

[17] *In Hoseam prophetam*, fol. 3(v)-4(v); 19(v); 20.
[18] *Ibid.*, fol. 122(v)-123; 67(v).
[19] *BAO*, II, 91-92.
[20] *De Operibus Dei*, fol. 3.

to remain together "like Theseus and Pirithous, David and Jonathan." [21]

Bucer, too, eventually saw the point, perhaps in further conversation with Capito. On June 24 he reported to Zwingli that Cellarius had left Strasbourg, and that he and Capito were reconciled. More importantly, he added what amounted to an endorsement of Capito's maligned commentary on Hosea. Regarding it and his own commentary on John he wrote,

> I beg of you one thing: Capito and I entrusted some books to your publisher Christopher [Forschauer] for forwarding to the brethern at Bern. On June 5 they received our letter offering the books but not the books. For Berchthold [Haller] wrote us about it that day. I beg you, I repeat, to do something about that, to see that the books are forwarded to Bern.[22]

Cellarius, too, was cleared. He later became professor of rhetoric and then of theology at Basel. Bucer's fright passed once he understood that Capito never favored the Anabaptists.

The disagreement between Bucer and Capito over the policy to be followed toward the Anabaptists nevertheless persisted. With the special memorandum that he wrote in 1530 Capito intended to protest a mandate that the city authorities issued that year against the radicals. He warned that in persecuting them "we may, I fear, have destroyed the entire judgment of the Spirit with so much bad judgment." Like so many others this decree was scarcely enforced, but late on the evening of April 17, 1531, three years after he published the commentary on Hosea, Capito reported to Musculus that Bucer was now supporting one of the senators, who was preparing another decree against the Anabaptists. "Daniel Mieg overhears the cruelty from the sermons of our brother Bucer ... who always contends that absolutely everything is to be taken away from them. I am resisting him, as I must in the sight of God. ... I have not yet been

---

[21] *ZW*, IX, 221; 487-488. The difference between Capito and Zwingli may be that, whereas Zwingli's predestinarianism in the *Elenchus* was intimately tied to his covenental theology, Capito's was not. Consequently, Zwingli saw baptism as taking the place of circumcision and Capito did not.

[22] *ZW*, IX, 492-493. Yet, Bucer's letter of April 1528 has determined past understanding of Capito's relations with the separatists. The only difference between the view of historians and Bucer's hasty judgment has been the discovery of Anabaptist "leanings" in Capito as early as 1524 and as late as 1531. The most extreme example is Strasser, *Beziehungen*, pp. 37-41. At the same time, scholars have ignored Bucer's recommendation of the Hosea commentary in June.

[23] *QGT*, VII, 331-332.

able to talk with Bucer at length, but it will be discussed between us
during the next days." [23] Although there is no report of further
talk between them on this subject, Capito was apparently successful,
for there was no new mandate against the radicals in Strasbourg in
1531. Religious dissenters in Strasbourg had Capito to thank for the
relative sanctuary they found there before 1533.

It is important to underline, nevertheless, that his comparatively
tolerant policy toward the radicals was not founded upon any theological agreement with them. Whenever he had kind words for
them, he was acknowleding only the depth and genuineness of their
personal piety, as did his humanist mentor Erasmus. And Capito
always coupled such approving judgments with an explicit condemnation of their teachings. His toleration was of a recognizably modern
sort, precisely because it was limited only by what he regarded as
expedient. He was unwilling to examine consciences, and he never
approved basing public policy upon what people believed. He was
willing to let people believe what they wished, so long as their
actions did not threaten the ecclesiastical and political order of
Strasbourg. On the other hand he not only actively tried to convert
individual Anabaptists but he also publicly refuted their teachings.
"He who contends with every nerve in this age for the repetition of
baptism after preaching ... is utterly removed from the Kingdom
of Christ," he declared even in the commentary on Hosea.[24]

It is possible to read the commentary on Hosea in particular and
to conclude that Capito listed powerfully toward the spiritualist
wing of Anabaptism.[25] His criticism of policy against the radicals was
frequently expressed as a defence of the spirit. "Now, the most
dangerous plague to the doctrine of Christ," he wrote, "is to consider oneself equal to everything and to usurp the entire role of the
Spirit. ..." He seemed in fact, to begin the work with frankly
spiritualist exegetical notions. Declaring that "The dead letters of the
Scriptures are not to be depended upon," he added, "Therefore,
more spiritual men do not depend at all upon the letter, which is
dead for posterity, but they rely upon the earnest-money of the Spirit,
which they emphasize and demonstrate in comparing the Scriptures."
At places he sounded even neo-Platonic, as in urging a symbolic

---

[24] *In Hoseam prophetam*, fol. 33(v)-34. On Erasmus, see Bainton, *Erasmus*,
pp. 260-262.
[25] The chief proponent of this argument is Strasser, *Beziehungen*, pp. 48-49;
92-93.

view of the sacraments: "For, under Christ's rule, one is to ascend from the earth, not to clutch at those earthly things and vain elements of the world—thus, if we would cleave to Christ properly." [26] There is little wonder that, upon casually reading passages such as these, Bucer might have pause about the reliability of his colleague.

And yet, Capito was no spiritualist, not even in the commentary on Hosea. A close reading of the passages quoted above reveals that when he spoke of "the spirit" or "the spiritual way" he always referred to Christ. He thus expanded upon his discussion of the letter and the spirit with the remark, "we hold to the mind of Christ. For the entire law, in so far as it is explained through all the prophets, is spiritual, and its end is Christ, of whose body and of whose flesh and bone we are members." [27] In the 1529 edition of his catechism he explained what "to ascend from the earth" meant in regard to the sacraments. A Christian "uses the sacrament and the signs for the good of his neighbor, out of love, for he has no command in addition, and he places no trust in outward acts, for he lives only in faith in God, to whom he comes through Christ Jesus, the one mediator." Consequently, whereas he might appear in the Hosea commentary to be concerned solely for "the role of the Spirit," the weight of his argument was that ever sharper confessional definition was "the most dangerous plague to the doctrine of Christ." [28] In contradistinction to the spiritualist wing of Anabaptism, Capito never saw the Spirit at work unless its sole content was Christ. The difficulty is merely that he sometimes used language he learned from Erasmus to express teachings he learned from Luther.

The most important consequence of this identification of the Spirit with Christ was Capito's argument that the Anabaptists transgressed the spiritualist principle by concerning themselves with the time and manner of baptism. In his 1530 memorandum he declared

---

[26] *In Hoseam prophetam*, fol. 2(v); 34; 68.

[27] *Ibid.*, fol. 1(v). "Omnia in figura contigerunt patribus, scripta uero sunt propter admonitionem nostri, ad quos termini aetatum inciderunt, hoc est, qui Christi regno paremus. Siquidem mentem Christi tenemus. Tota enim lex, quatenus per omnes prophetas explicatur spiritualis est, et finis eius est Christus, cuius corporis, et de cuius carne et ossibus membra dumus."

[28] *Kinderbericht-1529*, fol. 27(v). *In Hoseam prophetam*, fol. 68. "Peiculosissima enim pestis est doctrinae Christi, putare se omnia consecutum et usurpare partes spiritus omnes, qui unus in omnes quoslibet ueritatem et quandolibet inducet. Nam supra opinionem humanae sapientiae, hoc tempore dominus abditissima prodidit et amplius prodet. Bene illi igitur qui tranquillo spiritu praestolabiunter, uocantem unctionem."

that they were "more enslaved to the letter than to the Spirit." On November 18, 1525, he condemned them in a letter to Andreas Osiander, one of the preachers at Nuremberg.

> Now does it become those who profess Christ to depend upon a human trifle? I confess our faith to you and to the Lord in the presence of God. We believe in Christ Jesus, crucified for us, through whom the Lord promised salvation to the world and sacrificed himself; we always preach this one thing. We do not tolerate the rebaptizers who give power over Christianity to the element of water against the true sense of the Scriptures. . . .[29]

Capito's theology did have a spiritualist tendency, but this was more a matter of language than of substance, for he believed that the content of the Spirit was Christ alone. Capito's spiritualism amounted to an attack upon Anabaptist teachings, not an affirmation of them, because they, to his mind, did not cleave to Christ alone.

Capito also always defended the practice of baptizing infants. He was uncertain about the question when it first came to his attention in the feud between Carlstadt and Luther. In his treatise on the controversy he avoided the doctrinal issue with the declaration that "We do not question ourselves about which time and at what age one should baptize children. . . . Wherever we have no clear word, we cease to search; if something further should be necessary, God will surely reveal it." Two months later he wrote Zwingli only that "We will investigate the matter of infant baptism most carefully." But in January 1525, while writing Zwingli again, he defended the practice on prudential grounds:

> There were those (no, they still exist) who deny that infants are to be baptized; there are those who deny further that they are acknowledged by reason of baptism. We fight with the Word to keep necessity from insinuating something into liberty; we contend all the same that it is most useful that they be baptized, for it will be an opportunity in the remainder of life for the inculcation of religion.[30]

Cellarius' arrival in Strasbourg thus merely reinforced Capito's tendency to defend baptizing infants by reference to the law of love. He stated his argument explicitly in the 1527 catechism:

> *Question*: What command requires infant baptism?
> [*Answer*:] We have no outward command that is necessary, for love makes this of necessity without any other command; we are free from everything temporal.

---

[29] *QGT*, VII, 286; 48-49.
[30] *Von der Spaltung*, sig. Biii-Biii(v). *ZW*, VIII, 280; 300-301.

Question: How can baptism be given to children on the grounds of love if it does not serve to improve?

Answer: It improves greatly; for we witnesses are reminded of the gifts of God and the grace of the covenant that he wants to be our Father. The children are commended to the elders and to the community to bring them up now more as children of God, to the divine glory alone.

Capito's defence of infant baptism did not amount to Zwingli's argument that baptizing children was a divine command, nor did he agree that baptism took the place of circumcision under the old covenant. "Ceremonies are defined through the Scriptures to point more to the author than to the work among us," he wrote in the commentary on Hosea. "It is not baptism and the eucharist that have succeeded to their place but Christ, just as the body follows the shadow. . . ." [31] Nevertheless, even when Capito was most under the influence of Cellarius, he still taught that infants should be baptized.

Cellarius' predestinarian teachings in fact led Capito to be even more insistent upon baptizing infants. In the 1527 catechism he denied that the practice was "shameful" and that many of the damned were known as "Christians" because they had been baptized. It was impossible to determine the faith of anyone who presented himself for baptism, regardless of age, he argued, but some were Christians. Regarding infants he suggested that "we must hope that the kingdom of heaven is theirs and belongs to them of right, so that we accept them into the outward community with outward signs even as the ancients have done with circumcision." That was in 1527, before Cellarius' influence had made itself felt, but Capito added a section to the 1529 catechism in which he declared that "the kingdom of heaven does belong to elected children, but their covenant with God has not yet been revealed to them; that is, they have not yet experienced divine favor in themselves; we however should act in the ordinary fashion." He compared an infant to the son of a knight who does not yet know that he too is a knight. He might later in

---

[31] *Kinderbericht-1527*, sig. D. *In Hoseam prophetam*, fol. 155. In spite of Capito's suggestion to the contrary (see nn. 16, 21, above), the two did disagree on the nature of the covenant, for Capito saw little continuity between the old ceremonies and the new sacraments. He thus continued the argument in the Hosea commentary above by writing that Christ "has novas ceremonias instituit, ceu umbras earum rerum, quas ipse complecturus esset, nobisque elementa mundi non sunt, qui exaltatum Christum intelligimus."

life repudiate his status, but unless he did, he was entitled to the presumption, and the prerogatives, of knighthood. The church would err, Capito wrote, if it refused baptism "to *gläubigen Kinder*—believing children." [32] The very use of such a term would have horrified an Anabaptist. Cellarius' predestinarianism led Capito to insist more strongly upon baptizing infants.

Never once did Capito suggest that he approved the teachings of the radicals. But he was willing to outlaw only the practice of their beliefs, and he knew that separation was the great threat that they posed. He would never abide separatism, especially not on the grounds of baptism, for to him this was a sacrament of the church. "Therefore," he wrote in his confession for Bern in 1532, "it should not be done without the presence of the church, for whenever the church is not present, baptism is not a sacrament of the church but an ordinary child's bath." Baptism and the eucharist were very much the same for Capito. The church reached out with the sacraments; it did not exclude. In 1529 he added to his catechism a section in which he denied the catechumen's suggestion that by withholding baptism from infants "there might therefore be some division from the goats."

> People seek many such grounds to divide the two, which remain well mixed. But a pious, patient man looks up to God for love and improvement; he takes counsel for his deeds from the ground of faith and from that which is peculiar to Christianity, for God must purify his church. You will not accomplish it. What should be done in regard to the quarrel about water, upon which salvation does not depend? Hear me, dear child, and do not allow yourself to be heated up by anyone's talk; await God ... take hold of what serves peace and unity without detriment to the glory of God. ... One does not seek to erect a different community of God. ... Many who departed from the foulest blasphemy and stand in greater fear of God bring in quarrels and sects, to the destruction of the community of God. And, to be sure, their goal is to erect a pure community of God, which God himself will do in his own time by means that have been announced.[33]

Capito's very understanding of baptism led him to condemn Anabaptist separatism.

He equally deplored the other aspect of radical separatism. He rarely spoke of the Anabaptists without remarking on their opposition

---

[32] *Kinderbericht-1527*, sig. [Cviii]. *Kinderbericht-1529*, fol. 31-31(v).
[33] *Berner Synodus*, sig. eii(v)-eiii. *Kinderbericht-1529*, fol. 31(v)-32.

to the notion of a Christian magistrate. This was a myth to which Capito was deeply attached, and which he found particularly useful in the campaign against the Mass. To deny it, he suggested in the commentary on Hosea, was a mark of "fear of the Lord and zeal, but insufficient knowledge." In his judgment the Anabaptists failed to distinguish properly between the public and the private. "A private man may not resist evil. On the other hand, if the magistracy neglected the defence of widows and orphans it would incur the disgrace of the traitor." When he urged the city council of Horb to be merciful to Sattler's followers in 1527, he still condemned their belief that no magistracy was Christian. "Accordingly in whatever estate one trusts God through Christ and serves the neighbor, he is not against Christ. Now the authorities serve the commonality ... therefore, they are not unchristian. This is the order that there be an authority to reward good deeds and to frighten away evil deeds. Whoever resists this order resists the almighty God." [34] These words must have offered small comfort to the prisoners. But for Capito, as for the other reformers, the secular authority was divinely ordained, and every Christian must be obedient to it.

The mildness that Capito advocated toward the Anabaptists was thus based not upon any theological affinity for them but upon his own unwillingness to use force in matters of faith. He disagreed with Bucer only on the tactics that should be used to promote unity. One of the memoranda that he composed for Strasbourg's delegates to the Diet of Augsburg concluded with a plea that the princes eschew force. If they did not, Capito wrote, "much guiltless blood would be shed, there would be a contradiction between being a subject and being honorable that would drive one against the authorities. . . ." Civil war would result, and the consequences would be horrible. "The Imperial Majesty, the Electoral Princes, princes, and all estates— and with them all authority—would clearly be shattered." [35] The difference between Capito and the more warlike Zwingli and more forceful Bucer was that Capito included the Anabaptists in his proscription of force. He did the same for the followers of Luther when he was adviser to the Archbishop of Mainz.

The relatively permissive policy that Capito advocated toward the radicals eventually collapsed. It never had much likelihood for

---

[34] *In Hoseam prophetam*, fol. 18-18(v). *QGT*, VII, 84.
[35] Archives municipales de Strasbourg. Archivum S. Thoman, AA, 412, 79(v)-80(v).

success, because it depended finally upon the willingness of the sectarians not to act upon their religious beliefs. It was wishful thinking to suggest that rebaptism did not imply separation. Logically perhaps it did not, but in fact most people who practiced adult baptism held as a prime article of faith that they must not associate with an established church and must not serve temporal authorities. Capito could never bear the thought of further division in the church, and on January 10, 1531, he wrote Klaus Kniebis, one of the Thirteen, a memorandum in which he asserted that it was unchristian not to swear loyalty to the city authorities. Quite the contrary, Capito proclaimed, "To be sure, swearing in the fear of God is the highest honor to God." [36] But it was a fundamental belief of the Anabaptists that such swearing was to take the Lord's name in vain. As a reformer Capito was again seeking compromise in matters of faith, much as he did as adviser to the Archbishop of Mainz. And his policy of accomodation was no more successful with the Anabaptists than it was with Luther. Again Capito was forced to choose, this time between order and the unity of brotherly love.

A series of personal experiences in late 1531 and early 1532 helped convert Capito to Bucer's firmer policy toward religious dissenters. The first of these were staggering personal losses that struck Capito in fall 1531. Zwingli, with axe in hand, fell in the Battle of Kappel. And Capito's closest friend, Oecolampadius, died shortly thereafter. The measure of their intimacy was the reminiscence-filled biography of Oecolampadius that Capito published as an introduction to his commentary on Ezekiel in 1534. As if these deaths were insufficient occasion for grief, the plague reappeared in Strasbourg in early November 1531. Capito himself was bedridden for a month. His wife Agnes died. And he was deeply shaken. In the middle of December he began a letter to the preachers of Leonhard von Liechtenstein with an apology for not having written earlier, "for my dear sister and housewife, Gnese, my true helpmate in all service to God, lay sick and died ... with great quiet, peace, and submission to God, but not without my great distress and temptation (anfechtong). For I discerned well the punishment of God present and let my sin nearly get ahead of me. God pushed me to repentance through such means." [37] Capito did not proceed to a full confession of his sins in

---

[36] *QGT*, VII, 299.

[37] *QGT*, VII, 363-364. The letter will not bear the interpretation of Williams, *Radical Reformation*, pp. 255-257, that Capito interpreted his wife's death as

this letter, but Agnes' death seems to have served as a reminder of his own mortality. It almost led him to despair, and it may have prodded him to reconsider his reforming work.

Capito had plenty to reconsider, in particular his practice of allowing religious dissidents to believe what they wished so long as they did not act upon those beliefs. In 1531 he also had a brush with a man who held heretical notions and who was an undeniable threat to the reform party, even though he did not seek to establish a new church. The man was Michael Servetus, the famous antitrinitarian, and he arrived in Strasbourg while his *On the Errors of the Trinity* was being published in the nearby town of Hagenau. He may have been Capito's guest, and others began to suspect that Capito shared his beliefs. On July 18 Oecolampadius wrote Bucer that he first learned of the publication of Servetus' book from Capito. Oecolampadius was appalled by Servetus' teachings, and a month later he urged Bucer to rid the reformers of this blight immediately. He concluded with a curious note: "I will write Capito very soon so he will help you in repairing the church after putting that behavior of his behind him." On September 17 he did just that in a letter in which he sharply criticized Capito for providing hospitality to "enemies of the Church." Oecolampadius mentioned no names, but the story that Capito was involved with Servetus spread quickly. From Constance, Thomas Blaurer wrote his brother Ambrosius on December 9, "It is rumored here . . . that Capito agrees with the Jews concerning the divinity of Christ." Ambrosius repeated the story to Bucer on December 23. He urged caution for fear that Capito's reputation might be destroyed. On December 29 Bucer replied that he had attacked Servetus' book in his lectures. He put the rumors down to Capito's "imprudence" in matters of this importance.[38]

Bucer was right. Capito may have entertained Servetus' person but never his ideas. The stories nevertheless prompted Capito to act, especially when he received a lengthy exhortation from Berchthold Haller, one of the preachers at Bern.

> They say the Spaniard, Michael, has published an apology for the first book, full of monsters and errors by the thousands. It may not

"divine chastizement for his toleration of the Radicals." His remark must rather be read in the light of *In Hoseam prophetam*, fol. 6(v), "Nephario adulterio, pauperum oppressione, et nescientia D E I peccauit Ephraim peculiariter dilectus Deo. Igitur in periculo sum ego, ne similiter peccem. Quocirca mihi obseruatu necessarium est, ne uxorem et liberos charitate Dei anteponeam. . . ."

[38] *BAO*, II, 628; 636; 681-683. *BB*, I, 298; 304-307.

have occurred to you, who have devoured the mysteries of the matter from the sources, that it will not only discomfort the churches but also make you suspect, because you may either have been aware of it or have been involved in it. Accordingly, the brethren wish you to be warned and beg that you run to the aid of those whom so much of the light has not yet approached. . . .[39]

Capito did just as Haller requested. He was frightened by the prospect of antitrinitarianism. When the Strasbourg pastors petitioned the senate in November for a synod to define the city's teachings, Capito added a note in which he warned of the dangers of antitrinitarianism.[40] And in 1539 he concluded his commentary on the creation story with a "Refutation of the Dreams of the Jews" upon which he brought to bear his studies in the Talmud and in the Jewish commentators. "I have also been aided by the learned men among the Jews, not so something might be allowed them, but so I might rather refute their errors, or compare our religion to their testimonies." Haller was right when he wrote that Capito had "devoured the mysteries of the matter from the sources." [41] And the brush with Servetus offered evidence that it was not always prudent to allow people to believe what they wished.

The third impetus in Capito's change to Bucer's policy was a four-month trip in winter 1531-1532 during which he became involved for the first time in establishing organizational patterns for the new churches of the Reformation. The personal losses of late 1531 left him in deep melancholy, and Bucer suggested the trip with the hope that he would be improved "in body and soul" by the opportunity to be away from Strasbourg, and with other leaders of the reform party in Switzerland and southwest Germany. Capito began his tour on December 21 and visited Basel, Zurich, Bern, Esslingen, Memmingen, and Augsburg before returning home sometime after March 25, 1532.[42]

---

[39] Th. B., V, 48(v)-49. Strasser, *Beziehungen*, pp. 70-75, reads the letter exactly backwards to conclude that Haller was still suspicious of Capito's opinions after having talked with him in Bern in January.

[40] *QGT*, VII, 576. "Nun sein aber auch etliche, die frey wider die offentliche schrifft vnnd allen glauben sagen . . . das Christus nit sey worer von Maria der jungfrowen geboren; die andern, das er nit worer got sey. . . ."

[41] *Hexemeron Dei opus explicatum a Vuolphango Fa. Capitone Theologo* (Argentorati, 1539), fol. 283-286(v); a4(v)-a5. Capito had a copy of the Talmud from Pellican and was working on it as early as 1526, but he had difficulty with the vocabulary. He sent Pellican a "Gramara Babilonici Talmud" in 1538 and may have concluded his study then. See Capito to Pellican, 11 June 1526, Th. B., II, 258, and Riggenbach, *Chronikon*, p. 173.

[42] The itinerary is established by *BB*, I, 107, Th. B., V, 61-61(v); 57.

Bucer was badly mistaken if he thought Capito's trip would be a vacation, for in city after city he was drawn into consultations on the problems of the churches. Bern in particular provided a challenge. A crisis gripped the reform party there after the defeat in the Battle of Kappel. Caspar Megander, one of the preachers, was attacking the city authorities for insufficient zeal, and he was trying to incite the citizens to renewed war against the Catholic cantons. The preachers were taking sides on the issue, and those who opposed Megander feared that the city magistrates were about to turn against them all. According to Haller, the church had been "driven into the greatest danger" before Capito arrived on December 30, 1531. He was unaware that the city was about to hold a synod, but after being briefed by Haller, he asked the authorities' permission to remain and to take part. They granted both requests and cast him into the role of mediator. Within a week he prepared articles on doctrine and polity as an agenda for the synod.[43]

The first task was to ease the tensions that had built up among the city's pastors during the preceding months. Capito was extraordinarily evenhanded in acting as virtual chairman of the synod. The session of January 12, for instance, nearly exploded when Megander and Haller began shouting at one another over Megander's incendiary sermons. Capito broke into the argument, chastized Haller, and told the group that there should be no further wrangling over "outward things." He then turned on Megander and instructed him not to be offended personally by brotherly correction of his attitudes. These tactics were successful. On January 16 Haller wrote Bucer that Capito "brought forth the matter in words so blessedly, so felicitously, that he proved everything amazingly with the greatest wonder, just as Christ ought to be preached. . . ." Capito knew he had done well. A day earlier he reported to the Strasbourg senate that the synod of Bern was concluded with great honor for Strasbourg. "I know only . . . that God has led me," he confessed.[44]

Capito's success in settling this dispute in a formal synod probably made him less wary of Bucer's desire to dispose of the problem of the radicals in Strasbourg in a similar manner. More importantly, the position that Capito promoted at Bern contained implications for his policy toward the Anabaptists in Strasbourg. His "articles"

---

[43] Strasser, *Beziehungen, Beilage* II, 175. Steck and Tobler, *Aktensammlung zur Berner Reformation*, pp. 1491; 1493.
[44] *Ibid.*, p. 1496. Strasser, *Beziehungen, Beilage* II, 176. Th. B., V, 11-11(v).

were first published in Basel in late January. They were probably printed just as Capito read them to the synod, for he frequently employed the second person. The chief issue at stake at Bern was the relationship between the pastors and the city authorities, and by implication Capito criticized Megander for being disloyal. "In summary, no right is given a minister of Christ to subject other subjects or authorities to himself and to set himself forth as something," Capito declared. He agreed that "We should not understand that Our Gracious Lords should sit in the Pope's place," but he denied that they should be excluded from the church because they previously supported "the strivings of the Antichrist." Prudential reasons dictated to Capito that the reformers depend upon the magistracy to erect the true church, for, he said, "It is not well possible, Gracious, beloved Lords, for something fruitful to be ignited and maintained with outward ordinances by the teachers and ministers of the Word of the eternal God without the assistance and support of the temporal authority." [45] If Capito could condemn the disloyalty in Megander's sermons, what was he willing to do to the radicals who refused even the formality of swearing loyalty to the magistracy?

While Capito was concluding his tour, he could take pride in the work he had done to help order the churches of Switzerland and southwest Germany. But his domestic life was still unsettled, and Bucer, who urged him to take the trip, was paying attention to this problem too. He began to look for a new wife for his colleague less than a month after Agnes' death. On December 8 he wrote Margareta Blaurer and asked her to consider Capito. A new wife for Capito was a matter of high policy for Bucer. According to him, the sectarians in Strasbourg were trying to talk the widow of the "King of the Anabaptists" into marrying him. There were in fact few grounds for concern on that score. Although Capito may have employed her as his housekeeper, he was seeking to arrange her return to her family in Augsburg. But Bucer was wise in the ways of the heart, and he understood in particular that Capito consistently desired to care for the weak. So he persisted. To Blaurer he also suggested Wibrandis Rosenblatt, Oecolampadius' widow, who might cure Capito of his insomnia, which, Bucer thought, was the cause of his persistent melancholy. In passing, he suggested that perhaps Blaurer's

---

[45] *Berner Synodus*, sig. B-Biii; gii-gii(v).

sister, Margareta, would also be a suitable candidate. Bucer did not mention the means by which Wibrandis would end Capito's insomnia, but Blaurer was certain that she would be better for him than his sister. He replied that his sister would never marry. Moreover, he wrote, she served him quite well unmarried, and if she married, then he too would be compelled to find a wife in order to have a house-keeper.

A week later Bucer replied that a doctor in Bern had told Capito that marriage was essential to cure his melancholy. Ambrosius was right, Bucer replied. Wibrandis Rosenblatt would do nicely. He urged Ambrosius to suggest her to Capito when he arrived.[46] Then Bucer spread the net to include Haller in the plot. On March 16 Haller wrote Capito, "There is nothing else new with us, except that we admonish you to obtain from the Lord a fitting wife for yourself, unless you want to destroy yourself of your own free will by longlasting bad health brought on by your melancholy." Capito bowed to his friends' solicitations. He probably stopped by Basel on his way back from Augsburg to collect Wibrandis, along with Oecolampadius' literary remains.[47] When both Bucer's wife and Capito died in another outbreak of the plague in 1541, Bucer, the great unionist of the Reformation, married Wibrandis Rosenblatt himself, and she outlived him too.

Capito emerged from his experiences of 1531-1532 as Bucer's loyal ally in the plan to erect a church order for Strasbourg that would end toleration for the radicals. Toward the end of November 1532 he and Bucer petitioned the senate to call a synod for establishing doctrinal and organizational norms. There were apparently objections to their proposal, for they went out of their way to declare that "to make such commands and order is absolutely not, as some suggest, to compel belief, but to do away with clear abuse." On the contrary, they argued, much as they had in the campaign against the Mass, it was the authorities' duty to discourage false teachings, such as antitrinitarianism, and false practices, such as rebaptism.[48] This petition reflected the work Capito did with the Synod of Bern and

---

[46] For Bucer's correspondence with the Blaurer's, *BB*, II, 795; I, 317; 319-320. On the king of the Anabaptists widow, Arbenz, *Vadianische Briefsammlung*, V, 17-18.

[47] Th. B., V, 49.

[48] *QGT*, VII, 575-577, esp. 576. "Zu dem allen so were das fürgangen, das furgehn solle, vnnd hette die oberkeyt als auch die diener des worts das jr gethon, wie das die ordnung gottes erforderet. . . ."

the high position he granted temporal authority in the confession he composed there. But there was more to the matter, for it was also the logical consequence of the role he gave the senate in abolishing the Mass in Strasbourg. By 1532 Capito came over to Bucer's side on policy regarding the sectarians; he thereby chose order over the permissive unity of brotherly love.

The agreement of Capito and Bucer on the necessity of a synod was crucial to the plan's success. Strasbourg held no general synod of the church before Capito favored it. Nevertheless by 1532 Bucer was the chief pastor in Strasbourg, and the meeting and organization of the church were essentially his work.[49] Already in 1531 he persuaded the senate to create the office of elders, or *"Kirchenpfleger,"* for each parish. They joined with the pastors in the "convent" which represented the church as a whole. The petition with which Bucer and Capito requested the synod was presented to the senate by the pastors, but in the name of the convent. On April 12, 1533, when the authorities granted the synod, they changed its nature somewhat. In addition to the pastors and elders, they invited two representatives of each parish and anyone else who had complaints. They determined that the pastors and elders would meet before the synod to decide its business but Sturm was named chairman. The senate thus assured that its voice would be heard in the deliberations, but Bucer's influence was paramount. He composed the Sixteen Articles, which became the city's official doctrine. In the opening sermon to the pre-synodal meeting of pastors and elders between June 3 and June 6 Capito declared that the purpose of the gathering was to promote "unity of teaching, the ordering of the ministers, and the common management of the church." [50] But his position was purely honorific, for Bucer was the dominant figure in the meetings.

The synod met June 10-14. The first session, which included pastors and representatives of Strasbourg's rural dependencies, heard complaints against the rural pastors and then read and accepted the Sixteen Articles. Hearings of religious dissidents consumed the rest of the synod. Capito opened these meetings with prayer and then for

---

[49] François Wendel, *L'église de Strasbourg, sa constitution et son organization (1532-1535)* (Paris, 1942), esp. pp. 45-60, who neglects Capito's agreement with and support for Bucer. Chrisman, *Strasbourg*, pp. 201-232, recapitulates Wendel and extends the story to 1548. See also the superficial account of Eells, *Bucer*, pp. 146-159, who treats the Synod as entirely the affair of Bucer.

[50] *QGT*, VIII, 36.

the most part fell silent while Bucer debated Clement Ziegler, Claus Frey, Melchior Hofmann, and Schwenckfeld. This was the major reason for calling the synod. Bucer seemingly wrote the Sixteen Articles with the opposition in mind. He excluded opinions with great precision but made positive prescriptions almost casually. The first article condemned the teachings of "a Spaniard," and the seventh excluded all who "slander infant baptism as unchristian." Articles 14, 15, and 16 detailed the important role of the magistracy in religion and the responsibility of Christians to it. These articles and the decrees by which they were enforced ended the *ad hoc* policy that Capito previously favored and that allowed toleration of the Anabaptists to persist in Strasbourg.[51]

The Strasbourg Synod of 1533 accomplished much of what Capito opposed for six years from 1526 through 1531. In the petition in which they requested the synod Bucer and Capito denied that they intended to compel belief, but the hearings of the radicals in the presence of the civil authorities amounted to just that. To be sure, those who were examined had all committed acts that threatened public order, but they were examined about their beliefs. No longer would Bucer and Capito combat error solely through preaching the Word; they both also expected that the senate would expel those who refused to hear it. This was a critical issue. With the exception of the statement on infant baptism, the last three articles on the association of church and magistracy were the most hotly debated in Bucer's confession. Of course Schwenckfeld and Hofmann objected, but so did Anton Engelbrecht, the pastor at St. Stephen's. He and two other pastors charged that the synod was unchristian because it mixed the temporal with the spiritual. June 6 in the pre-synodal meeting was consumed with their objections; and the dispute continued well into November.[52] Engelbrecht, who eventually left the city, took up the cudgels when Capito dropped them.

Capito wholeheartedly approved Strasbourg's new church order. In the examination of the city pastors he graciously accepted the criticisms of the vicar of Bucer's church and of his old student Hedio for his "special weakness for foreign guests" and for his financial interest in a printing establishment. These reprovals were just. Capito provided hospitality to such notables as William Farel

---

[51] *QGT*, VIII, 25-32. See the judgment of Wendel, *L'église de Strasbourg*, pp. 129-130.

[52] *QGT*, VIII, 54-63. Wendel, *L'église de Strasbourg*, pp. 72-73.

and the French humanist Jacques Lefèvre d'Étaples in addition
to an assortment of radicals. And he probably wished he had never
become involved with Matthew Apiarius' press, for two years later
he was indebted with Apiarius for the sum of 2000 gulden, which was
rather much for a preacher whose annual income never exceeded
300 gulden. Capito was so desperate to get out of this misadventure
that he once withheld a theological manuscript from Apiarius because he wanted him to concentrate on easily salable items, among
which he numbered history.[53]

Although unwilling, or unable, to default on his financial obliga-
tions, Capito did cease being hospitable to foreigners. In November
and December 1533 he joined Bucer in examining three radicals, one
of whom tried to shout him down while he was preaching. And in
July 1534, after Schwenckfeld returned to Strasbourg, he and Hedio
asked the senate to authorize a disputation with his former house
guest, so they could quash rumors that the pastors mistreated him at
the synod. Instead of granting their request, the authorities ordered
Schwenckfeld to leave the city, and Capito approved. Two months
earlier he warned Jacob Truchsess, an adviser to Duke Ulrich of
Württemberg, not to tolerate people like Schwenckfeld in reforming
the church of Württemberg. Bucer was delighted. On October 10,
1533, he wrote Blaurer, "Capito is wholly ours and he is well acquainted with the hair-splitting of these people. . . ." Bucer could
hardly contain himself. A month later he wrote Blaurer again,
"Capito is wholly ours now; if only he had always been so!" [54]

Bucer had good reason to be pleased with his colleague's behavior,
for Capito supported Strasbourg's new church order as vigorously
as he once agitated against the Mass. Bucer, Capito, Hedio, and
Zell remonstrated with the senate on January 28, 1534, about the
failure of enforcing decrees to appear even after agreement was
reached on implementing the decisions of the June meeting at a
second session of the synod in late October 1533. Finally on March 4
the authorities declared that the Sixteen Articles, together with the
Tetrapolitana, were the official doctrine of the city, and on April
13 they decreed that all who did not hold to them must leave the
city. But Capito was still not satisfied. In November 1534 and again
early in 1535 he petitioned the senate to decree "the abolition of
the sects" through municipal enforcement of excommunication. On

---

[53] *QGT*, VIII, 49; 52. *BB*, I, 675.
[54] *QGT*, VIII, 367. Th. B., VII, 109e-109i. *BB*, I, 432-433; 441.

February 7, 1535, the authorities promulgated a final decree that sharpened earlier mandates against the radicals and threatened excommunication for those who did not observe Sundays or who exhibited loose morals.[55] This decree was as much the work of Capito as of any other reformer in the city.

Nothing could have been more opposed to Capito's policy from 1526 through 1531 than Strasbourg's new church order. All citizens were now required not to give aid to those who attacked the city's doctrine or preachers but to report them to a committee of five elders, who would investigate. With the advice of the pastors this committee was empowered to declare excommunication. Control of this formidable authority lay firmly in the hands of the senate, which appointed the elders. The pastors themselves were subject to investigation or excommunication if citizens complained about their lives or teachings. Far from objecting to such ordered temporal control, Capito and the other pastors wanted the senate to be more vigilant in supervising the citizens' moral and religious lives. On August 7, 1535, the pastors complained that the citizens, including the authorities, were not attending services or partaking of the Lord's Supper. They demanded that the senate require parents to bring their children to the sermons, in particular to those on the catechism. They suggested that the elders could administer any new mandate on the subject.[56]

The true measure of Capito's commitment to such close association between the temporal authorities and the church was that he tried to extend Strasbourg's church order to other areas in the Rhineland. On February 8, 1535, Bucer, Blaurer, and Simon Grynaeus, who were in Tübingen, wrote Capito a letter in which they urged him or Hedio to go to Frankfurt and restore order in the church there.[57] The Strasbourg senate asked Capito to undertake the mission. Trouble had been brewing in Frankfurt long before Capito arrived on February 25. For years Dionysius Melander preached zealously against the Mass, and when the city council refused to abolish it, he turned his attack on the authorities. By 1535 circumstances in Frankfurt paralleled those that prevailed in Bern three years earlier. As Capito recalled in the report to the Frankfurt city council that he wrote after he returned to Strasbourg on March 7, "I have never found

---

[55] *QGT*, VII, 392; 416-420; 421-430. Wendel, *L'église de Strasbourg*, pp. 117-123.
[56] *QGT*, VIII, 473-474.
[57] *BB*. I, 672.

more willfulness and irritation among the preachers of our Gospel. . . .
And yet both sides, in so far as I could determine, are pious, loving
men. God, however, wants to lead you (I trust) to a fuller knowledge
and following of Christ through such anxieties." [58]

In his report Capito assumed that the temporal authorities, rather
than the pastors, were responsible for church order in Frankfurt.
He addressed his memorandum to the city council but made no such
report to the pastors. He suggested that the council could retain
Melander in office with guarantees, or it could force him to leave the
city on the grounds of the common good. Capito advised it to
dismiss Melander. He failed even to imply that the pastors should
be consulted on a matter of such importance.

Capito also outlined a church order for Frankfurt in which he
closely involved the temporal authority in the affairs of the church.
At the beginning of his memorandum he summarized it:

> In the first place, that the unrest and difficulties among the preachers
> would be clearly set aside. On the other hand, that the main issues
> would be recognized so that an Honorable Council might ward off
> partisanship in civil matters, even if a misunderstanding appears on
> account of religion. In the third place, that *seniores ecclesiae*, elders
> of the church, and other invested persons be created concerning
> spiritual management. In the fourth place, that municipal schools be
> erected, and that able Frankfurt children be educated in learning and
> especially in the Holy Scriptures.

Capito was most persistent in regard to his third point, arguing that
"Therefore in this period the church has ordered itself as under
Moses, that elders be elected from all tribes; therefore elders, who
are called *Kirchenpfleger* elsewhere, should in this time also be elected
from all classes of the people." Through the institution of the elders,
Capito argued, the public disputes that earlier wracked the Frankfurt
church could be avoided.

He was trying to transplant Strasbourg's church order into Frankfurt. The elders would consist of three members of the city council
and six citizens. He also commended the office of deacons, who would
visit the sick and administer alms and church property, but real
authority rested with the elders, who should serve no longer than
three years. They would meet with the pastors in a "council of the
churches," "a meeting of the church," or a "conventicle of the pastors" every two weeks. Regarding this body's powers Capito wrote

---

[58] Ritter, *Evangelisches Denkmahl*, pp. 329-330.

only, "In sum, nothing should be excluded." With this advice he
revealed how much the apostle of order he became in his declining
years. If the Frankfurt city council did as he suggested, it would
create the institutions of the church, take part in their deliberations,
and enforce their decisions. He recommended even the establishment
of a "civil police" to watch over the morals and beliefs of the citizens.[59]

The religious role of the civil authorities became an ever more
pressing issue throughout Germany in the years after the Diet of
Augsburg, as one principality and town after another dismantled
the local institutions of the Roman Church. The question also came
to occupy more and more of Capito's own thought and energies
after the Strasbourg synods. On March 5, 1532 he bluntly gave it
the form that agitated many clergymen. Writing Bullinger, who
was confronted by an increasingly aggressive city council in Zurich
after Zwingli's death, he advised, "Here it is necessary that you take
care that the magistracy do neither too much nor none at all of those
things that pertain to the kingdom of Christ." [60] Here was the problem
that underlay much of Capito's own practical work in Strasbourg,
whether it was the campaign against the Mass, or policy toward the
Anabaptists, or the formation of a new church. Most reformers
agreed that the civil authorities, in their roles as Christian magistrates,
were responsible for the religious life of their subjects, within limits.
But here was the problem: what were the limits?

Capito confronted the question directly in a book that he finished
by December 1535 and then published in 1537. He was responding
to a request from Duke Ruprecht of the Palatinate-Zweibrücken,
whose chancellor, Jacob Schorr, had recently advised that the prince
had no authority to regulate marriage, to outlaw concubinage
among the priests, or to abolish the mass. In his prefatory letter to
Ruprecht, Capito charged that Schorr's policy threatened "the
tranquillity of your kingdom." Here was the argument he used
against the Mass in Strasbourg. And he indicated the direction of
his opinion in this case by adding another dedicatory epistle, to
Henry VIII of England, on March 9, 1537. There he declared, "A
Christian prince is one that not only conducts affairs by making
laws for good morals but also secures genuine piety among the

---

[59] *Ibid.*, pp. 330-342.
[60] Th. B., V, 39. "Hic opus est, ut caveas, ne Magistratus neque nimirum
neque nihil agat earum rerum quae sunt regni Christi."

people according to the Word of God—nay, he makes this the first concern, that true religion prosper among the people." [61]

This book reveals the close connection between Capito's campaign against the Mass in Strasbourg and his view of church order. He was seeking to persuade Duke Ruprecht to reform the church in his territory when he charged, "Let any magistracy that has accepted some power . . . from God faithfully employ it according to the will of the supreme Lord against the petty contempts of men; if it should cease, it should be adjudged guilty of perfidy." [62] Much in the manner of Luther, he was here granting Ruprecht emergency episcopal powers.

On the surface, Capito's mature views on the nature of temporal authority were strikingly similar to Luther's. They were a bit more clearly developed in that he distinguished more sharply between sorts of temporal authority. Following Aristotle, there were to Capito's mind first tyrants, who ruled without laws for their own gain, then legitimate authorities who ruled with laws for the benefit of their subjects. Finally, there was the "Christian magistracy." [63] Although he clearly favored the Christian magistrate, all three types of authority were directly ordained by God, who had regard for humanity's need for good order. Consequently, there was no right of resistance, not even for Christians. Capito was also in agreement with Luther in that, while granting religious responsibilities to the Christian magistrate, he witheld from the tyrant and from legitimate authority any relationship with the church.[64] For Capito as for

---

[61] *Responsio*, sig. [ii-vii], fol. 6(v). Henry VIII was pleased. See Cranmer to Capito, [late 1537], Th. B., X, 206-206(v). This work has been virtually ignored by scholars. Wendel, *L'église de Strasbourg*, pp. 11-23, for instance, fails to mention it in his discussion of sources.

[62] *Responsio*, fol. 207.

[63] *Ibid.*, fol. 6-6(v). "Ordinata autem potestas triplex est, tyrannica, legitima ac Christiana. . . . Prima se quarit, et affectibus rapitur, soluta legibus. Altera populi externam utilitatem et civiles mores, et legibus tenetur. Tertia salutem animae per uerbum Domini. . . ." For the first two types of authority see Aristotle, *Politics*, III, 6; V, 10.

[64] The test case is the tyrant. See *Responsio*, fol. 7, where he argued that God "tales tyrannos saepius in potestatem inaugurat propter populi peccata, ut pro meritis ea uia publice puniatur," and fol. 5(v), where, much in the manner of Luther, he argued, "Quod si pergit uiolare, etiam Deum et Christum in nobis, hic ea plane propter conscientiam timenda non est, dum pro loco iuxta nostram ipsorum uocationem, et absque libidine nouandi aduersus tyrannidem ueritatem asseveremus," and fol. 6(v), "Cui tamen per seditionem repugnandum non est, sed potius a pijs toleratur, iuxta illud, Ne resistatis malo."

Luther, the Christian prince had religious duties chiefly by virtue of being Christian rather than by virtue of being prince.

And yet there was an important difference in the tone of Capito's pronouncements, a difference that calls to mind more a Zwingli than a Luther. It was already evident in the argument Capito used to persuade the Strasbourg senate to abolish the Mass, and it was repeated in the book he wrote to Duke Ruprecht:

> I freely confess that whatever is conducted within souls and minds is outside the competence of the magistracy. A legitimate magistracy has never usurped control over what is hidden and secret, nor do we attribute an investigation of the thoughts of men to an evangelical prince; but rather he is concerned with what is out in the open, with what all can see, with what offends inexperienced simplicity and opposes the Word of God.

Yielding to the Christian prince all externalities gave him considerable latitude in ordering religious affairs. Toward the end of his book Capito directed Duke Ruprecht's attention to the example of Henry VIII with the declaration, "The prince is the head of the church on earth." He thus placed the administrative, as distinct from the doctrinal and sacerdotal, authority of the medieval bishop squarely in the hands of the Christian magistracy. "The governances of the prince are whatever pertains to the outward ruling of the people of God," he wrote, and added, "He who is prince, the same is pastor, the same father, the same external head of the church on earth." [65] Whereas Luther gave the Christian prince the right, during an emergency, to intervene in the affairs of the church, Capito, more in the manner of Zwingli, obliged him to do so. Consequently, an argument that Ruprecht had the authority to abolish the Mass became a justification for continuing temporal supervision of the Church.

At first glance it appears that Capito so rejected the radicals' vision of a separate believers' church that he adopted an Erastian position on the relationship between church and temporal authority. In his last published work, a commentary on the first six chapters of Genesis, he approached the same problem from the standpoint of discipline. "There is no effective ministry outside the church," he declared. For him "the ministry of the Gospel" consisted of "doctrine, keys, baptism, and the eucharist." He defined the power of the keys as an office of "admonition, encouragement, reprimanding, public rebuking, the summoning of witnesses, reporting to the

[65] *Ibid.*, fol. 59-59(v); 198(v)-199.

church, and withdrawal, or, if you wish, excommunication." And he
assigned this formidable authority to a body that was similar to the
Strasbourg *Kirchenconvent*, "the senate of that churchman, that is,
of the pastor and the chosen elders." [66] According to Capito's recommendation to the Frankfurt city council, and as it really existed in
Strasbourg, the convent well represented the secular authority.
Besides lay elders, members of the city council participated as fully
constituted members in its deliberations. And he had in mind the
sectarians when he so closely associated the church with temporal
authority in the exercise of discipline. "Certainly the church, now
born of the Word," he wrote, "could hardly have been held together
in any way if it were not somehow maintained by discipline, as if
by chains." [67] The metaphor was well chosen.

Yet Capito proclaimed in the *Responsio* that "The entire ecclesiastical authority is in the possession of the church. . . . It was given
to the church and not handed over to the lust of perverse men,
neither of a monarch nor of a universal bishop." In the commentary
on the creation story he judged in fact that "Without discipline the
church of Christ degenerates into the civil administration and an
iron tyranny at the same time; it does not await the kingdom of the
Spirit." [68] How could he maintain such a position, when he devised
and defended church orders in which members of the temporal
magistracy played such an important role? The answer is that city
councilmen and the representatives of princes did not participate in
the use of the keys as members of the secular order but as ministers
of the church. For Capito the ministry of the church included not
only ordained pastors but also "deacons, subdeacons, and anyone
believing in Christ, according to the measure of received gifts."
In the *Responsio* he argued that when the Christian prince participated
in the rule of the church, he participated as a member of "one body
of one head—Christ," one of whose "received gifts" was the duty
of governing.[69]

To be sure, Capito carefully hedged the role the Christian magis-

---

[66] *Hexemeron Dei opus*, fol. 164-164(v).

[67] *Ibid.*, fol. 186(v)-187.

[68] *Responsio*, fol. 195(v). *Hexemeron Dei opus*, fol. 177-177(v). "In hac autem
pastor aut Episcopus praesidet, qui dux verbi et sacramentorum distributer,
cuius est tota clavium administratio. Huic agenti secundum uerbum domini,
quasi ad diaconi, subdiaconi, et quisque Christo credentium pro accepti doni
modulo."

[69] *Ibid.*, fol. 183(v). *Responsio*, fol. 6-10(v).

tracy played in the church as magistrate. He emphatically denied that, even in exercising the ban, the church was proceeding with force. In his catechism he asked, "Is the ban not an exercise of power in the churches?" and received the answer, "No, it is on the contrary a work of love. . . ." Consequently the sword was entirely inappropriate to the church, and those who were also civil magistrates were to leave it outside the meeting of pastors and elders.[70] For Capito, the ban itself was not even a separate sign of the church; "And so the evangelical stewardship, which we call the keys, has two parts. The one is the authority to preach the Gospel and to announce the remission of sins, the other publicly to ward off criminals who are clearly offensive to the church. . . ." [71] The ban was thus related to the office of preaching the Word, and there was no question of who controlled that office. In the *Responsio* he remarked, "Because the Kingdom and the remission of sins is offered and shown to a believing soul through the external Word and sacraments, we desire to show what and how much may be permitted a pious magistrate regarding Word and sacraments. Here we will easily answer that there is no power either to add or to subtract anything from the Word." [72] Moreover, it was the Word that constituted the church in the first place. "Hence it is evident," he concluded in the commentary on Hosea, "that the external church of Christ is properly the city of those who sincerely declare faith and common love through the spirit of Christ." The church, he wrote in 1529, is "wherever the faithful are." [73] And no magistracy had any religious authority over the faithful.

And yet, throughout, the tone that marked Capito off from Luther and put him into the reformed camp clearly persists. It is not so much that he failed to protect the authority of the church in Word-

---

[70] *Kinderbericht-1527*, sig., Cv(v). See also *Kinderbericht-1529*, fol. 27-27(v)., where he argued that, although the excommunicate was barred from the sacrament and Christians were not to have close relations with such a person, "Aber in ander burgerlicher beywonung, sollen wir jhn nit flichen als eyn feindt, sonder lieb gegen jhn, als eym Heyden erzeygen, zur besserung, oder begeren als eyn irrenden bruder wider auff die pan zu bringen, wo nurt ettwas zeychen des sonnen Gottes erscheynen."

[71] *Hexemeron Dei opus*, fol. 166(v)-167.

[72] *Responsio*, fol. 25(v)-26.

[73] *In Hoseam prophetam*, fol. 278(v). *Kinderbericht-1529*, fol. 26-27(v). See also *Responsio*, fol. 28, where he summarized Augustine, "Ideoque sentit, et ecclesiam et eius authoritatem existere a uerbo Dei, quod initio sine hominum authoritate diuinitus revelatum est. . . ."

related matters as that he exalted the role of the Christian magistracy
into a continuing, rather than an emergency, responsibility for the
church. And he did so on the basis not only of his experiences during
the campaign against the Mass but also of views about the civil
authority that he shared with Erasmus. In brief, he gave the temporal
authorities the same high moral position that Erasmus gave them in
his famous *Education of a Christian Prince*. To Capito, David was the
great example of a king who provided not only peace without and
harmony within but also by his example led his people to the true
honoring of God. Like Erasmus, Capito looked to government
to provide not only protection but also moral and religious leadership.[74] Consequently, he was less suspicious of the temporal authorities than was Luther and more inclined to heap upon them the
burdens of the church, as in the manner of Zwingli.

There was one other distinction that Capito made and that put
him more in the line of Erasmus and Zwingli than of Luther on the
subject of church order. He too was limiting the church to *spiritualia*
while granting all *temporalia* to the civil authority. In spite of all
his careful defence of the autonomy of the Word, he had a very
limited view of what constituted Word-related matters. Thus, he
wrote the Frankfurt city council,

> The Lord is the proper ruler of the world. Now he rules in a temporal
> and a spiritual way. Life and property and all outward things belong
> to the temporal; for a believing people, the outward rule of the church
> is also in this way. The spiritual concerns only the conscience and
> erects itself through the Word, sacraments, brotherly admonition and
> that sort of thing. The temporal rule concerns Your Worthinesses;
> the spiritual concerns the churches. . . .[75]

---

[74] *Ibid.*, fol. 16. "Haec prudentissimus rex, non propter pacem externam ef-
fecit, neque ut populum sibi deuinceret, sed ut exemplo suo, et retuum ueneratione
populum ad sacra facienda, et ad uerbum domini audiendum amplius incenderet,"
and fol. 13, "Itaque finis administratae Reipublicae inter Ethnicos est publica
pax ad civiles mores faciens. . . . Inter pios autem et Christianos, publicata gloria
Dei, finis est. . . ." On Erasmus, see Wilhelm Maurer, *Das Verhältnis des Staates
zur Kirche nach humanistischer Anschauung, vornehmlich bei Erasmus* (Giessen, 1930),
esp. pp. 19-25, who makes too much of the modernity of Erasmus' viewpoint.

[75] Ritter, *Evangelisches Denkmahl*, p. 334. For a remarkable parallel, see James
M. Estes, "Church Order and the Christian Magistrate according to Johannes
Brenz," *Archiv für Reformationsgeschichte*, LIX (1968), 5-23. The one possible
difference is that Capito argued that pastors acted in the church "cum assentu
publico," which could refer to some congregational call, or to their being installed
by the Christian magistrate. *Hexemeron Dei opus*, fol. 173-173(v).

In the 1527 catechism he had the catechumen confess, "I believe in the Christian community so long as it may not be seen by physical eyes." And in the commentary on Hosea he maintained that "The internal compact of the Spirit maintains us, without which the external church is not a church but the congregation of Satan." [76] The essence of the church was therefore spiritual to such an extent that all outward matters, including public morality, were the proper preserve of the civil authorities. They might by their example lead people to moral lives and to the church. But all the church did was to preach the Word, to administer the sacraments, and to exercise brotherly discipline. When hedged in by the Christian prince's authority over all *temporalia*, the Word became a limiting rather than an expanding principle for the activities of the church.

In both his work and his writing Capito did pay more attention to church order after 1531 than he did before. The personal experiences of that year certainly encouraged him to support Bucer's efforts to organize the church in Strasbourg. And his remarks on church order in the *Responsio* and in the commentary on the first six chapters of Genesis were similar to the views that Bucer propounded when he published his first treatise on church polity, *Von der wahren Seelsorge*, in 1538. [77] Both men envisioned a church that was closely associated with, but theoretically separate from, the temporal authority. On April 4, 1538 Capito sent Bullinger a copy of Bucer's treatise with the recommendation, "Without this care, I do not believe that either order or system could have remained in the churches." Yet, if Bucer influenced Capito to advocate a more highly structured church than existed in Strasbourg before 1533, he did so in unrecorded conversations. Although Capito repeated Bucer's views on discipline in 1539, he finished writing his *Responsio*, in which he taught the same close association between church and magistracy, in 1535. And in the catechism of 1529 he queried, "Is the ban necessary?" and had the catechumen answer,

---

[76] *Kinderbericht-1527*, sig. Ciiii(v). *In Hoseam prophetam*, fol. 278.

[77] Jacques Courvoisier, *La notion d'église chez Bucer dans son développement historique* (Paris, 1933), esp. pp. 97-115. Because he did not use Capito's *Berner Synodus*, Wendel, *L'église de Strasbourg*, pp. 15-16, can suggest that Capito did not yet agree with Bucer on the need for a close association between church and magistracy. This is common doctrine among historians who ignore Capito's role in the campaign against the Mass. Gerbert, *Sectenbewegung*, pp. 182-192, entitled his last chapter, "Capito's conversion to Bucer's ecclesiastical-political camp." Strasser, *Beziehungen*, pp. 167-169, and *Pensée*, p. 6, asserts that he "finally became 'the man of the church' " only after 1533.

"Without the ban there can be no Christians. The church must defend itself from false teaching, false spirits, and evil livers." [78]

Capito's vision of intimate cooperation between an established true church and a Christian magistracy did not derive from a post-1531 dependence upon Bucer. It was rather the natural consequence of the view of magisterial spiritual duty that guided his campaign for reform between 1524 and 1529. Even in the commentary on Hosea, while he vigorously defended the freedom of the Spirit from temporal intrusions, he so desired the authorities to abolish the Mass that he wrote,

> Nevertheless, it is not enough for a pious magistrate to desist from tyranny and force and to have ceased to prohibit the true worship of God, which may exist simply by reason of the Word of the Lord: but if it wishes to be considered as having performed its duty, it must do away with wooden calves, the Idols of Baal, that is, all little offenses, so it will not be destroyed through imprudence. . . . [79]

He could not have it both ways. He could not have both a permissive unity based upon brotherly love among those who believed that Christ alone was the source of salvation, and a highly ordered church that depended upon the power of the secular authorities. He finally chose order over tolerance. In doing so he was true to the call for reform from above that he issued as a humanist in Basel. He was true to his pleas for orderly procedure as an adviser to the Archbishop of Mainz. And he was true to the methods by which he saw the Mass abolished in Strasbourg. The difference between him and Luther derived not so much from theological disagreement as it did from the high moral status that Capito continued to attribute to the temporal authorities.

[78] Th. B., XI, 85. *Kinderbericht-1529*, fol. 26-27(v). See also *In Hoseam prophetam*, fol. 134. For repititions of Bucer's view of discipline in his scheme, see *Hexemeron Dei opus*, fol. 172(v)-173; 177-177(v).

[79] *In Hoseam prophetam*, fol. 104-104(v).

CHAPTER EIGHT

WOLFGANG CAPITO, FROM HUMANIST TO REFORMER

Labors for the concord and unity of the true church were the swan song of Capito's reforming career. There was no concord among the reformers, and the Strasbourg senate, to which he gave such far reaching spiritual duties, would not allow the ban to be exercised. From 1529 his health began to fail. For several weeks that year he was ill with what Bucer called "the English sweats," a peculiarly debilitating disease, and poor health kept him from his work for another period in 1531. In February and March 1534 Bucer reported to Blaurer that "physical weakness" was forcing Capito to limit his activities again. In April he contracted another fever, which Bucer declared to be the fault of Apiarius, who had defaulted on his debts. On April 10 Margareta Blaurer sent Capito some apples, and a month later he wrote her brother, Ambrosius, that the fever had passed. He hoped to resume his full duties soon, and he did.[1]

But he remained a weak man. Seven years later the plague returned to Strasbourg. "Oh, my Myconius," wrote Jacob Bedrot, one of the pastors, on October 24, 1541, "pray with us for our Capito, who began to suffer two days ago with the gravest illness. . . ." Bedrot added a sad postscript: "In the last half year about 1200 persons have died in our city." On the same day Bucer was begging Blaurer to pray for divine intervention. A week later Bedrot reported that Capito is "failing dangerously." When he did die on November 2, none of his colleagues, neither Bucer, nor Hedio, nor Zell, was present to record his last words. The deacon of Capito's parish told Hedio, who passed the sad news to Bucer by letter. He closed with a judgment that may serve as Capito's epitaph: "He was certainly a true father to all of us, and to the church." [2]

Capito seems never to have realized what a profound religious change he underwent between spring 1522 and 1524. He translated Erasmus' *On Mending the Unity of the Church* into German in 1533, and, appropriately enough, took the occasion of writing a dedicatory letter to Albert of Mainz as an opportunity to reflect upon his career. "And I am accordingly inclined even as before in Your Princely

---

[1] *BB*, I, 196-197; 468; 476; 487; 489; 495-496.
[2] Th. B., XIII, 100; 105; 113. *BB*, II, 88. Sturm, *Luctus ad Camerarium*, sig. Bii.

Grace's Service," he wrote, "although, God be praised, the understanding is brighter and my activity is more public. . . ." [3]

Perhaps he was merely striking a pose in this dedication, but there was something to Capito's judgment that he changed little from 1520 to 1533. It is true that he desired reform no less as a humanist in Mainz, or Basel, than he did as a reformer in Strasbourg. And some aspects of his life after 1524 revealed his humanist background. His campaign for concord between the Swiss and the Saxons, and his relative toleration for the radicals evidenced the same concern for religious harmony that partially lay behind his humanist critique of the scholastics and his accommodating policy toward Luther. Capito's anxious attempts to enlist the secular authorities in the work of purifying the church harkened back to his tenure at Mainz and to the religious elitism and love of peace and order that he shared with Erasmus. And the language that Capito used to describe the sacraments and with which he discussed church polity testified to his abiding indebtedness to Erasmian spiritualism. These were matters of style and attitude in thought and deed that made of Capito a peculiar kind of reformer. After all, he learned Luther's message second-hand without Luther's intense spiritual struggles. His reforming style naturally contained elements of his earlier life as a humanist.

Style and attitude are nevertheless elusive qualities that may operate without the subjects' being aware of them at all. A far more revealing measure of the degree to which Capito ceased to be a humanist after he converted to the Reformation comes from changes that transpired in his cultural and religious values. He was primarily a thinker, and although the man remained very much the man, he changed not only his understanding of the way to salvation but also his view of the religious worth and place of learning. By virtue of his conscious values, as well as of his deeds, he spanned the epoch-making transition from humanism to the Reformation.

The outward aspects of Capito's intellectual life remained in the humanist mold, as did those of most reformers. To a casual observer, his daily activities as a reformer in Strasbourg were identical with those he pursued as a humanist in Basel. He preached daily, he promoted the work of reform, and, above all, he studied the Old Testament. He published original commentaries on Habakkuk, Hosea, and the first six chapters of Genesis. In 1527 he became the

---

[3] *Von der kirchen lieblichen Vereinigung*, sig. iii(v).

first reformer to translate Hosea from Hebrew into German, and he edited and completed Oecolampadius' commentaries on Ezekiel and Jeremiah. Although Strasbourg had no university, Capito lectured on Habakkuk, Hosea, Malachai, Jonah, Isaiah, and some of Paul's letters.[4] In the preface to the commentary on Habakkuk, he reported that he and Bucer began lecturing with the thought that they would have small classes. "But because it seems proper to turn away no one, in a short time the listeners were there in throngs, many more than we had guessed there would be, in fact so many that my upper room holds them only painfully." They then began also to lecture "among the monks of the Dominican Order, where we have done everything, within the limits of our mediocrity, somewhat more fully and more accurately than among our friends alone." [5] The three years at Mainz apparently did not dull Capito's skill as an academic lecturer.

He also continued to cultivate his own scholarly speciality. He published a third edition of his Hebrew grammar in 1525, and the Erasmian humanist still spoke in the dedication. "Having turned back from the court, I devoted myself to the review of the languages," he wrote, as if he had done nothing else. He expressed the hope that the new grammar might still find readers in the midst of "all the new tragedies," and he added that these studies "may have progressed, unless I err, with less trouble for me and much more value for the reader" than his polemical works. In the best scholarly tradition he used his knowledge of Hebrew to compare "the Latin and the Lutheran translations" of the Bible, and he was impressed with Luther's work. "Luther has superbly restored the power and vigor [of the Hebrew], which is the duty of the distinguished translator he is able to become. Now I advise that you neither venerate his words more superstitiously than a common thing nor that you spoil with misrepresentation what has been most splendidly translated by him." [6] This was high praise from one whose knowledge of Hebrew literature was far deeper than Luther's. By 1526 Capito also was studying the Talmud, although, he complained to Pellican, he was finding it very difficult because he had no teacher. He asked Pellican to send him a "Talmudic dictionary" if he had one, but he may have

---

[4] *De operibus Dei*, fol. [7(v)]. *BB*, I, 585.
[5] *In Habakvk prophetam*, fol. 2-2(v).
[6] *Institvtionvm Hebraicarum Libri Duo* (Argentorati, 1525), sig. aii(v); [bvii-bviii(v)]. (Hereafter cited as *Institvtionvm-1525*.)

given up the project in 1538, because that year he sent Pellican a copy of the Talmud itself. Nevertheless, twelve years of labor produced some fruit, for in 1539 he published a commentary on the creation story in which he referred to the Talmudic commentators. [7] Just as in Basel, he continued to use the ancient languages and to press his studies back to the sources.

He also continued to read and to admire the authors of classical antiquity, although if references in his own works are any guide, he preferred the ancient political writers to the philosophers. On several occasions he commended the value of histories. He had read Demosthenes' *Orations*, as well as Cicero's *Letters to Atticus*, but he was particularly attracted to Cicero. In 1521 he vainly tried to secure Aldus' portable edition through Luther's virulent opponent, Cochlaeus, and when that channel was closed, for obvious reasons, he turned to Boniface Amerbach. If Aldus' edition was unavailable, Capito suggested in November 1534, then the Amerbachs themselves ought to republish "the philosophical works and orations of Cicero." The only two philosophers of a speculative bent to whom Capito referred positively were Plato and Aristotle, but it was the Plato of the *Republic* and the Aristotle who wrote the *Politics*. Capito used Aristotle to buttress his argument that peace was the goal of pagan government, and he employed Aristotle's means of distinguishing between "tyranny" and "legitimate authority" on the basis of whether government ruled with laws and for the sake of the public good. Capito continued to value classical, as well as Christian antiquity. [8]

Traces of humanist values may also be found in the form of his Reformation writings. His works, particularly those in Latin, were always composed in the most lucid Ciceronian style. And he continued to pay close attention to the peculiarly human aspect of religious scholarship and instruction, even when he was at his most didactic. In his catechisms, for example, he wrote genuine dialogue:

> *Question*: From all this I understand that you believe that all things are free to the Christian, who should not entangle himself in any particular thing but remain free, even as the Lord freed him.
>
> *Answer*: Yes, in this God uses him to the purpose he wishes.

---

[7] Th. B., II, 258. Riggenbach, *Chronikon*, p. 173. *Hexemeron Dei opus*, fol. 150-150(v).

[8] See, *inter alia*, Th. B., VII, 292. *In Hoseam prophetam*, fol. 15(v). *In Habakvk prophetam*, fol. 6(v). *Responsio*, fol. [i-vii]; 6-10(v); 13. *Entschuldigung*, sig. CCiii(v). Ritter, *Evangelisches Denkmahl*, p. 343.

Question: From this it follows that a Christian may do anything that he pleases.[9]

The student had no difficulty extricating himself from this conundrum. Yet, how different such an exchange was from Luther's catechism, in which the catechumen invariably responded with the most technically correct answer. Capito still preferred the sweet reason of rhetoric to the compelling rigor of dialectic.

The most enduring manner in which the reformers transplanted humanism into the Reformation was through educational reform. In *To the Councilmen of All Cities* of 1524 Luther himself urged the establishment of public schools in which students would learn above all grammar, rhetoric, and the Bible. But the practical work of establishing and reforming public education fell for the most part to reformers who were once humanists. Melanchthon was the most famous among them, but Capito was also part of this general pattern. In their first major reform petition, which he probably composed, the Strasbourg pastors included a request that the Senate appoint "pious, learned schoolmasters" to teach the children of the city, so that "thereby God's glory may be furthered and piety and good for the whole city may be obtained." In about April 1525 the reformers returned to the question of schools in a petition in which they asked the authorities to suppress the Mass, abolish the monasteries, enact sumptuary laws, and limit public begging. Schools, they declared, would serve "the common need, well-being, and peace," and also would aid in "furthering the Word of God the almighty." [10]

Wherever Capito went, he urged the necessity of an education for all. At the end of their meeting after the Diet of Augsburg, he and the Swiss reformers resolved to pressure the authorities of their cities to spend the income from secularized ecclesiastical properties on public schools. The fourth point in his memorandum to the Frankfurt city council was "that municipal schools be erected, and that able Frankfurt children be educated in learning, and especially in the Holy Scriptures." He offered even the shrewd advice that

---

[9] *Kinderbericht-1527*, sig. [Aviii(v)]-B.

[10] *BDS*, II, 397-398. Th. B., II, 208-210. The assertion of Kohls, *Die Schule bei Bucer*, pp. 50-52, that Bucer composed the petition of August 1524 is untenable. In the absence of paleographic evidence, the arguments applied to the entire petition in Chapter V, n. 14, apply also to the section regarding schools. Moreover, there can be no doubt that Capito was the leader of the reform party in Strasbourg in 1524, as Bucer himself acknowledged when he asked him to respond to Treger.

the city not open its schools to outsiders, as was common before the Reformation. "Frankfurt youths have much more charm to their fatherland," he suggested, possibly remembering his own treatment as a youth at Pforzheim. And he was true to his pledge after the Diet of Augsburg to pressure the Strasbourg senate on schools. In March 1530 he and Hedio exhorted the senate to use all ecclesiastical properties for "school masters, especially for the maintenance of the young, the poor, the stewards, and the servants, and also for other uses." [11] He was as insistent about schools as he was about abolishing the Mass. Strasbourg's public school system, which the famous educator Johannes Sturm established in the 1530's, became a model for Germany, and Capito was one of the forces behind it.

When he was a humanist, educational reform was one of Capito's deepest concerns. After he became a reformer, he naturally favored not only the establishment of public schools but also a peculiarly humanistic curriculum. In July 1525 he engineered a petition from the canons of St. Thomas in which they requested the senate to found lectureships in Hebrew, Greek, and rhetoric, for the strengthening of the Church. In the preface to the new grammar he wrote Huldrich Varnbuller, a secretary at the Imperial Court, that he was urging the authorities to provide for "the study of good letters and eloquence." [12] He indicated what sort of education he intended for the new schools of the Reformation, when he wrote in the 1529 catechism,

> *Instructor*: Further you should learn the Hebrew, Greek, and Latin languages.
>
> *Youth*: That is too much for me. I will learn Latin with time; also my father says I should not become a pastor.
>
> *Instructor*: Dear child, you may learn Greek and Hebrew alongside Latin because there is so much of necessity in them. The languages fortify one another, and they contribute a healthy understanding; you may well be a man of the world, even though you have learned the divine languages well, for the world is never better than when it is ruled by a godly leader. [13]

---

[11] Virck and Winckelmann, *Politische Correspondenz*, I, 495. Ritter, *Evangelisches Denkmahl*, pp. 342-343. Th. B., III, 193-197, esp. 196, where he argued, "Man mocht mit einem Canonicat zu St. Thomann, zum jungen oder alten St. Peter, vil lermeister vnderhalted do mitt sÿ den armen burgern jer kinder dester truwlicher leren möchten, welche ÿtzend zum thijl mit grossen arbeÿt, grosznot vnd hunger liden."

[12] *Institvtionvm-1525*, sig., aiii. For the petition see Th. B., III, 165(v).

[13] *Kinderbericht-1529*, fol. 40(v).

Not once as a reformer did Capito recommend the study of Aristotelian logic or physics. In this respect he was, perhaps, even more the humanist than he was in Basel.

From Basel to Strasbourg, from humanist to reformer, he continued to espouse the humanist cultural and educational program to which he was converted as a university student. In the preface to the new grammar he reported that the Strasbourg "senate is considering the establishment of tri-lingual colleges and the study of good letters and eloquence, since they were taught by experience, just as we daily urge: that ignorance is the worst disease of the republic and the mother of superstition, even of tyranny, by whose evil deeds the gluttony of the Antichrist has seized Germany, indeed the whole world. . . ." The lack of learning meant "extinguished piety, human profligacy, and the obliteration of every talent for goodness." On the surface such remarks echoed the praises of learning he proclaimed in the first two Hebrew grammars and in the second preface to Summenhart between 1516 to 1518. His continued religious elitism showed when he stated his fear that the reformers could not "renew something, touch up for the better, as it were, those things that had collapsed for the worst" without assuring through education that "the lawlessness of the commoners" would not wreck their efforts. He still believed that learning was essential to religion, as well as to the proper governance of this world. "With the same support," he concluded, "let us nourish an honest and prudent citizenry within the republic, moreover a populace spontaneous for Christ, and, unbound to harmful laws, of free spirits, which the Lord set free by his death." He accordingly looked forward to "that happy day when it will be given to see the Strasbourg child being taught sound letters and even piety." [14]

In 1525 Capito was, if anything, more insistent upon the religious, as well as the social and political, utility of education than he was in 1518. In this sense there was no difference between his views as humanist and as reformer. But the sort of education he had in mind as a reformer was different. As a humanist he judged that true piety would follow naturally from good learning based upon Christian

---

[14] *Institvtionvm-1525*, sig. aiii-av(v), esp. aiii(v)-aiiii, where he saw political advantages to mass education: "Reip. detrimentosum experimur, paucos e multis sapere, quorum arbitrio res dependet, popularis status in oligarchian, et hinc in monarchian facile transit, cui proxime adfinis est tyrannis. Mediocrem igitur eruditionem non solum populo optamus sed etiam plebi et opificibus. . . ."

and classical antiquity. But as a reformer he no longer intended simply to inculcate enlightened piety. In the preface to the new grammar he described education as one means of combatting "the non-sensical and barbaric inventions of papist impiety, by which they held the whole world captive. . . ." [15] There was a great difference between depicting scholastic learning as barbaric and uncultured, and bluntly calling it "the inventions of papist impiety." Capito no longer intended to lead the student through good learning to inward piety, but to teach him true doctrine. Throughout the dedication to the 1525 grammar he viewed schools as another weapon for the reformers. However much he continued to espouse humanistic methods of education, he turned them to the dogmatic ends of the Reformation. In this, he was at one with Luther and Melanchthon.

Theological education was the point upon which Capito's new understanding of good learning bore especially heavily. If he gave to secondary education the religious function of teaching true doctrine, he scarcely could ignore this task when he turned to the training of theologians. When he became a reformer he accordingly moved theology from the scholar's study to the sacristy of the church. In the commentary on Hosea of 1528 he went so far as to maintain that "The name of doctor is therefore to be attributed to no mortal in the church of Christ, because it is taught entirely by God. . . ." [16] This was an uncharacteristic and extreme position that he took only momentarily. It nevertheless expressed the spirit in which he viewed the task of the theologian.

Capito revealed the concerns that guided his new thinking about theological education when he offered advice in the 1530's on disputes over the theological faculty of the University of Basel. In 1529 Oecolampadius restructured the University, whose functioning was virtually suspended during the uproar of the 1520's. For the old series of courses in theology he substituted two professorships, one on the Old Testament, which he held, and one on the New Testament, which Paul Phrygio, the pastor at St. Peter's occupied. To support Biblical studies, Oecolampadius established lectureships in the arts faculty in Hebrew and Greek. Problems yet remained. In September 1531 the preachers and professors gathered to consider futher reforms. In this connection Oecolampadius wrote Capito on October 22 to

---

[15] *Ibid.*, sig. aiiii(v), "fabulis et barbaris commentis papisticae impietatis, quibus orbem captiuum . . . tenuerunt."

[16] *In Hoseam prophetam*, fol. 2(v). But see n. 26 below.

thank him for recommendations "concerning the reform of schools and concerning laurels and titles." The suggestions are no longer extant, but from Oecolampadius' letter it may be inferred that Capito urged no major changes. In any event, the problems continued, perhaps because of Oecolampadius' untimely death in November. In March the following year Phrygio asked Bucer to pressure Capito into intervening in the controversy over the University. According to Phrygio the church was moving speedily toward "ruin" because "studies are being neglected." [17]

While Oecolampadius was living, the chief difficulty of the University and the Basel municipal school system was funding. The city fathers were reluctant to part with the income of secularized ecclesiastical foundations. But with Oecolampadius' death and with no one of great moral authority to take his place, a new dispute appeared, this time among the pastors and professors. In January 1535 Myconius, one of the preachers, complained to Capito that an unnamed agitator was insisting that all pastors hold the doctorate. Myconius was referring to Capito's old irritant, Carlstadt, who was one of the few Basel pastors to hold the degree. On January 1 he asked Bucer, whose highest degree was the M.A., to support his project.[18] Myconius did not find Capito's response satisfying. In February he wrote, "I therefore give great thanks to you. You write obscurely." [19]

Myconius had every reason to be upset. He was referring to a "Disputation concerning the doctorate. . . . Whether the name or title of a doctor may exist in the community of God." As the title implies, while Capito did not require the doctorate of all preachers, he did reverse his earlier repudiation of learned titles. Moreover, he cast his response in the form of an academic disputation. He began it by dividing all questions between the earthly and the heavenly, the temporal and the spiritual. In heavenly matters he allowed no class of teachers, no implication that the learned were more amenable

[17] Ernst Staehelin, *Das Theologische Lebenswerk des Johannes Oekolampads*. XXI, *Quellen und Forschungen zur Reformationsgeschichte* (Leipzig, 1939), pp. 541-552. *BAO*, II, 699-700. Th. B., V, 35.

[18] Carlstadt to Bucer, 1 January 1535, Th. B., VIII, 1: "Ego certe destinavi instigare ut ad nos de jurisrandi formulis in quas Theologos jurare oporteat et de aliis referatur," in regard to reinstituting disputations. Myconius to Capito, 20 January 1535, Th. B., VIII, 22-22(v): "Erecta igitur hac gloriae vanitate in Ecclesia nostra Satano obtinuit, cujus tu caussa potissima quod nolim. Habeat Academia suos Doctores, ministerium verbi ne polluatur vanitate."

[19] Th. B., VIII, 48.

to the kingdom of heaven than their unlettered brethren. But here on earth, he declared, the doctorate was necessary. There must be some way of knowing which men were trained to interpret the Scriptures. Capito considered the title especially necessary in theology as an outward sign of an inward commitment. If the public insisted upon titles for physicians and lawyers, he queried, why should they not wish to know who was qualified in theology?

Once again Capito was defending the place of learning in religion. But while retaining learned titles in theology, he emphasized more the church's formal certification of the right to teach, than the learning of its recipient. In the prophetic and Apostolic Ages, he suggested, teachers held no academic titles. They were, however, "called" to teach, and even Paul travelled to Jerusalem to receive formal acceptance from the church before he began his missions. "But we should and may not depend upon such special works of God" as Paul's revelation on the road to Damascus, Capito wrote, "but upon his ordinary ordination (*uff seinem gemeyne ordnung*). . . ." For him the doctorate in theology was now a degree that the church granted. He accordingly maintained that the granting of degrees in theology and what he called "the *herrampt der Kirchen* should be fastened together and should not be torn apart from one another. . . ." Like Calvin later, Capito viewed the calling of teacher more as an office of the church than as a recognition of great learning.[20]

Capito consistently maintained this twofold understanding of the place of learning in theology during his last involvement in the dispute. This episode began in spring 1539 when another Basel pastor, Simon Grynaeus, expressed fears that the University would control the Church. In May, in a letter to Meyer, the same official with whom Capito corresponded regarding the sacramentarian controversy, he defended the settlement he suggested four years earlier. He wrote that he sympathized with Grynaeus' concern, but he still insisted that the University and the church should have the same governance.

---

[20] Ein disputation vom Doctorat. D. Wolfgang Capitons. M. C. xxxv. Darum dise frag erwegen und gehandelt wirdt. Ob in der Gemein Gottes möge der name oder titel eines Doctors sein. Archives municipales de Strasbourg. Varia Ecclesiastica, XVIII, 329-343(v), esp. 330(v): "Die antwort steht in dem was das Doctorat in der Theologi seie vnnd ob es etwas nutze zur besserung des leibs Christi. Dann so es nur ein schein vnd pracht were, müste es bei den Christen nit gerhümet, sonder verdammet sein." On Calvin, see Robert W. Henderson, *The Teaching Office in the Reformed Tradition. A History of the Doctrinal Ministry* (Philadelphia, 1962), esp. pp. 24-31.

If they were divided, he declared, "the University will become heathen and stand in eternal enmity to the churches, with undoubted evil consequences to the churches." [21] This was one side of Capito's view. He expressed the other when he and Bucer traveled to Breisach in late July and learned that Grynaeus was arguing that pastors should not serve as rectors of the University because that would mix the two institutions. "Oh my dear sir," Capito wrote Meyer, "what harm is it to a pastor that he is a member of the society of the learned and the learning? We absolutely require everything that we have been taught; why should it be a shame that I have learned in school those things that God has given others by spiritual understanding?" [22] Capito did not have free religious inquiry in mind while he was defending learning, for in August he sent Meyer some "Articles," which are no longer extant, but which, he wrote, would guarantee that the church would control the University.[23] While maintaining learning within the church, Capito unequivocally relegated it to a secondary position.

In his advice on ordering the University of Basel, Capito was giving insitutional expression to his new view of the religious function of learning. After he became a reformer, he considered his own Biblical scholarship less an intellectual pursuit whose end was deepened piety and improved morals, and more a vital function of the church. In his commentary on Habakkuk of 1526 he wrote,

> For the judging of teachings is necessary; nor does it grieve Christ to prescribe that. Now he who demands that we carefully watch the wolves while they don sheep's clothing . . . demands that we carefully consider all doctrine. If in fact they deceive the simple spirits with pernicious teachings, they will be infected with errors; they spread, they attack, they devour. Hence, judgment is the greatest necessity. . . .[24]

---

[21] Th. B., XII, 53-54.

[22] Th. B., XII, 63. "Ach lieber her, was schate es dem diener, das er in der geselschafft der gelerten und lernenden ist? Wir bedurffen doch alle das wir gelert werden, worumb solte es ein schand sÿn das ich in der schul zuhöret was Gott vom geistlichen verstand andere geben hatt?"

[23] Th. B., XII, 73-74(v). He concluded with an appeal, "Daruff ist unser yetzlich bitt umb gottes willen, Ir wollen mit allem flisz sampt allen guthertzigen handelen, dasz die universitet nit widder abgeton. . . . Es ist ein besondere gab gottes und wurt obern dütschen landen zu nutz und euer statt zu eren dienen mögen. . . ." See Capito to Boniface Amerbach, 19 April 1540, Th. B., XII, fol. 147, for the same argument he used in the disputation: "Nam quod tibi et juresconsulto tribuunt eruditorum judicia, id illi ut philosopho ac Theologo. Quare existimo officii esse ut hactenus ei credatis, modo titulum habeat Doctoris, quacunque ratione habeat."

[24] *In Habakvk prophetam*, fol. 3.

It was this all-important task of "testing the spirits to see if they be from God" that he had in mind when he wrote Erasmus in July 1523, "Any good men meanwhile limit the freedom of a Christian to the breadth of the Scriptures." Capito would no longer abide religious scholarship that did not occur within the church and for the benefit of the church. In 1539 he attacked the sects with the declaration, "Now, fickle interpretation, which does not cling to the faith won by the ministry of the church, is deluded from the very beginning and deviates utterly and totally from the prescribed way, which initially leads to obtaining salvation within the church. . . ." [25]

Capito had the sects in mind when he condemned theological studies that were conducted without regard for true doctrine. But he was also attacking much of the Renaissance tradition of religious speculation, and he knew it. He dedicated his commentary on Hosea to Marguerite de Navarre, the Neo-platonist patronness of Lefèvre d' Étaples. Capito noted that "a long time ago" she offered him her patronage and that "At first you were being driven about, stimulated by various works of superstition, which is something I know from secret testimony." Then, he remarked, Maguerite transferred her attentions to "the discipline of the contemplation of God." In this conjunction he reported that he had seen two letters that were translated into French for her, and that "philosophize about the essence and power of God in the manner of Nicholas Cusanus." Capito probably knew of Marguerite's journey of soul from Lefèvre himself, who was then his guest, and who edited Cusanus' works. But Capito did not let Lefèvre's presence restrain him. He urged Marguerite to put aside "that worthless multiplication of works and regard for merit that you so often had without the Spirit. . . ." According to him, her problem was with "the weakness of human nature, with whose will the Spirit does not cooperate, because it is the free gift of God at his own measure of place and time, without which nothing is blessed by God." [26]

In these remarks to Marguerite de Navarre, Capito was turning the same criticism upon the amateur Renaissance theologians that

---

[25] *EE*, V, 305. *Hexemeron Dei opus*, fol. 170-170(v). On private reading see also *In Hoseam prophetam*, fol. 1., "Neque privata interpretatione uicianda est, sed eodem spiritu enarranda, quo impulsi, locuti sunt sancti Dei homines."

[26] *Ibid.*, fol. 4-4(v); 6-6(v), where he urged, "Christumque Iesvm et hunc crucefixum tibi solum reseruas. . . . ." It was in this context that he rejected the notion of "learned" people having a special place in the church. On Lefèvre in Strasbourg, see *ZW*, VIII, 430-431.

Luther employed against the scholastics. He returned to the question
of the "philosophical God," as he called it, in his commentary on
Genesis of 1539. "God is not to be taken in this for a philosophical
God, whom they very likely preach as *optimum maximum* and *extremum
bonarum* . . . but he is to be accepted as his own God (*pro eo Deo*) who
gave himself up in pacts for the sake of the covenanted people." [27]
Capito also sounded very much like Luther in condemning astrology
and astral magic. Under the rubric, "The astrologists are rebuked,"
he declared, "The boasted power of the stars does not move us at
all. For we know that in the produce of the earth, the work of the
Lord of the third day is to be contemplated by faith. . . ." [28] While
dismissing the Cabbala as "those worthless thoughts," he broke
with the Renaissance occult tradition by dating its composition at
the time of translating the Septuagint into Greek. He condemned
these various forms of speculation with explicit reference to "a
Spaniard" and to Pico. "Now there are some persons who are eager,
even to the point of vanity, to make a subtle interpretation. Their
ill-judged diligence in philosophizing about nature and the stars,
or else in otherwise making an untimely ostentation of their wide
reading of the profane authors, has brought together on this first
chapter the biggest mishmash of nonsensical opinions—but the
spiritual meaning is neglected." [29] No longer would Capito abide
a theology that did not have as its main point and determining
principle the central Reformation doctrine that salvation came
through Christ alone.

The attempt to create from classical and Christian antiquity one
norm for contemporary thought and life was characteristic of the
Northern humanists. And even when Capito became a reformer,
he continued to agree with this program insofar as it pertained to
temporal affairs. In 1529 he asked his catechumen about his prayers
and his attendance at worship services, and then he queried,

Instructor: What do you do with the time that remains?

Youth: I go to the schoolmaster and learn to write and to read.

---

[27] *Hexemeron Dei opus*, fol. 102(v), to which he added, "Necque priscorum
pietas, in se deum incertum speculata est, sed semper in hac promissione foederis
cognitissimum: Ego sum Deus tuus."

[28] *Ibid*, fol. 236; 226(v), where he argued, "Hic notandum, terrae suam con-
tigisse foecunditatem astris nondum conditis. Quare quod fertilitate eius alamur,
non est ullis creaturae sed uerbi Dei potentia. . . ."

[29] *Ibid.*, fol. 9; 16-16(v). He did employ the Cabbala, but only on linguistic
points. See *In Hoseam prophetam*, fol. 5.

Instructor: What do you read especially . . . ?

Youth: The New Testament and a German edition of Titus Livius, but mostly the New Testament. When I read Livy, I recall that I am a Christian and given over to God, and I read with fear.

Instructor: That should be the most important to you which refers you to God, to the neighbor. But yet . . . you may also learn other books. They bring a worldly understanding, exercise the reason, work on the other powers, and to believing hearts they also give to understand that nothing besides faith and love are sure and standing profit.

He still considered humanistic learning autonomous in the affairs of the world. In the preface to the 1525 grammar he urged the Strasbourg senate to assure that the public was "moderately learned" so that through "the lawlessness of the commoners" they would not be "formed into an oligarchy and then easily move to a monarchy, whose next-door neighbor is tyranny. . . . We therefore wish moderate learning not only for children of highly-placed families but also for the lower classes and artisans. . . ," he concluded.[30] After becoming a reformer, he continued to read Cicero and Livy, and he considered that sort of learning essential to the proper conduct of political affairs. His own career as a practical reformer suggests that he applied such secular wisdom to the work of purifying the church in Strasbourg.

Capito was, however, no longer a humanist after 1523. He rejected the close association between good letters and sacred letters, between learning and piety that he affirmed as an Erasmian humanist in Basel. When he turned the theologian to the task of teaching true doctrine, he also declared that good learning had no religious authority. In 1532 he urged the Bernese pastors to read together extensively in the Bible but he warned them "to read worldly books with care:"

> To be sure, worldly books, such as histories, may also be read with good understanding and judgment, and with such a point of view: that they serve to exercise the reason and to point out the nature of the flesh, but above all they serve neither to improve us inwardly nor as an example for the common people. Therefore all teaching, exhortation, criticism, and correction should be taken from the spirit of Christ and the divine Scriptures, no matter how appealing it might be to demonstrate a little something from a heathen history with a few words, so that we do not deviate and consider that it is the custodian of the mystery of Christ and the servant of his spirit, and use carnal more than divine writings.[31]

---

[30] *Kinderbericht-1529*, fol. 40. *Institvtionvm-1525*, sig. aiiii.

[31] *Berner Synodus*, sig. i(v)-[i-iiii].

Such a sharp division between sacred and secular literature could not be found in Capito's writings before 1523. Moreover, here he was not attacking the incursion of Aristotle into theology, but the religious use of the humanists' favorite authors, the poets, historians, and orators. These were the writings that in 1517 he commended for the education of the young theologian. Although he retained his earlier preference for grammar and rhetoric in temporal affairs, and as tools for the theologian, he condemned the close association of classical and Christian antiquity that he once espoused. In this regard he was no longer a humanist.

The change in Capito's perspective on cultural and intellectual questions derived from a new answer he gave to the critical issue of human religious capabilities, or free will. All humanists did not agree with Erasmus' position on the matter, but there did lie behind their program of cultural and religious renovation the common assumption that at least the man of letters could restore the purity of the Christian faith through his scholarship. Capito shared this assumption when he was a humanist, and in October 1521 he even told Melanchthon "that he approved of Luther's teachings, except that there might be something about the free will that would be open to dispute at the outset." [32]

He cast aside such doubts when he became a reformer. In 1524 he privately criticized Erasmus' *Diatribe on the Free Will*, and in the commentary on Hosea of 1528 he attacked Erasmus' teaching. "So much foul arrogance is an insult to God and easily the foulest example of idolatry," he declared. He pointed to Hosea 5:6, "With their flocks and herds they shall go to seek the Lord, but they will not find him; he has withdrawn from them," and explained, "Being convinced of a free will cheats them, because they consider the judgment of blessedness and the promise to depend upon themselves alone." Like Luther, Capito believed that the Fall did not merely lame human nature but turned it profoundly perverse. In regard to Hosea 5:4, "Their deeds do not permit them to return to their God. For the spirit of harlotry is within them and they know not the Lord," Capito exulted, "This is an outstanding passage against the fiction of a free will. Now, to turn to God and to true worship, it is necessary that, having discarded your energies, you hope for divine motion." [33]

---

[32] *CR*, I, 464.

[33] *In Hoseam prophetam*, fol. 196; 94(v)[*sic!* 104(v)]-105.

Capito's mature teaching on human religious capabilities at the same time summarized his new cultural values and mirrored Luther's position. Fittingly, Capito wrote his most balanced statement about the will in the introduction to his translation of Erasmus' *On Mending the Unity of the Church*:

> Now our understanding is therefore, namely: in regard to the free will, we say that man does good and bad with a free will. However, because his heart is dark and evil, he has no will or capacity in himself for sincere, true piety and genuine good; he is, then, illuminated and driven by the spirit of Christ. . . . Therefore, it is true; man is capable of nothing from his own powers.

In the manner of Luther, Capito distinguished between "good and bad," which men did with a free will, and "sincere, true piety and genuine good" of which "man is capable of nothing from his own powers." He thus granted men a certain natural morality while maintaining that reason was the highest authority in temporal affairs. But human goodness was evil in the presence of God. As he argued in the commentary on Hosea, "Now no one may share [in the covenant] without faith, because no one will be able to please God without faith." [34]

All natural morality was, thus, at base selfish. As Capito noted in a letter to the preachers of Leonhard von Liechtenstein in December 1531, "Cicero did great deeds for Roman authority in his office as consul, but he was seeking a good reputation from it. . . ." In the commentary on Hosea, he charged that "Among the people of works there can be no truth; on the contrary, they are all mendacity, tricks, smoke, and a mere shadow of what is true." He continued the same theme in the 1529 catechism, having the catechumen declare that non-christians "always sin unto death. . . . But the Christian sins only because of the necessity of the flesh and against his will." Capito was unwilling to grant anything of true value to fallen mankind. "The Lord is the one who takes away impiety," he added in the Hosea commentary; "we are not at all capable of it, because we are insufficient to think that anything at all is from us ourselves; and if we are capable of anything important, it is from God, who implants

---

[34] *Von der Kirchen*, sig. a. *In Hoseam prophetam*, fol. 151. The entire passage reads, "Nam quod cum uno Abrahamo pactus sit, sed de uno illo pactus scribitur, in exemplum credentium, hoc est participantium foedere. Nam sine fide nemo participat, quia sine fide placere Deo nemo poterit."

in us a heart of flesh instead of stone." [35] Such a statement was more than momentary hyperbole. In the introduction to Erasmus' essay he maintained, "Whatever good we will and with which we freely and willingly cooperate is the work and gift of God alone. . . ." For Capito goodness and evil in divine terms were questions to which human reason had no answers. In regard to the command that Hosea marry a prostitute, he commented, "Is it possible for the Lord to command something so absurd . . .? I respond that the just is whatever the Lord wills, of whose will justice is entirely composed. . . ." [36]

To Capito's mind human reason contained the same tragic flaws as natural morality. Just as he had while lecturing on Romans in 1518, he taught that men could know there was a God without the aid of revelation. In 1527 he asked the catechumen, "But for what reason do you know that there is an almighty God?" and received the answer, "I discover the foregoing in the heart and in daily experience." [37] In the commentary on the first six chapters of Genesis, he wrote that "The knowledge of God is two-fold, natural and divine." This natural knowledge, he added, "is either handed down in philosophical writings or is acquired by reading the Scriptures according to human reason without the illumination of the Spirit. . . . Allow me to call it speculative knowledge," he concluded. Like Luther, whose commentary on Galatians he was here following, Capito taught that all men could know there was an all-powerful God who created everything.[38] Moreover, he assigned this knowledge a positive place in the process of salvation. "I think it is to be conceded that we are first caused by the visible works of the six days to comtemplate God's invisible works," he suggested in the commentary on Genesis.[39]

---

[35] *QGT*, VII, 381-382. *In Hoseam prophetam*, fol. 25(v); 58(v). *Kinderbericht-1529*, fol. 10.

[36] *Von der Kirchen lieblichen Vereinigung*, sig. a. *In Hoseam prophetam*, fol. 7(v).

[37] *Kinderbericht-1527*, sig. aiii(v), which Strasser, *Beziehungen*, pp. 49ff., quotes out of context to demonstrate Capito's "subjectivism" between 1524 and 1532. In distinction to the Romans lectures, Capito did not, however, draw the speculative conclusion that all were obligated to know God by faith, however ill-formed. See Chapter II, above.

[38] *Hexemeron Dei Opus*, fol. 100(v)-101. "Duplex est cognitio Dei, Naturalis et diuina. Illa quidem aut literis philosophicis traditur, aut legendis scripturis humana ratione sine illuminatione spiritus comparatur. . . . Eam liceat ut appelem speculatiuam." Compare Luther in the commentary on Galatians, WA, XL^i, 607, "Duplex est cognitio Dei, generalis et propria." On Luther's views in this work, see B. A. Gerrish, *Grace and Reason. A Study in Luther's Theology* (Oxford, 1962), esp. pp. 100-113.

[39] *Hexemeron Dei opus*, fol. 115.

On the other hand, such natural knowledge was not only imperfect but also profoundly wrong. In 1531 he declared that "among those without the Law, it is self-seeking, inquisitive, unprofitable, and frivolous thought—no permanence, no loyalty, no God above all things; the more they trouble themselves about God, the less they know or hold of God." [40] It was in this context that he renounced the close manner in which he earlier associated profane with sacred learning. Now he taught that men, unaided by revelation, could know only God the omnipotent creator:

> Besides, such knowledge which grows through the Scriptures is two-fold, because while we know God from his works, they are propounded in two ways in divine letters—works of creation and works of restoration. . . . On the one hand, creation declares the power and infinite capacity of God. Restoration, on the other hand, declares also his mercy and kindness in addition to his omnipotence. [41]

Capito thus followed Luther in teaching that God's mercy was hidden in his omnipotence and righteousness. "If you should ask by what means it was hidden, I will answer with one word—universal carnality, that is, the reason of men. . . . The reason of men cannot grasp the mystery of redemption. . . ." And this mystery was the only knowledge that was worthwhile. "Moreover, the natural knowledge of God disquiets men and, out of a sense of sin, it stirs up, as we say, desperation, which is the first avenue to salvation. . . . Now that natural knowledge knows God in a creaturely manner, but, stupified, it shrinks from him; it shuns and hates him." [42] Again Capito was repeating Luther's teachings.

Capito was fully evangelical in his understanding of the knowledge of God. "The knowledge of God that we call revealed is different. . . . It is not so much sought by reason as it is accepted as a special gift of God." According to him, "divine or revealed" knowledge always existed under "the tutelage of the Spirit." It was a "practical knowl-

---

[40] *QGT*, VII, 382.

[41] *Hexemeron Dei opus*, fol. 101-101(v).

[42] *Ibid.*, fol. 86(v); 119-119(v). Earlier on fol. 119, "Itaque haec naturalis Dei cognitio per conditionem rerum intellectam comparata poenos inferorum in hac uita praelibat. Necque tamen illi, quamuis exedit curis animum, atque hominem abijcit in desperationem." This was a fairly consistent understanding in Capito. Compare *In Hoseam prophetam*, fol. 51(v). "Ordo igitur iustificationis hic est ut principio ad nostri displicentiam adversis rebus exerceamur, quem usum et lex habet conscientiam de peccato convicens. Secundo vacuum bonis euandis animum, hoc est attritum confractumque atque ex desperatione mortuum, pater amicissime compellit. . . ."

edge" that was "not so busy with thoughts as it is with use and practice, the diligent and assiduous driving to permitting oneself for God, to calling upon him, to accepting all things from him, and to holding the grace of this one. For it is a certain persuasion that God, according to his Word, can and wishes to guard and conserve us." Eleven years earlier he commented on the passage in Hosea, "I will betrothe you to me in faithfulness, and you shall know the Lord," by explaining, "Observe the sequence of the words: 'because we are betrothed and adopted by the Lord,' by faith in Christ. Then the true knowledge of God follows." [43]

While he underscored the anxieties that the uncertainty of natural knowledge caused, Capito praised the certainty of revealed knowledge. "This, implanted by the Spirit, moves outside from the inner heart, softly strengthens the soul, dispels the clouds of doubt, and gives peace to those illumined by faith." This was not a matter of learning or erudition, he wrote, for "Even the simplest Christian, if only he be learned by the cross of Christ, now perceives with a tranquill spirit the tasting of eternal life. He knows with certainty that God the father is true God and he whom he sent, Jesus Christ. . . . Without the Word of God, knowledge is uncertain." For Capito, God's unwillingness to accept men's works was a sign of his mercy. "Yet, so faith may not depend upon the goodness of human talents or the use of human teachings and would thus not be impeded either by weakness of reason or by inexperience, it is a gift of God." [44]

In all his discussion of human inability to perceive the abscondite, gracious God, Capito was following Luther. And denying the freedom of the will had profound consequences for Capito's once humanistic stand on cultural issues such as the place and worth of education and the religious value of profane literature. In the manner of Luther he now began to give distinctly theological answers to these questions. He drew a heavy black line to separate the temporal from the spiritual. He affirmed free will and the autonomy of reason and humanistic study in the affairs of this world. But in theology the chief considera-

---

[43] *Hexemeron Dei opus*, fol. 101-101(v); 119(v). *In Hoseam prophetam*, fol. 61(v).

[44] *Hexemeron Dei opus*, fol. 119(v)-120; 142; 46. That these thoughts marked a fundamental break with his past is evident from fol. 118, where, next to the marginal note, "Facere quod in se est," he wrote "Hic [fear] est fructus pessimus pessimae stirpis, hoc est, humani cordis, quem homo ut optime institutus, faciendo quod in se est, sibique instando, pro uirili nunquam non producit, siquidem sensus aliquis legis adest. . . . Vbi igitur de uiribus liberi arbitrij gloriatio? Ubi merita et opera supererogationis in tam impotente hominis natura?"

tion was spiritual understanding, as he replied to Treger, "It is clear that we do not explain the Scriptures according to our own understanding. We bring clear passages to the dark and the obscure, and we consider the context of the passage; we keep in view the central meaning of the Holy Spirit and judge accordingly even as God gives it, and still we may err." [45] Capito left room in theology for reason, but it was the illumined reason of faith that led the theologian always to teach true doctrine.

Capito's rejection of his earlier humanist values penetrated his own scholarship. He remained throughout his life a student of the Old Testament, but in his three commentaries, on Habakkuk (1526), on Hosea (1528), and on the first six chapters of Genesis (1539), he gradually became so concerned to teach true doctrine that he came virtually to ignore his earlier preoccupation with the linguistic problems of the text. He put into practice his assertion that theology should be studied for the benefit of the church and his belief that the task of the theologian was to teach true doctrine. "Thus," he wrote in the commentary on Genesis, "whoever prays for the gifts and grace of Christ in any other way than through the ministry of the church and from the church itself, through which and in which alone the spirit of Christ wishes to be efficacious, will yet appear to have received nothing." [46] From a humanist grammarian Capito became a Reformation theologian.

His earliest Biblical scholarship as a reformer naturally contained the most evidence of Capito's humanist past. In the preface to the commentary on Habakkuk he insisted that the exegete master the tools of the humanist. The Biblical scholar must, he argued, "be thoroughly experienced in an exact knowledge of the histories of that time, with also a moderate knowledge of languages and especially of Hebrew, and with the knowledge of Christ and the faith." In a prefatory "method of explaining the prophets," he argued that if an exegete proceeded without a knowledge of history, "Whatever plan he has built up on top falls; he will ramble around in uncertain places and amuse himself with his allegories." Soon "five languages will be necessary" to comprehend the Scriptures, he predicted. "A rich abundance of words is available to the Hebrew language and a remote form of saying something. What Latin somehow says in one way, it . . . says in many different ways with various corresponding voices."

---

[45] *Antwurt*, sig. Oiij(v).
[46] *Hexemeron Dei opus*, fol. 224.

In 1526 Capito not only stressed the necessity of languages and history but also still judged that the lack of these humanistic skills doomed the commentaries of the most pious scholar. "For the sense of Christ, which they introduce everywhere, falls flat in the treatment of their scribblings. A soul a little more dedicated to elegance shrinks from the perusal of the Scriptures. . . ." He wrote that he doubted neither "the integrity nor the faith" of the medieval exegetes; the source of their error lay elsewhere. "First, ignorance of history, then contempt for languages, third the confusion of the prophetic faith with our fiction. These three delusions obscure, and they entangle everything in foul darkness; we, however, proceed piously." [47] Capito did include in his catalogue of scholastic sins the schoolmen's failure to teach "the prophetic faith" in unalloyed form, but he left the impression that only a scholar with the skills of the humanist was equipped to find that faith.

The commentary on Habakkuk would be the most attractive to modern readers, partly because Capito followed his own advice. He began with a brief history of the Babylonians and remarked that the prophecy of Habakkuk "depends upon the substance of Isaiah 21, Jeremiah 30, and other prophets." He then observed that Habakkuk contained three parts: first, a section in which he deplored the destruction of Jerusalem, then, following verse twelve of the first chapter, "the vengence of the Lord" against the Babylonians, and "in the third place, he preaches Christ as if he were already to come. . . ." Throughout the commentary Capito evidenced great interest in the textual and linguistic problems of the prophecy. In commenting on the first verse he noted that the reference to "the oracle of God" really meant "the oracle of Jahweh," and that in Hebrew "you were unable to speak about God, etc." Later he explained that Hebrew had no future tense, and at another point he discussed the conjugation of a Hebrew verb with the suggestion to the reader, "Look in our grammar." [48] Capito's first commentary remained in the humanist mold by virtue of its emphasis upon literary and grammatical questions alongside theological issues.

Capito employed history and the languages in all three of his published commentaries, but gradually his dogmatic concerns overcame his linguistic and grammatical interests. Frequent attempts to explain the precise sense of a Hebrew expression are missing in the

---

[47] *In Habakvk prophetam*, fol. 4-5(v).
[48] *Ibid.*, fol. 11-14.

commentaries on Hosea and Genesis. More importantly, he began to employ an exegetical tool that he rejected when he was a humanist. This was allegory, a method commonly used by the medieval commentators. In the commentary on Habakkuk, he remained true to his earlier evaluation of this method with the remark that some erred by reading the Old Testament without Christ.

> On the other hand, too many are pious for the sake of appearances; these are those who bring in not only the faith of the prophet but, I would imagine, they also even add in things they have begotten. They are the ones who make light of the weighty authority of Christ . . . with inappropriate allegories, as if the everlasting truth needs our lying.[49]

In this commentary Capito scrupulously practiced what he preached. His was a straightforward explication of the text in which he emphasized the prophet's trust in the promises of God.

In later commentaries Capito still avoided the often fanciful allegory of the medieval exegetes. On the other hand, he changed his evaluation of the method. He discussed allegory again when he came in the commentary on Hosea to God's command that the prophet marry a prostitute. Some commentators, he noted, glossed over this affront to morality with allegories. On the contrary, he insisted, "every point is to be accepted in so far as it was spoken by the Spirit." Capito urged his readers to consult his remarks on the subject in the commentary on Habakkuk, and then suggested that the Scriptures contained metaphors "in single words" and "allegories of history." In the latter case, such passages "are explained no more fully than to the measure of the glory of God," he decreed. They "belong to the Spirit," for they showed Christ in the Old Testament. Above all, Capito wrote, "The authority of the Scriptures is little established by allegories, however much they may be born of the Spirit. . . . In truth the external Word testifies most happily concerning such works of God with the elect; let no one therefore insolently reject the Scriptures by which . . . the Apostles . . . exhort and console themselves in turn." [50] Capito nevertheless held a more ambivalent

---

[49] *Ibid.*, fol. 7(v).

[50] *In Hoseam prophetam*, fol. 7(v)-9; 76; esp. 8, "Nam ea est proprie allegoria, quemadmodum metaphora in uerbis singulis est. Sed et historiae interim, ut ita dicam, allegoriae sunt spiritus, quod pleraeque praeter seriem rei gestae, qua quidem bonitatem Dei electis declarant, ut in minuta quapiam re exhibitam, etiam ordinem Dei se explicantis, per dona spiritus insinuat." Reading with the "spirit" was thus reading to find Christ. Consequently one must reject the assertion of Strasser, *Beziehungen*, pp. 48-49, that in 1528 Capito did not value the Scriptures as "an objective ground of faith."

judgment of the allegorical method in 1528 than he had in 1526.

Regardless of his wavering judgment on their value, Capito did use allegories in his last two commentaries. In regard to Hosea 1:7, "But I will have mercy on the house of Judah," he noted that "Judah signifies the pious ones who, having been placed on the path of God, embrace it, so he may have mercy upon them. . . ." Where Hosea declared that the houses of Israel and of Judah would be united, he saw a prophecy of brotherly love among all men "conciliated by the cross." [51] Such a use of "single-word metaphors" was even more pronounced in the commentary on the creation story. When Capito discussed the waters that covered everything before creation he declared, "Therefore the waters are the Holy Spirit, the long-standing new creation, the grace of adoption, the gift of faith, the continuous and perpetual action of the heart, where, grasping God through Christ, we find pleasure in one God sweetly and with the proper gratitude of the soul." This was rather much to find in one word, nor was it all. After a lengthy discussion of the church, he returned to the text and remarked that the gathering of the waters into one place was "a simile concerning the unity of the church." Then, writing about the division of the seas on the third day, he noted, "Moreover, this sea is the church of Christ. . . ." [52] By the time he had finished, the seas in the creation story symbolized nearly every aspect of the Christian faith. Such practice was far from his humanist condemnation of allegory.

It is not difficult to ascertain Capito's motives for employing a method that he proscribed even after he became a reformer. He allowed reason of dogma to compel him to allegorize in spite of himself. In the commentary on Hosea he desired most to teach a doctrine of rigorous predestination. And when he wrote the commentary on the first six chapters of Genesis, his greatest concerns were to rebut Servetus' antitrinitarianism and to guard the unity and order of the new churches of the Reformation. He therefore used the text to promote these dogmatic issues whenever he had the chance. Theological considerations overrode the exegetical principles that he embraced as a humanist. Most reformers did not employ allegory, but Capito did, and for reasons that had very much to do with his conversion to the Reformation. He was very much the reformer in giving first place in his commentaries to teaching true doctrine.

---

[51] *In Hoseam prophetam*, fol. 27; 31.
[52] *Hexemeron Dei opus*, fol. 162(v)-163; 222-224.

The use of the allegorical method was a narrow sense in which theological concerns overrode Capito's earlier humanistic attitude toward the text. There was also a broader and more important way in which he shed his humanistic values as a Biblical scholar. This was in his view of the Bible itself. While he was still under Erasmus' tutelage, he viewed the Scriptures as merely the most important among several sources for Christian life and faith. But after he became a reformer, he naturally insisted, particularly in the books against Treger, that the Scriptures alone were authoritative. To this he added Luther's teaching that they explained themselves on essential matters of faith. There was no room for doubt about their content.

Such questions were major issues in the Reformation, and it could be expected that Capito would side with Luther and the other reformers on them. It is more noteworthy, as evidence of Capito's changing values, that his earlier humanistic understanding of the Scriptures' content and canon perished with his conversion. While he was still a humanist, he followed Erasmus in believing that the central message of the Bible was one of inward piety and brotherly love. When he became a reformer, he adopted Luther's teaching that Christ was the sole content of the Scriptures. "For Jesus is the end of the Law and the Scriptures," he responded to Treger. "We say that, in so far as it is necessary to know, the Scriptures are bright and clear. For who is so dull that he does not understand this Word— Jesus Christ came into the world to make sinners blessed, to call sinners and not to judge them?" In 1528 he wrote a short defence of reform in Strasbourg in which he declared that "our teaching and preaching . . . are completely in accord with and measured by the divine Scriptures, which are the only source from which they have been taken." According to him this fact meant that the city's doctrine and practice depended "entirely upon our Savior Jesus Christ." To Treger he replied four years earlier, "Oh, how burdensome it is to hear that our faith should depend upon the masses and not be founded on the Word of God. It is true that no one can stop you; you may say and believe otherwise if you wish, but you reveal yourself to be a non-Christian when you do not believe in the Word of God in the Scriptures." [53] According to Capito, not to accept the sole authority of the Scriptures was not to believe in Christ.

Like Luther, Capito was professionally an Old Testament scholar,

---

[53] *Antwurt*, sig. Mii-Miij. *Kurtze Summ*, sig. [A(v)].

and like Luther he saw Christ as the content of the Old, as well as the New, Testaments. He decreed in the introductory "method of explaining the prophets" to the commentary on Habakkuk of 1526,

> Now with all the prophets there is that one objective: that they declare the glory of the Lord, that is, goodness in having mercy on the pious and severity in judging the impious. Paul in all the letters and Christ himself—nay, all the pious—look back in like manner. . . . Moreover, everything is concluded in Christ. For he is the glory and splendor of the Father and he proclaims the glory of the Father to men, which was obscured by the yeast of the Pharisees and by human doctrine. Thus the sayings that the magnificent Scriptures speak for the illumination of God are interpreted by Christ and speak in the same manner to us. [54]

In 1524 Treger argued that one could never be certain, without the authority of the church, that "the Apostles' writings come from the Apostles."

> I say that this was never doubted by the Fathers and that their [the Apostles'] spirit had been authenticated by the writings of the Old Testament, and therefore they should still be accepted as authentic. I have not seen the Apostles, but even today I see the same spirit in the writings of the Apostles, uniform with the old writings of Moses and the prophets. . . . There has never been any doubt about the Old Testament, to which we compare all succeeding writings. [55]

Capito was so certain of Christ's centrality in the Old Testament that he used it to establish the proper reading of the New Testament.

Capito was following Luther in teaching that Christ was the content of the Scriptures, both Old and New Testaments. He also depended upon Luther in declaring that the content of the Scriptures was their canon. In 1524 Treger challenged the principle of *sola scriptura* with the argument that because the Epistle of James was part of the canon the Scriptures were contradictory, because James taught that Abraham was justified by works. And if James were not canonical, asked Treger, how then could the reformers retain Matthew, Mark, Luke, and John without also accepting "the Gospels of Bartholomeus and Nicodemus?" In either case, the authority of the church was obviously prior to the authority of the Scriptures. Capito took the substance of his reply from Luther's preface to the New Testament of 1522:

---

[54] *In Habakvk prophetam*, fol. 5.
[55] *Antwurt*, sig. Mii(v)-Miij.

That the letter, which one calls Saint James, is termed an 'Epistle of
Straw,' in comparison to the Gospel of Saint John, is not new; for
the Fathers have certainly rejected it, and have accepted this because
it says that Abraham was justified by works. . . . Accordingly it does
not have an apostolic nature, which always urges faith in Christ and
orders the Scriptures according to the true understanding of the
Spirit. To be sure, one nevertheless allows it to remain a true and
useful Letter, although of little importance in comparison to the
Letters to the Romans, Galatians, etc. Do not say therefore that the
Holy Spirit contradicts itself, or has forgotten itself, for this letter
was never considered by the Fathers to be Saint James' and worthy
of faith.[56]

Capito did refer here to the authority of the Fathers in establishing
the canon of the Scriptures, but the weight of his argument fell upon
Luther's doctrine that Christ was the canon of the Scriptures. Capito
thus discarded the medieval presupposition that the authority of
the Scriptures was based upon their antiquity or upon public agreement. Like Luther, he returned the canon of the Scriptures to the
Scriptures. In doing so, he even used Luther's words.

Capito also agreed with Luther that Christ must be the main
exegetical principle for the Old Testament scholar. In the preface to
his German translation of Hosea in 1527 he remarked, "On the way
to Emmaeus, Christ our Lord expounded to his disciples beginning
with Moses and all the way through the prophets, and he pointed to
himself. For he is the end of the Law and the prophets; accordingly,
I have determined to expound a prophet, namely Hosea, in a Christian
manner, that is, according to the limits of the truth. . . ." [57] At the
beginning of the commentary on the first six chapters of Genesis he
wrote, "In this book I have set forth one Christ; seeing that it is
directed to him, I certainly thought it possible that he could be the
rule of my commentaries." Here Capito was writing against Servetus'
denial of the Trinity, and declared, "I think, on the contrary, that I
have found in this explanation the hidden, tripartite power and
nature of God, while having retained the historical sense . . ." of
Genesis. He employed all his imagination in finding Christ in the

---

[56] *Ibid.*, sig. Mii-Miij. For Luther's use of the figure, "epistle of straw" see the
1522 preface to the New Testament. *WADB*, VI, 11. On Luther's hermeneutics,
see, *inter alia*, Paul Althaus, *Die Theologie Martin Luthers* (Gütersloh, 1962),
pp. 71-89, and Heinrich Bornkamm, *Luther und das Alte Testament* (Tübingen,
1962), esp. pp. 86-103.
[57] *Hosea der Prophet, der Kirchen zu Strassburg verteutscht* (Strassburg, 1527),
sig. [A(v)].

creation story, arguing that a comparison of the opening lines of Genesis with those of John revealed that the proper reading of Genesis was "In Christ, God created the heavens and the earth." [58] Like Luther, Capito found Christ throughout the Old Testament.

Because he was a convert to the Reformation, it could be expected that his views on such critical topics as the canon and content of the Scriptures would reflect Luther's teachings. What is noteworthy is how very faithful he was to Luther, even on technical points on which he might have deviated. For example, he used Luther's language in speaking about the Law. By itself, he argued, "the Law points out sin, arouses anger, kills and damns, and it creates hated of God." Capito repeated Luther's teachings again when he denied Erasmus' belief that the Law concerned only outward acts. " 'On the contrary,' he says," according to Erasmus' report, " 'the Law condemns the whole man.' " [59] But this was not the Law's true function, for it was "the hidden Gospel (*verborgenen Evangelium*)" or the "obscured Gospel (*involutum Evangelium*)." Capito also echoed Luther in 1531 when he declared that "Whenever the Law is considered against the Gospel, it is usually nothing more than the letters of Moses without Christ and without the Spirit. . . ." [60] It was necessary to understand the Law "not according to the letters of Moses, for such an outward Law is imperfect until Christ writes it on the heart itself in the Holy Spirit, which shows and imparts not just sin but also the forgiveness of sin." For Capito as for Luther, the Law showed Christ because it was an instance of God's glory and graciousness; it led men to Christ because it convicted them of their sins. As he explained in the commentary on Genesis, "Thus Moses disseminates the Word of the Lord, so that it may perform the duties of instructing the people about Christ. . . ." [61]

---

[58] *Hexemeron Dei opus*, sig. a4; fol. 42-44. He summarized the argument on fol. 42(v): "Verbum quod erat in principio inuenies si exordium illud Mosi ad regulam fidei ponderis hoc modo: Si Deus in principio, coelum et terram, ut tam erant, creauit, necesse est ut concedam quod ea per verbum creauit."

[59] *Responsio*, fol. 30. *EE*, V, 382.

[60] *Responsio*, fol. 70. "Hinc natum Augustino et Patribus ut dicerent legem esse inuolutum Euangelium, et Euangelium apertam ac declaratam legem." Compare the discussion in Chapter II, above. Even while at Basel he sought the "lex evangeliis explicata," but its content differed, for it was the law of love. For precisely the same mature useage, see Capito to the preachers of Leonhard von Liechtenstein, mid-December 1531, *QGT*, VII, 371. "Daruff antwurten Augustinus und die vätter gewonlich also, das das gesetz ist das verborgen euangelion vnd das euangelion das erkleret gesetz. . . .". Cf. Aug. Quaestionum in Heptateuchem II. 73 (CCSL 33. 106).

[61] *Ibid.*, VII, 370-371. *Hexemeron Dei opus*, fol. 90-90(v). Several times he

Capito was also faithful to Luther in the manner in which he found Christ in the Old Testament. Like Luther, he read the Old Testament as a *Heilsgeschichte* in which Christ was always present. From the act of creation Capito interpolated, "The persuasion follows that the universe was created by the Word of God. . . . His providence presses on unconcernedly and in his [Christ's] presence he established the mainstay of the salvation that is to be grasped from the Gospel that was proclaimed." [62] For Capito, as for Luther, the Old Testament was more a foreshadowing of Christ's mission than it was the source of predictions regarding his coming. As he explained in the commentary on Habakkuk, "Now, whereas Christ is the brightness of the glory and the clear image of God the Father, it follows that whatever describes his glory expresses Christ." Capito repeated even Luther's exegesis of specific passages on this point. In discussing Abraham's vacillation and then his faith in God's promise, he explained, "Abraham believed God and he was reputed to justification by him. With this promise to make Abraham's seed muliply, he refers to that great healing later, which pertains to Christ." According to Capito, "the covenant of God always involved Christ, and he is the end and the complement of the covenant who is expressed in the word, 'In your seed shall all nations be blessed.' He does not say 'in seeds' but 'in seed,' which, in fact, is Christ." [63]

As a Biblical scholar Capito faithfully followed Luther's teachings. He had recourse to Luther again, mentioning him by name, in the commentary on Genesis, when he summarized his hermeneutics. He insisted that in seeking Christ throughout the Scriptures, the exegete was finding the literal sense of the text. "And accordingly we permit no section of the Scriptures, especially not this sacred arranging of things, to be expounded other than according to the rule, the analogy of faith, hard by the full power of the natural understanding of the words." He granted that the proper under-

---

repeated his view that the Law led to Christ, as at fol. 87, "Nam lex paedegogia ad Christum est," and *Responsio*, fol. 30, "Nam leges Israeli multas promulgauit, ut ad Christum essent paedegogia. . . ."

[62] *Hexemeron Dei opus*, fol. 99(v)-100.

[63] *In Habakvk prophetam*, fol. 23(v). *Hexemeron Dei opus*, fol. 99(v). "Christum igitur semper involuit foedus dei, et finis atque complementum foederis est, qui sermone interim exprimitur: Vt in semine tuo benedicemur omnes gentes terrae. Non in seminibus, sed in semine, inquit, quod quidem est Christus." Compare the emphasis upon God's promise with the emphasis in the Romans lectures upon God's acceptance of Abraham's partial faith as if it were the real article. See the discussion in Chapter II, above.

standing of the Scriptures "does not inhere in the letters without the proper knowledge of the Spirit." But, he charged, finding Christ in the Old Testament forced nothing on the text, for "we are sold on nothing except the simple sense of the Scriptures, in the same manner that the grammarians commonly understand profane authors." [64]

Seeking the spiritual sense of the Scriptures meant for Capito to penetrate the author's point of view, which was always Christ. It no longer amounted, as it had when he was a humanist, to spiritualizing the text in search of a hidden meaning. "Christ is the end of the Law. The Law is spiritual, it is the law of the Spirit and of life," he declared in 1535. The exegete must not consider the Old Testament merely the history of the people of Israel, "just as now the most learned in this age do not seek to grasp Cicero's letters to Atticus by means of a history of that period. . . ." This was the failure of the Jewish commentators. "They are unable to discover one shred beyond history; they do not see, nor do they wish to see, anything beyond Moses in the camp at Moab, always learning more to the end (which they do not believe) of knowledge, that is, to Christ Jesus. . . . Thus it is concerning the Jews and those similar to them, who read the prophets without the spirit of the prophets." [65] This spirit was God's complete graciousness, for "there is no true mention of God that was outside the Word of Promise. Nor will there be any invocation, any action of graciousness if the Word of Promising is not present." [66] For Capito, as for Luther, the simple sense, the grammatical sense, and the spiritual sense of the Scriptures all met in the *sensus propheticus*, which was Christ. "Now the simple sense, which our party usually calls the grammatical sense, is the one and unique sense of the Spirit to us," Capito wrote in the commentary on Genesis. "The simple sense of the Scriptures always squares with the faith." [67] He was repeating Luther's views again.

Capito's conversion to the Reformation went so deep that he adopted in great detail a new way of viewing and accomplishing his work as a Biblical theologian. He knew he had changed. As he remarked in the introduction to his commentary on Habakkuk,

---

[64] *Ibid.*, fol. 15; 23.

[65] *Responsio*, fol. 65. *In Habakvk prophetam*, fol. 6(v)-7(v).

[66] *Responsio*, fol. 29. Compare *Hexemeron Dei opus*, fol. 95. Beside the marginal note, "Nulla promissio sine Christo firma est," he wrote, "Sine einim Christi beneficio, Deum secura fide nemo inuocauerit . ."

[67] *Ibid.*, fol. 15.

I was so carefully examining it [the text] that it would not yet have determined me in accordance with a method of explaining the Old Testament. Now it has been more pleasing. By the favor of the Lord I have been able to attempt a little something in his wrestling-house with a definite method instead of trying nothing. So I said to myself, 'Now I am in a position to dictate a specific work for myself.'

A few pages later he confessed, "I would speak vainly about the most important matters after Luther and Melanchthon, as well as others, much more skilled than I." He decided rather to "borrow happily" from the work of "the leaders." [68] He wrote these words in 1526 at the height of the sacramentarian controversy, when it would have served partisan purposes not to acknowledge his debts to Luther. But Capito was too candid for that. He learned to expound the Scriptures from Luther, and he admitted it.

Luther was the great abiding influence on Capito's thought after he became a reformer. There were certainly elements in his theology (his understanding of the eucharist, for example) that differed from Luther's but in regard to principles he was fully evangelical. He followed Luther. In 1535 he included in his *Responsio* a section he titled "Martin Luther, doctor of the liberty of faith," in which he praised Luther as "the man of God, memorable in all ages, who explained Christ so excellently as to be without example in the memory of all time." In September 1536 he termed Luther "the learned lord." [69] Capito knew that Luther made of him a reformer.

More importantly, Capito penetrated through the formulae and the catch-words of Reformation thought to the substance of Luther's evangelical message. For him, as for Luther, the one crucial point was that in Christ, God became "*Deus nobis*, God for us," as he put it in the *Responsio*. He was using Luther's language here, and he did so again in the commentary on the creation story, when he wrote that "faith in the remission of sins by Christ occurs for us, when we men, who were corrupted by the sign of Adam, are next perfected by the grace of adoption, while we are initiated by the sacraments of Christ and by hearing the Gospel." [70] As a reformer Capito consistently ordered his theology according to the central doctrine that salvation came only through God's grace in Christ. In 1527 he asked his cate-

---

[68] *In Habakvk prophetam*, fol. 2(v); 7(v)-8.

[69] *Responsio*, fol. 77-77(v). Th. B., IX, 209-209(v). See also *Antwurt*, sig. Miii(v), "Christlich freyheit ist von natur vnd wesen des glaubens, on welche der christlich glaub nit steet."

[70] *Responsio*, fol. 64. *Hexemeron Dei opus*, fol. 277-277(v).

chumen whether being saved by faith alone meant that he had no need for Christ. "*Answer*: I cannot truly believe in God except through Christ alone. *Question*: Give the reason for this. *Answer*: God can be known without Christ, but not as my father. On the contrary as my strictest judge. . . ." Trust in God through Christ was the master concept in Capito's theology, as it was in Luther's. In 1529 Capito's catechumen said, "I have heard some say, 'I am not certain of God's election . . .' " to which Capito replied, "Answer them in this way 'Believe truly in Christ and then you will be sure. . . .' "[71] Even the doctrine of predestination was subsidiary to Christ's sole sufficiency.

When he became a reformer, Capito substituted Luther's theology of the cross for Erasmus' philosophy of Christ. Luther's doctrine that salvation came through Christ alone became Capito's guiding principle as a reformer, and he knew that this doctrine made impossible a return to the medieval cultural and religious order. He did suggest in the preface to Erasmus' *On Mending the Unity of the Church* that he changed little since the years he served Archbishop Albert, and he wrote that he sympathized with Erasmus' desire for concord on the basis of a common desire for salvation and unity. But he added that the freedom of the will, the Mass, prayers for the intercession of saints, the veneration of images and relics, and all else that distracted the sinner from trusting in Christ alone were intolerable. "This heavenly man Christ . . . does everything in the here and now that constitutes eternity for God and that can bring mortal men to eternal life. We therefore maintain that only this resurrected Christ should be set forth in the preaching of the Word, in the sacraments, and in the entire management of the church. . . ." The substance of these remarks destroyed utterly Erasmus' irenic appeal. "For we insist only upon the necessary justification through faith in the one Christ . . . and upon the true worship service that leads everyone to the Lord Christ." [72] That insistence was the great dividing line between humanism and the Reformation in Capito's life. In so far as it turned upon the core of his religion, a humanist died when Capito became a reformer.

---

[71] *Kinderbericht-1527*, sig. aiii. *Kinderbericht-1529*, fol. 19. There is no discussion of predestination in the 1527 edition.

[72] *Von der Kirchen*, sig. [iiii-aiiii(v)].

AFTERWORD

Building generalizations about the relationship between humanism and the Reformation upon the career of one individual is a risky business. On the other hand, Capito's life ought to be particularly instructive, for he moved between the two giants of his age, Erasmus and Luther, and his transition from humanist to reformer is more open to analysis than that of many others. In the 1510's he was the most accomplished scholar among the younger humanists, more so even than the precocious Melanchthon. And his career during the vital, fluid years between 1520 and 1524 was a very public one, in spite of his attempts to camouflage his activities. He became a reformer in an important Free Imperial City, one that experienced all the problems, religious, political, and social, of the Reformation era. Were it still fashionable to do so, he might be considered an "ideal type" of the humanist-turned-reformer. At the very least, his career suggests issues of general import that deserve to be underlined.

The life of Capito tends in one sense to confirm the long-standing judgment, in the words of Gerhard Ritter, that the converted humanists discovered in the reform movement "what had eluded them to this point: the powerful incentive of a new religious movement that gave them the strength to put their newly-acquired possession of classical culture once more into the service of the Christian ideal. . ." [1] The drama of Capito's life did lie far more in the realm of ideas than of real circumstances. He was driven to convert under the impetus of Luther's theology when all his personal instincts led him to remain within the Old Church. Even after he hesitatingly adopted Luther's teachings in 1522, he delayed joining the struggle for reform until mid-1523. And then he continued to guard his prebend and his middle position until the crisis of the married priests drove him in 1524 to the view that he could not embrace the Gospel and remain within the Church of Rome. Changed behavior thus awaited a change of religion. In Capito's case as well as his own, Luther's evangelical theology was the cutting-edge of change.

Capito's career also underscores the gulf between northern humanism and the Reformation that has been so clearly delineated by

---

[1] Ritter, "Geschichtliche Bedeutung," *Historische Zeitschrift*, CXXVII, 451.

modern scholarship.[2] There was a certain outward similarity between his drive to restore Christianity on the basis of the antique sources and Luther's insistence upon *sola scriptura*, between his critique of empty formalism and Luther's emphasis upon faith, between his delight in history and languages and Luther's use of such knowledge as exegetical tools. Yet Capito's sense of comradeship in arms with Luther was based upon a poorly perceived but fundamental disagreement. His humanistic ideals and religious attitudes finally inhibited his development as a reformer. The superficial correspondence of their views obscured Luther's theology and led Capito not only to support Luther but also to criticize him for intemperance and to threaten on occasion to withdraw his support. The conflict over the reliquary at Halle in 1521 revealed finally that at base Capito's humanism and Luther's evangelical theology had little to do with one another. Only then could Capito come to grips with Luther, and, as it happened, finally convert to his party.

Yet, the fate of Capito during the Reformation era also suggests ways to sharpen and to criticize the received view of the relationship between humanism and the Reformation. In the first place, viewing Capito in his own terms, rather than against preconceived standards of what constituted a humanist or a reformer, reveals that his activities and loyalties really did change. Although he never suffered it, he richly deserved excommunication after 1523. And he deserved it not only by virtue of his deeds but also of his thoughts. In 1516, for example, he advised Erasmus not to criticize penance and indulgences and the Mass; in 1521 he begged Luther not to "snatch at small points." After 1523 he considered these matters blasphemous rather than merely superstitious. Even his habits of thought changed. In 1518 he asserted that passages in Genesis and Deuteronomy that spoke of the "seed of Jacob" as the "seed of all men of the world" referred to Christ "in accord with a precept of Latin from Erasmus." In 1539 he no longer founded theological doctrines upon linguistic arguments. He gave these passages the same interpretation, to be sure, but this time he asserted that "the covenant of God always involved Christ."[3] From a humanist grammarian with skeptical assumptions he became a Reformation theologian who asserted boldly.

---

[2] In addition to *ibid.*, pp. 434-435, see Moeller, "Humanisten," *ZKG*, LXX, 47-50, and Spitz, *German Humanists*, pp. 280-293.

[3] *Institvtionvm-1518*, fol. 23. *Hexemeron Dei opus*, fol. 93(v).

In a very real sense, Capito's transition from humanist to reformer provides a critical incident within which these key terms take on sharpened meanings. Whatever may be made of the exactness with which he appropriated Luther's teachings, it is undeniable that Capito became a reformer in the sense that he began to concern himself with true doctrine and right practice as he never had before. (Much the same may be said of many of the others who became reformers, be it Bucer, Melanchthon, Zwingli, or Oecolampadius.) The very core of Capito's life as a humanist becomes, then, a basic skepticism about the knowability and worth of doctrinal assertions. Like the Italian humanists in other areas of intellectual activity, and like Erasmus, Capito the humanist regarded doctrines as being basically unworthy of a struggle, verbal or physical. The other side of the coin is, then, that the essential element in his conversion was coming to agree with Luther, even before the famous dispute on the freedom of the will, that "The Holy Spirit is not a skeptic," and ordering his activities in accord with this precept.

Capito's life reveals, therefore, that, just as the precise religious or philosophical doctrines an individual held had little to do with whether he was a humanist, so too the precise doctrinal position a sixteenth-century "religious activist" held may have little to do with his being among the class of people historians may justly call reformers. His career surely calls into doubt the "humanist or reformer" issue that has so ensnared Zwingli scholarship, and to a lesser extent research on Bucer and Melanchthon.[4] Finally, Capito's transition should establish that there is little to be gained, except confusion, from considering the converted humanists reformers only to the extent that they conformed in some degree to Luther's doctrinal standard. When they became reformers, Capito and the others no longer intended to inculcate enlightened piety but to preach true doctrine. This change of intentions was in itself epoch-making. It corresponded to the beginning of the Reformation era.

Such an analysis should help to establish the true value of research that seeks to characterize the precise theological positions that the various reformers occupied. In Capito's case, his prior incarnation

---

[4] See the intriguing survey of Zwingli research in Christoph Gestrich, *Zwingli als Theologe. Glaube und Geist beim Zürcher Reformator. XX, Studien zur Dogmengeschichte und Systematischen Theologie* (Zurich, 1967), pp. 13-19. For more recent work, Gäbler, "Zwingli-Forschung," *Theologische Literaturzeitung*, XCVI, 482-488. See also the foreword above, n. 3.

as a humanist had little abiding significance for his formal theology; he was remarkably true to the essentials and even some of the details of Luther's evangelical religion. Recent work has suggested that Zwingli too approximated Luther's views more than once had been thought.[5] Accordingly, studies of the thought of such figures reveal best the extent to which a community of theological agreement developed among the first generation of reformers, the extent to which Luther may properly characterize Reformation thought, and the extent to which these communities, or the community, of theological agreement drew upon prior traditions. Here, Capito marks a more abrupt break with the past than Zwingli, Bucer, or even Melanchthon.

It is not surprising, then, that the example of Capito demands a second hard look at common assertions regarding the consequences of the conversion of so many young humanists to the reform party. It cannot be maintained that his having been a humanist meant increased attention to sanctification, a tendency toward Protestant Scholasticism, and a swelling of the ranks of those who favored a spiritualist view of the eucharist.[6]

In the first instance, Capito was as single-minded as Luther on the subject of justification and faith. Although he never used Luther's famous formula *simul iustus et peccator*, there can be no doubt that for him too the only progress for which Christians could hope was a *progressio fidei*. Even in the *Antwurt* to Treger he confessed, "We fall daily and sin attacks us daily. . . ." [7] He viewed the good works of

---

[5] Gottfried Locher, "Zwingli und Erasmus," *Scrinium Erasmianum* (Leiden, 1969), II, 325-350, and "Change in the Understanding of Zwingli," *Church History*, XXIV, 3-24. Gestrich, *Zwingli*, pp. 144-146, has countered with the suggestion that while Luther emphasized above all the Word, Zwingli stressed faith. But, is it possible to distinguish between "faith" and "Word" in either instance?

[6] Ritter, "Geschichtliche Bedeutung," *Historische Zeitschrift*, CXXVII, 450-451, was the first to suggest that Protestant Scholasticism originated with the converted humanists. Moeller, "Humanisten," *ZKG*, LXX, 59-60, repeated Ritter and added the emphasis upon sanctification and a spiritualist view of the eucharist to the converts' distortions of Luther. Spitz, *German Humanists*, p. 292, concludes, "The result [of the humanists' conversion] was a gradual reversion in later years to a synergism and a spiritualized view of the Sacrament, so that both Luther's teaching on justification and of the real presence in the Sacrament encountered resistance due in no small part to the early conditioning of many churchmen in the religious thought of the German humanists." In defence of these scholars, it should be added that this issue lay outside the focus of their research, and that, with the exception of Calvin, Zwingli, and, to a lesser extent Melanchthon, scholars are just now studying the converted humanists.

[7] *Antwurt*, sig. F(v).

a Christian in precisely the manner of Luther. "We declare that faith makes sinners just," he replied to Erasmus in 1533; "that faith cannot exist without love, even as flames do not exist without light and heat." [8] Capito's very use of the term *sanctificatio* reveals that for him sanctification and justification were the same act. "It is the deepest sorrow for an upright soul to contemplate God's being cheated of his glory," he wrote in 1528. "Brought to its senses, it considers the absolutely certain and eternal power of God, one with the sanctification by which he cleansed and saved us; aroused by an unconquerable faith, it exclaims, 'Are you not my Lord God from eternity?' " For him as for Luther, then, the entire life of the Christian was a life of faith. "Faith requires no works, but . . . it requires standing the watch so you may know what the Lord says to you; that is, it requires obedience to the Word of God, for which purpose this promise was given, that the just man shall live by his faith, that is, the life of the just . . . depends upon the expectation of the promise of the merciful God. . . ." [9] To obey God was, then, to believe God's promises. There is no evidence that Capito emphasized sanctification during his years as a reformer.

On the basis of his career one must also question the view that the converted humanists brought to the Reformation a tendency toward later Protestant Scholasticism. Not even Luther despised the intrusion of Aristotle into theology more thoroughly than did Capito. And like Luther, he never wrote a systematic work, while he never tired of repeating the central themes of evangelical theology. Contrary to the common view of the development of Protestant Orthodoxy, it appears that Capito was in fact far too much the humanist to allow dogma to become the sum of Christianity. As he declared to the Bernese in 1532, "all beneficial doctrine is nothing other than the one eternal Word of God, the Fatherly gifts and affection that he has imparted to us through Christ. . . ." [10] There is no trace of

---

[8] *Von der Kirche*, sig. a.

[9] *In Habakvk prophetam*, fol. 18(v), 29(v)-30, and 24(v), where he depicts a Christian as knowing an "internum morbum" in spite of being saved. See also *Responsio*, fol. 97(v)-98, where he followed Luther in locating one of the grounds of secular authority in the continuing existence of sin even within Christians.

[10] *Berner Synodus*, sig. Biii(v). The confessional interests of figures such as Chemnitz, Marbach, or Flaccius were utterly inconsistent with the typically Erasmian critique of scholastic "quibbling." In fact, the development of Lutheran, and Calvinist, Orthodoxy may have more to do with such figures' having been trained as Lutherans or Calvinists than with any vestiges of the humanist movement.

later Protestant Scholasticism in Capito's works, and there was no
reformer who was once more the humanist.

It cannot be maintained even that Capito's spiritualist view of the
Lord's Supper derived from his years as a humanist. Although his
tutelage to Erasmus may have reinforced the development of his
eucharistic theology, its point of departure was the teachings of
Wyclif. According to Capito, the same may be true of the most
famous spiritualist of them all—Zwingli. In 1524 he reported to the
Zurich reformer, "I wrote Pomeranus Bugenhagen that earlier you
agreed with Wyclif but hesitated to broadcast it among the common
people, because they have the reasoning power of a dimwit." [11]
Capito's humanistic values did lead him actively to pursue concord
during the Sacramentarian Controversy, but they did not lie behind
his theology of the Lord's Supper.

Yet, it is almost self-evident that in Capito the humanist movement
influenced the Reformation in spite of how closely he appropriated
Luther's evangelical religion. But, as may be expected, given the sort
of humanist he once was, this influence existed more in attitudes and
values that shaped his reforming work than in theological doctrines
that led him to join the reform party in the first place. As his role in
the *Sakramentstreit* suggests, the abiding influence of humanism lay in
the arena of action rather than the realm of formal thought. If his
career is any guide, the humanist movement survived into the
Reformation by not only broadening the scope of reform but also
determining the manner in which reform was accomplished.

The scope of Capito's reform program did go beyond changes in
religion and the church to which it might well have been limited.
It affected the most basic social institutions as well. Nearly every
reform petition with which he was associated gave equal weight with
religious reforms to appeals for public schools, a closer supervision
of morals (sexual behavior in particular), and to public welfare
legislation. In fact he pressed such reforms in the broader social
sphere in the name of creating a godly, civil community. [12] Luther

---

[11] *ZW*, VIII, 304.

[12] Otto Winckelmann, *Das Fürsorgewesen der Stadt Strassburg vor und nach der
Reformation bis zum Ausgang des sechszehnten Jahrhunderts.* V, *Quellen und Forschungen
zur Reformationsgeschichte* (Leipzig, 1922), pp. 75-87, establishes that the basic
welfare ordinance was passed by the civil authorities without the pastors' advice.
Yet, in a defence of the reform movement in Strasbourg, Capito—with Jacob
Sturm's approval—included this ordinance among "die erneverong vnd verende-
rong . . . in die ceremonien vnd kirchen pruchen." Memorandum for Strasbourg's

too prized such reforms, but he never placed upon them the priority that they held in Capito's mind. Education and morals were issues that agitated the humanists, and Capito in particular, long before the beginning of the Reformation. Their inclusion among practical reforms to be accomplished had to do in part with the centrality of religion in sixteenth-century culture, but it also had to do with the wishes of the converted humanists.[13]

Moreover, Capito and reformers like him all over Europe happily made such social functions the duty of the secular authority, and they thereby sharply diminished the position of the institutional church within society. The standing of the church and its clergy was the central issue in the conflict with the canons of the collegiate churches in 1524 and 1525, and Capito aligned himself as always with the secular authorities. In part he had no choice, but he was also acting in accord with the high moral stature most humanists conferred upon the state. Luther too wished the authorities to take upon themselves a more active responsibility for such things as public welfare and education, but he was less naive about the motives of princes and city councilmen, and, therefore, about the benefits that would accrue from their increased purview. Through Capito, humanism broadened the impact of the reform movement in Strasbourg from the narrowly religious focus it might have had.

Humanistic values may also have shaped the very way the Reformation happened. The facts speak for themselves. All over Germany the new institutions of the Reformation were established without revolution! In part this had to do with the German social and political situation, for at least the acquiescence, if not the positive approval, of the secular authorities was the *sine qua non* for such far-reaching changes. But that reforms did occur may have had also to do with the fact that the reformers were in the main converted humanists. Capito's political activities in the campaigns to abolish the Mass and to establish a new church in Strasbourg are particularly illuminating. He, for one, remained so fearful of public unrest throughout his life that he gave civil government and only civil government the authority to

delegates to the Diet of Augsburg, 1530. Archives municipales de Strasbourg, AA 415, 6, fol. 88.

[13] For individual examples, see Kohls, *Die Schule bei Bucer*, esp. pp. 121-129; Staehelin, *Oecolampadius*, p. 357; Irmgard Höss, *Georg Spalatin, 1484-1545. Ein Leben in der Zeit des Humanismus und der Reformation* (Weimar, 1956), esp. pp. 328-330, 369-370; Erich Roth, *Die Reformation in Siebenbürgen* (Graz, 1962), pp. 59-62, and others.

legislate reforms. He never once favored congregational autonomy. He always looked disfavorably upon popular initiative. "Give peace to our time, oh Lord," was the hymn in which he expressed in 1524 his abiding indebtedness to Erasmus' abhorrence of disturbances and the common man's proclivity to create them. Such solicitude for the established order undoubtedly made the popular Reformation more palatable to the magistrates of Strasbourg. If Capito's career is any guide, the religious elitism and pacifism of the converted humanists was vital to the success of the Reformation as it really happened.[14]

The most important consequence of studying the career of a man such as Capito may be to cast the figure of Luther into bolder relief. It is true that Luther and his doctrines played the leading role in the conversion of Capito and many others from humanists to reformers. On the other hand, few sixteenth-century figures were quite so single-minded about their religious insight as was Luther. Much of what has been said of Capito's activities could be replicated from the career of Zwingli,[15] for example: non-theological attitudes, values, and circumstances shaped their work. Moreover, one of the most basic realities of the Reformation era is that Luther did little actual reforming. For the most part, this work was done by men of Capito's stripe, and they accomplished a very different reform from that attempted by the likes of Carlstadt, the Zwickau Prophets, or the Anabaptists. Just as Luther influenced men like Capito, so they shaped Luther's message on its way to creating and altering institutions. If Capito and the other humanists who became reformers are studied in their own terms, it may become apparent that they were the rule among religious leaders of the sixteenth-century, while Luther, like all geniuses, was the exception. Perhaps, then, they should be the standard for judging the spirit of the age.

---

[14] For a more extended treatment, see Kittelson, "Capito," *Archive for Reformation History*, LXIII, 126-140.

[15] Walton, *Zwingli's Theocracy*, esp. pp. 30-49.

BIBLIOGRAPHY

MANUSCRIPTS

Article on the eucharist. AA. 420. Archives municipales de Strasbourg.

Article on the eucharist. Archivum S. Thoman, 45:1. Archives municipales de Strasbourg.

Article on the eucharist. Varia Ecclesiastica, IX, 101-106. Archives municipales de Strasbourg.

Diarium Gerbelli. Archivum S. Thoman. 38. Archives municipales de Strasbourg.

Lectures on Romans. D. 96. 741. Zurich Zentralbibliothek.

Letter to Bonfiacius [Wolfhart], [mid-1521]. 25a, fol. 244-245(v). Kirchenarchiv Basel.

Letter from Jakob Sturm, June 28, 1520. Collection Labouchère, 756. Bibliothèque de l'histoire du protestantisme français. Paris.

Memorandum for Strasbourg's delegates to the Diet of Augsburg. 1530. AA. 412. Archives municipales de Strasbourg.

Memorandum for Strasbourg's delegates to the Diet of Augsburg, 1530. AA. 415. Archives municipales de Strasbourg.

Memorandum on the doctorate. Varia Ecclesiastica, XVIII, 329-343(v). Archives municipales de Strasbourg.

Protocollum Wurmserianum. Archivum S. Thoman. 192. Archives municipales de Strasbourg.

Simler'sche Sammlung der Zentralbibliothek Zurich. V. Microfilm copy, Foundation for Reformation Research. St. Louis, Missouri.

Thesaurus Epistolicus Reformatorum Alsaticorum. (copied by Johann Wilhelm Baum, *et al.*) Bibliothèque nationale et universitaire de Strasbourg.

CAPITO'S PUBLISHED WORKS

Afterword. *Conradi Summenhart Commentaria in Summam physice Alberti magni. In Conradam Summenhardum Theologum secularem Alberti magni interpretem Exasthycon Jacobi Wymphelingi.* Hagenoiae, 1507. Zurich Zentralbibliothek.

Institvtivncvla in Hebream linguam. Autore Volphango Fabro Professore Theologiae. Basileae, 1516. Basel Universitätsbibliothek.

Philosophia Natvralis Conradi Svmmenhardt Absolutissima. V. Fabritii Capitonis Concionatoris Basiliensis Epistola, de formando a pueris Theologo ad nobilem Ioannem Rudolphum Halvilerum. Basileae, 1517. Zurich Zentralbibliothek.

Preface. *Elvcidatorivm Ecclesiasticum, Ad Officium Ecclesiae Pertinentia Planivs Exponens, Et Quator Libros Complectens. Ivdoco Clichtoveo Explanatore.* Basileae, 1517. Zurich Zentralbibliothek.

V. Fabritii Capitonis Hagenoii Theologiae Doctoris et concionatoris Basiliensis, Hebraicarum Institvtionvm Libri Dvo. Basileae, 1518. Bibliothèque nationale et universitaire de Strasbourg.

Preface. *Resolutiones disputationum D. Martini Lutheri de virtute indulgentiarum.* [Basileae, 1518]. Basel Universitätsbibliothek.

Ad Reverendissimvm atque illustrissimum principem, D. Albertum Archiepiscopum Moguntinum Cardinalem etc. epistola V. Fabritii Capitonis. Paraenesis Prior Divi Io. Chrysostomi ad Theodorum lapsum, V. Fabritio Capitone interprete cum praefatione ad eundem D. Albertum Archiep. Mogunt. Card. Basileae, 1519. Basel Universitätsbibliothek.

Divi Io. Chrysostomi Homilia, De Eo Qvod Dixit Apostolus, Vtinam Tolerassetis Pavlvlvm Qviddam Insipientiae Meae. V. Fabritio Capitone Interprete. Basileae, 1519. Basel Universitätsbibliothek.

An den Hochwürdigen fürsten vnd herren Wilhelmen Bischoffen zu Strassburg vnd Lantgrauen zu Elsas. Entschuldigung D. Wolffgangs Fa. Capito. Zeigt an ursach Warumb er Burger worden Gepredigt Und ein offenliche Disputation Begert habe. Strassburg, 1523. Bibliothèque nationale et universitaire de Strasbourg.

Appellatio sacerdotum maritorum, Urbis Argentinae, adversus excommunicationem Episcopi. Argentinae, 1524. Bibliothèque nationale et universitaire de Strasbourg.

Appellatio der Eelichen Priester von der vermeinten Excommunication des hochwirdigen fürsten herrn Wilhelmen Bischoffen zu Strassburg. [Strassburg, 1524]. Bibliothèque nationale et universitaire de Strasbourg.

Verwarnung der diener des worts und der Brüder zu Strassburg An die Brüder von Landen und Stetten gemeyner Eydgnoschafft. Wider die Gotslesterige Disputation brüder Conradts Augustiner Ordens Provincial. Strassburg, 1524. Bibliothèque nationale et universitaire de Strasbourg.

Antwurt D. Wolffgang Fab. Capitons auff Brüder Conradts Augustiner ordens Provincials vermanung so er an gemein Eidgnoschafft jüngst geschriben hat. Strassburg, 1524. Bibliothèque nationale et universitaire de Strasbourg.

Was man halten vnnd Antwürtten soll von der Spaltung zwischen Martin Luther vnnd Andres Carolstadt. [Augsburg, 1524]. Bibliothèque nationale et universitaire de Strasbourg.

Das die Pfafheit schuldig sey Burgerlichen Eyd zuthun On verletzung irer Eeren. Strassburg, 1524. Bibliothèque nationale et universitaire de Strasbourg.

Der Stifft von sanct Thoman zü Straszburg uszschryben vnd protestation Wider ettliche vngüttliche handlung Jüngst vor Keyserlicher Maiestatt Regiment zü Esslingen fürgenomen. Strassburg, 1524. Bibliothèque nationale et universitaire de Strasbourg.

Institvtionvm Hebraicarum, Libri Duo. V. Fabritio Capitone Autore. Argentorati, 1525. Bibliothèque nationale et universitaire de Strasbourg.

Doctor Capito Mathis Zellen vnnd ander Predicanten zu Strassburg warhafftige verantwortung vff eins gerichten vergicht jüngest zu Zabern aussgangen. Item von Hans Jacob der zu Straszburg gefierteylt und dem Büchlein das zu Freyburg im Brissgaw verbrannt worden ist. [Strassburg, 1525]. Bayerische Staatsbibliothek, Munich.

Von drey Straszburger Pfaffen Vnd den geüsserten Kirchengüttern. Das Lateinisch singen, lesen, meszhalten erung der bildnuss anrüffong der heyligen fürbitt S. Aurelien grab vnnd anders billich inn der Kirchen zu Straszburg abgethon sey. Strassburg, 1525. Bibliothèque du seminaire protestante, Strasbourg.

In Habakvk Prophetam V. Fabritii Capitonis enarrationes. Argent[orati], 1526. Bibliothèque nationale et universitaire de Strasbourg.

Epistola V. Fabritii Capitonis, ad Huldrichum Zwinglium, quam ab Helvetiis forte interceptam D. Ioan. Faber Constantiensis, in germanicam versam depravavit, una cum duabus epistolis, quibus illum concionatores Argentinenses ad Collationem scripturarum provocarunt. Argentorati, 1526. Bibliothèque nationale et universitaire de Strasbourg.

An gemeyne stend des heyligen Römischen reichs: yetzung zu Speyer versamlet wider D. Hanns Fabri Pfarrherren zu Lindaw, etc. Missiven und Sendbrief Wolffgang Capitons. Strassburg, 1526. Bibliothèque nationale et universitaire de Strasbourg.

Kinderbericht und fragstuck von gemeynen puncten Christlichs glaubens. Strassburg, 1527. Bibliothèque nationale et universitaire de Strasbourg.

Hosea der Prophet der Kirchen zu Straszburg verteutscht durch Capitonem. [Strassburg,] 1527. Bibliothèque du seminaire protestante, Strasbourg.

Preface. *De Operibus Dei Martino Cellario authore.* Argentorati, 1527. Zurich Zentralbibliothek.

In Hoseam Prophetam V. F. Capitonis Commentarius. Argentorati, 1528. Bibliothèque nationale et universitaire de Strasbourg.

Kurtze Summ aller Lere und Predig so zü Straszburg gelert und gepredigt würt mit erbieten der Prediger doselbst an einem gewalthaber Key. Mai. kurtzlich beschehen etc. Strassburg, [1528]. Basel Universitätsbibliothek.

Kinderbericht und fragstuck von glauben. Wolff. F. Capitons. Strassburg, 1529. Bibliothèque nationale et universitaire de Strasbourg.

Preface. *Apologia vnd erclerung der Schlesier das sy den leyb und blut Christi im Nachtmal dess Herrn und im geheimnuss des hailgen Sacraments nit verleugnend auf das angeben und buchlein damit ettliche in disem artikel der Rü. Maii. zu Ungern Beheim, etc. seind beschuldigt worden.* [Strassburg], 1529. Bibliothèque nationale et universitaire de Strasbourg.

Dess Conciliums zu Basel satzung und Constitution wider prrunden handel und Curtisanen practick mit auszlegung aller puncten inn geystlichen Rechten gegrundet und warhoftigem beriecht wie ferrden concilien zeglauben sei. [Strassburg], 1530. Zurich Zentralbibliothek.

Berner Synodus Ordnung wie sich pfarrer und prediger zu Statt und Land Bern in leer und leben halten sollen mit wyteren bericht von Christo vnnd den Sacramenten. [Basel, 1532]. Bibliothèque du seminaire protestante de Strasbourg.

Preface. *Von der kirchen lieblichen Vereinigung, und von Hinlegung dieser zeit haltender Spaltung in der glauben leer geschriben durch den hochgelerten und weitheriempten herren Des. Eras. von Roterdam.* Strassburg, 1533. Bibliothèque nationale et universitaire de Strasbourg.

Responsio, De Missa, Matrimonio et Ivre Magistratus in Religionem. Vuolfgango Capitone autore. Argentorati, 1537; 1540. Basel Universitätsbibliothek.

Hexemeron Dei Opus explicatum a Vuolphgango Fa. Capitone Theologo. Argentorati, 1539. Bibliothèque nationale et universitaire de Strasbourg.

OTHER CONTEMPORARY IMPRINTS

Münster, Sebastian. *Opus Grammaticum consummatum, ex variis Elianis libris concinnatum.* Basileae, 1556. Bibliothèque nationale et universitaire de Strasbourg.

Sturm, Johannes. *Ioan. Sturmii et Gynasii Argentoratensis Luctus ad Joachimum Camerarium.* Argentorati, 1542. Bibliothèque nationale et universitaire de Strasbourg.

Supplication des pfarrhers vnnd der pfarrkinder zu sam Thoman eim ersamen Rath zü Straszburg am. XII Decembr. uberantwurt Anno M. D. XXiii. Basel [Strassburg], 1524. Bibliothèque nationale et universitaire de Strasbourg.

Treger, Conrad. *Ad Reverendum in Christo. P. Et Illvstrem Principem Fabianum de monte Falcone Lausanensem Episcopum paradoxa Centum fratris Conradi Tregorii Helvecii Augustinione familie per superiorem Germaniam provincialis de ecclesiae Conciliorumque auctoritate.* Argentorati, 1524. Bibliothèque nationale et universitaire de Strasbourg.

Warhaftige handlung der disputation in obern Baden des D. Hans Fabri Jo. Ecken vnnd irs gewaltigen anhangs gegen Joan Ecolampadio und den dienern des worts Angefangen auff den XIX. tag Maii. An. 1526. Zwingly antwurt auff Ecken daselbst in geleyt schluszreden. In torheit wurt offenbar werden. [Strassburg, 1526]. Bibliothèque nationale et universitaire de Strasbourg.

PUBLISHED SOURCES

Henrici Cornelii Agrippae ab Nettesheym, armatae equitis aurati, et iuris utriusque ac medicinae Doctoris Opera. 2 vols. Lugduni, n. d.

Allen, P. S. and H. M. Allen, eds. *Opus Epistolarum Des. Erasmi Roterodami.* 12 vols. Oxford, 1906-1956.

Arbenz, Emil, ed. *Die Vadianische Briefsammlung der Stadtbibliothek St. Gallen,* 7 vols. St. Gallen, 1890-1913.

Böcking, Edvardvs, ed. *Ulrichi Hutteni Equitis Germani Opera Quae Repervi Potuerunt Omnia.* 7 vols. Leipzig, 1859-1864.

Bretschneider, Carolus Gottlieb *et al.*, eds. *Corpus Reformatorum. Philip Melanchthonis Opera Quae Supersunt Omnia.* 28 vols. Halle, 1834-

Clemen, Otto, ed. *Melanchthons Briefwechsel.* Sechste Abteilung, *Supplementa Melanchthoniana. Werke Philip Melanchthons die im Corpus Reformatorum Vermisst Werden.* I, Leipzig, 1926.

Dacheux, L., ed. *Fragments des Anciennes Chroniques d'Alsace,* III. *Les Chroniques Strasbourgeoises de Jacques Trausch et de Jean Wencker. Annales de Sebastien Brant.* Strasbourg, 1892.

Dürr, Emil and Paul Roth, eds. *Aktensammlung zur Geschichte der Basler Reformation in den Jahren 1519 bis Anfang 1534.* 6 vols. Basel, 1921-1950.

Egli, Emil *et al.*, eds. *Corpus Reformatorum. Huldreich Zwinglis Sämtliche Werke.* 13 vols. Leipzig, 1905-1935.

Ferguson, Wallace K., ed. *Erasmi Opuscula, A Supplement to the Opera Omnia.* The Hague, 1933.

Franz, Günther, ed. *Quellen zur Geschichte des Bauernkrieges.* II, *Ausgewählte Quellen zur Deutsche Geschichte der Neuzeit. Freiherr vom Stein-Gedächtnisausgabe.* Munich, 1963.

Friedensburg, Walter, ed. "Beiträge zum Briefwechsel der Katholischen Gelehrten Deutschlands in Reformationszeitalter." *Zeitschrift für Kirchengeschichte,* XVI (1896), 470-499; XVIII (1897), 106-131.

Hartmann, Alfred, ed. *Die Amerbach Korrespondenz.* 5 vols. Basel, 1942-1958.

Hekelius, Jo. Fredericus, ed. *Manipulus Primus Epistolarum Singularium.* Plaviae, 1695.

Herminjard, A.-L., ed. *Correspondance des Réformateurs dans les Pays de Langue française.* 11 vols. Geneva and Paris, 1866-1897.

Holborn, Hajo and Annemarie Holborn, eds. *Desiderius Erasmus Ausgewählte Werke.* Munich 1933.

Horawitz, Adalbert and Karl Hartfelder, eds. *Briefwechsel des Beatus Rhenanus.* Leipzig, 1886.

Kalkoff, Paul, ed. *Die Depeschen des Nuntius Aleander vom Wormser Reichstage 1521.* Halle, 1886.

Kawerau, Gustav, ed. *Briefwechsel des Justus Jonas.* 2 vols. Halle, 1884-1885.

Kolde, Theodor, ed. "Gleichzeitige Berichte über die Wittenberger Unruhen im Jahre 1521 und 1522." *Zeitschrift für Kirchengeschichte,* V (1882), 325-333.

Krafft, Karl and Wilhelm Krafft, eds., *Briefe und Dokumente aus der Zeit der Reformation im 16. Jahrhundert nebst Mittheilungen über Kölnische Gelehrte und Studien im 13. und 16. Jahrhundert.* Elberfeld, [1875].

Krebs, Manfred and Hans Georg Rott, eds. *Quellen zur Geschichte der Täufer.* VII, *Elsasz, I. Teil: Stadt Straszburg, 1522-1532;* VIII, *Elsasz II. Teil: Stadt Straszburg, 1533-1535.* 2 vols. Gütersloh, 1959-1960.

D. Martin Luthers Werke. Kritische Gesamtausgabe. 99 vols. Weimar, 1883-.

Mayer, Hermann, ed. *Die Matrikel der Universität Freiburg im Breisgau von 1460-1656.* 2 vols. Freiburg im Breisgau, 1907-1910.

Pollet, Jacques-V., ed. *Martin Bucer. Études sur la correspondance avec des nombreux textes inédits*. 2 vols. Paris, 1958-1962.

Riggenbach, Bernhard, ed. *Das Chronikon des Konrad Pellikan*. Basel, 1877.

Rott, Jean, ed. "Un recueil de correspondances strasbourgeoises de XVIᵉ siècle à la bibliothèque de Copenhague." *Bulletin philologique et historique*. (Paris, 1971), pp. 749-818.

Schiess, Traugott, ed. *Briefwechsel der Brüder Ambrosius und Thomas Blaurer, 1509-1548*. 3 vols. Freiburg, 1908-1912.

Schwebellius, Henricus, ed. *Centuria Epistolarum Theologicarum ad Johannem Schwebelium*. Biponti, 1597.

Staehelin, Ernst, ed. *Briefe und Akten zum Leben Oekolampads*. X, XIX, *Quellen und Forschungen zur Reformationsgeschichte*. 2 vols. Leipzig, 1927-1934.

Staehelin, Rudolf, ed. *Briefe aus der Reformationszeit*. Basel, 1887.

Steck, R. and G. Tobler, eds. *Aktensammlung zur Geschichte der Berner Reformation, 1521-1532*. Bern, 1923.

Stupperich, Robert, et al., eds. *Martin Bucers Deutsche Schriften*. 4 vols. Gütersloh, 1960-

Virck, Hans and Otto Winckelmann, eds. *Politische Correspondenz der Stadt Straszburg im Zeitalter der Reformation*. 5 vols. Strassburg, 1887-1898.

Vogt, O., ed. *Dr. Johann Bugenhagens Briefwechsel*, Stettin, 1888.

Wackernagel, Hans Georg, ed. *Die Matrikel der Universität Basel*. 3 vols. Basel, 1951-1962.

Wittmer, Charles and J. Charles Meyer, eds. *Le Livre de bourgeoisie de la ville de Strasbourg, 1440-1530*. 2 vols. Strasbourg, 1948-

Wrede, Adolf, ed. *Deutsche Reichstagsakten unter Kaiser Karl V*. II, *Deutsche Reichstagsakten, Jüngere Reihe*. Gotha, 1896.

SECONDARY MATERIALS

Adam, Johann. *Evangelische Kirchengeschichte der Stadt Straszburg bis zur Französischen Revolution*. Strassburg, 1922.

Adamus, Melchior. *Vitae Germanorum Theologorum, qui superiori seculo ecclesiam Christi voci scriptisque propagarunt et propugnarunt*. Heidelbergae, 1620.

Althaus, Paul. *Die Theologie Martin Luthers*. Gütersloh, 1962.

Bainton, Roland H. *Erasmus of Christendom*. New York, 1969.

Barge, Hermann. *Andreas Bodenstein von Karlstadt*. 2 vols. Leipzig, 1905.

Bauer, Johannes Joseph. *Zur Frühgeschichte der theologischen Fakultät der Universität Freiburg I. Br. (1460-1620)*. XIV, *Beiträge zur Freiburger Wissenschafts- und Universitätsgeschichte*. Freiburg, 1957.

Baum, Adolph. *Magistrat und Reformation in Strassburg bis 1529*. Strassburg, 1887.

Baum, Johann Wilhelm. *Capito und Butzer, Strassburgs Reformatoren*. III, *Leben und Ausgewählte Schriften der Väter und Begründer der Reformierten Kirche*. Elberfeld, 1860.

Bizer, Ernst. *Studien zur Geschichte des Abendmahlstreits im 16. Jahrhundert*. Darmstadt, 1962.

Bornkamm, Heinrich. *Luther und das Alte Testament*. Tübingen, 1948

Bouwsma, William J. *Venice and the Defence of Republican Liberty*. Berkeley, Calif., 1968.

Brady, Thomas A., Jr. "Jacob Sturm of Strasbourg and the Lutherans at the Diet of Augsburg, 1530." *Church History*, XLII (1973), 183-202.

Clemen, Otto. "Ein Strassburger Sammeldruck von 1523." *Zeitschrift für Kirchengeschichte*, XLIII (1924), 219-226.

Chrisman, Miriam Usher. *Strasbourg and the Reform. A Study in the Process of Change*. New Haven, Conn., 1967.

Courvoisier, Jacques. *La Notion d'église chez Bucer dans son développement historique.* Paris, 1933.

Douglass, E. Jane Dempsey. *Justification in Late Medieval Preaching. A Study of John Geiler of Keisersberg.* I, *Studies in Medieval and Reformation Thought.* Leiden, 1966.

Eells, Hastings. *Martin Bucer.* New Haven, Conn., 1931.

——. "The Genesis of Martin Bucer's Doctrine of the Lord's Supper." *Princeton Theological Review,* XXIV (1926), 225-251.

——. "Sacramental Negotiations at the Diet of Augsburg, 1530." *Princeton Theological Review,* XXIII (1925), 213-233.

Estes, James M. "Church Order and the Christian Magistrate according to Johannes Brenz," *Archiv für Reformationsgeschichte,* LIX (1968), 5-23.

Ficker, Johannes, ed. *Thesaurus Baumianus. Verzeichniss der Briefe und Aktenstücke.* Strassburg, 1905.

——, and Otto Winckelmann, eds. *Handschriftenprobe des Sechszehnten Jahrhunderts nach Strassburger Originalen.* 2 vols. Strassburg, 1902-1905.

Franz, Günther. *Der Deutsche Bauernkrieg.* Darmstadt, 1956.

Freys, E., and H. Barge. "Verzeichniss der gedruckten Schriften des Andreas Bodenstein von Karlstadt." *Zentralblatt für Bibliothekswesen,* XXI (1904), 153-179; 209-243; 305-331.

Gäbler, Ulrich. "Zwingli-Forschung seit 1960," *Theologische Literaturzeitung,* XCVI (1971), 482-488.

Gerbert, Camill. *Geschichte der Strassburger Sectenbewegung zur Zeit der Reformation, 1524-1534.* Strassburg, 1889.

Gerdesius, Daniel. *Introductio in Historiam Evangelii seculo XVI. Passim per Europam Renovati Doctrinaeque Reformatae. Addedunt Varia Quibus ipsa Historia Illustratur, Monumenta Pietatis atque Rei Litterariae.* 4 vols. Groningae et Bremae, 1744-1752.

Gestrich, Christof. *Zwingli als Theologe. Glaube und Geist beim Zürcher Reformator.* XX, *Studien zur Dogmengeschichte und Systematischen Theologie.* Zurich, 1967.

Ginzburg, Carlo. *Il Nicodemismo: Simulazione e Dissimulazione Religiosa del'500.* Torino, 1970.

Gothein, Eberhard. *Pforzheims Vergangenheit. Ein Beitrag zur deutschen Städte- und Gewerbegeschichte.* IX, *Staats- und Socialwissenschaftliche Forschungen.* Leipzig, 1889.

Greschat, Martin and J. F. G. Goeters, eds. *Reformation und Humanismus. Robert Stupperich zum 65. Geburtstag.* Witten, 1969.

Gussmann, Wilhelm. *Quellen und Forschungen zur Geschichte des Augsburgischen Glaubensbekenntnisses.* Leipzig, 1911.

Heath, Terrance. "Logical Grammar, Grammatical Logic, and Humanism in three German Universities." *Studies in the Renaissance,* XVIII (1971), 9-64.

Heberle, [   ]. "W. Capitos Verhältnis zum Anabaptismus." *Zeitschrift für die Historische Theologie,* XXVII (1857), 285-310.

Herrmann, Fritz. *Die Evangelische Bewegung zu Mainz im Reformationszeitalter.* Mainz, 1907.

Hoffet, Jean-Charles. *Ésquisse biographique sûr Capiton.* Strasbourg, 1850.

Höss, Irmgard. *Georg Spalatin, 1484-1545. Ein Leben in der Zeit des Humanismus und der Reformation.* Weimar, 1956.

Hubert, F. "Strassburger Katechismen aus den Tagen der Reformation." *Zeitschrift für Kirchengeschichte,* XX (1900), 395-413.

Kalkoff, Paul. *W. Capito im Dienste Erzbischof Albrechts von Mainz. Quellen und Forschungen zu den entscheidenden Jahren der Reformation (1519-1523).* I, *Neue Studien zur Geschichte der Theologie und Kirche.* Berlin, 1907.

——. *Die Entstehung des Wormser Edikts. Eine Geschichte des Wormser Reichstages vom Standpunkt der Lutherischen Frage*. Leipzig, 1913.

Kittelson, James M. "Wolfgang Capito, the Council and Reform Strasbourg." *Archive for Reformation History*, LXIII (1972), 126-140.

——. "Martin Bucer and the Sacramentarian Controversy: the Origins of his Policy of Concord." *Archive for Reformation History*, LXIV (1973), 166-183.

Klaustermeyer, William H. "The Role of Matthew and Catherine Zell in the Strassburg Reformation." Unpublished doctoral dissertation, Stanford University, 1965.

Knod, Gustav. *Die Stifftsheren von St. Thomas zu Strassburg, 1518-1548. Ein Beitrag zur Strassburger Kirchen- und Schulgeschichte*. Strassburg, 1892.

Köhler, Walther. *Zwingli und Luther, Ihr Streit über das Abendmahl nach seinen politischen und religiösen Beziehungen*. 2 vols. Leipzig and Gütersloh, 1924-1953.

Kohls, Ernst-Wilhelm. *Die Schule bei Martin Bucer in Ihrem Verhältnis zu Kirche und Obrigkeit*. XXII, *Pädagogische Forschungen. Veröffentlichungen des Comenius-Instituts*. Heidelberg, 1962.

——. *Die Theologie des Erasmus*. 2 vols. Basel, 1966.

——. "Humanisten auf dem Reichstag zu Worms." *Der Reichstag zu Worms von 1521: Reichspolitik und Luthersache* (ed. by Fritz Reuter). Worms, 1971.

Kreider, Robert. "The Anabaptists and the Civil Authorities of Strasbourg, 1525-1555." *Church History*, XXIV (1955), 99-118.

Kristeller, P. O. *Renaissance Humanism. The Scholastic, Classic, and Humanist Strains*. New York, 1961.

Krodel, Gottfried G. "Wider den Abgott zu Halle." *Lutherjahrbuch*, XXXIII (1966), 9-87.

Littell, Franklin Hamlin. *The Anabaptist View of the Church. A Study in the Origins of Sectarian Protestantism*. Boston, 1958.

Locher, Gottfried W. "Zwingli und Erasmus." *Scrinium Erasmianum* (ed. by J. Coppens). Leiden, 1969.

——. "The Change in the Understanding of Zwingli in Recent Research." *Church History*, XXIV (1965), 3-24.

Looss, Sigrid. "Butzer und Capito in ihrem Verhältnis zu Bauernkrieg und Täufertum." *Weltwirkung der Reformation* (ed. by Max Steinmetz) Berlin, 1969.

Luchsinger, Friedrich. *Der Baselbuchdruck als Vermittler italienischen Geistes, 1470-1529*. XLV, *Basler Beiträge zur Geschichtswissenschaft*. Basel, 1953.

Lutz, Jules. "Les Reformateurs de Mulhouse." *Bulletin de Musée historique de Mulhouse*, XVII (1904), 10-68.

Massaut, Jean-Pierre. *Josse Clichtove, L'humanisme et la réforme du clergé*. CLXXXIII, *Bibliothèque de la faculté de philosophie et lettres de l'Université de Liège*. 2 vols. Paris, 1968.

Maurer, Wilhelm. *Der Junge Melanchthon*. 2 vols. Gütersloh, 1967-1969.

——. *Das Verhältnis des Staates zur Kirche nach humanistischer Anschauung, vornehmlich bei Erasmus*. Giessen, 1930.

Mieg, Philippe. *La Réforme à Mulhouse, 1518-1538*. Strasbourg, 1948.

——. "Capiton, le réformateur strasbourgeois. Quelques details biographiques à propos de ses armoiries." *Societé de l'histoire de Protestantisme français. Bulletin*, LXIV (1926), 177-187.

Mitchell, Charles Buell. "Martin Bucer and Sectarian Dissent: A Confrontation of the Magisterial Reformation with Anabaptists and Spiritualists." Unpublished doctoral dissertation. Yale University, 1960.

Moeller, Bernd. *Johannes Zwick und die Reformation in Konstanz*. Heidelberg, 1961.

——. "Kleriker als Bürger." *Festschrift für Hermann Heimpel*. XXXVI, *Veröffentlichungen des Max-Plank-Instituts für Geschichte*. Göttingen, 1972.

——. *Reichstadt und Reformation.* CLXXX, *Schriften des Vereins für Reformationsgeschichte.* Gütersloh, 1962.
——. "Die deutschen Humanisten und die Anfänge der Reformation." *Zeitschrift für Kirchengeschichte,* LXX (1959), 46-61.
Nauert, Charles G., Jr. *Agrippa and the Crisis of Renaissance Thought.* LV, *Illinois Studies in the Social Sciences.* Urbana, Ill., 1965.
Oberman, Heiko Augustinus. *The Harvest of Medieval Theology: Gabriel Biel and Late Medieval Nominalism.* 2nd ed. Grand Rapids, Mich., 1967.
Oyer, John S. *Lutheran Reformers against Anabaptists. Luther, Melanchthon, and Menius and the Anabaptists of Central Germany.* The Hague, 1964.
Payne, J. B. "Toward the Hermeneutics of Erasmus." *Scrinium Erasmianum* (ed. by J. Coppens) Leiden, 1969.
Raeder, Siegfried. *Die Benutzung des masoretischen Textes bei Luther in der Zeit zwischen der ersten und zweiten Psalmenvorlesung (1515-1518).* XXXVIII, *Beiträge zur Historischen Theologie.* Tübingen, 1967.
Rittelmeyer, G. H. A. "Die evangelische Liederdichter des Elsasses." *Beiträge zu den Theologischen Wissenschaften,* VI (1855), 137-220.
Ritter, François. *Histoire de l'imprimerie alsacienne aux XVe et XVIe siècles.* Strasbourg, 1955.
Ritter, Gerhard. *Erasmus und der deutsche Humanistenkreis am Oberrhein.* XXIII, *Freiburger Universitätsreden* (Freiburg im Breisgau, 1937), pp. 8-14.
——. "Die geschichtliche Bedeutung des deutschen Humanismus." *Historische Zeitschrift,* CXXVII (1923), 393-453.
Ritter, Johann Balthazar. *Evangelisches Denkmahl der Stadt Frankfurth am Mayn.* Franckfurth am Mayn, 1726.
Röhrich, Timotheus Wilhelm. *Geschichte der Reformation im Elsass und besonders in Strassburg.* 3 vols. Strassburg, 1830-1832.
Roth, Erich. *Die Reformation in Siebenbürgen.* Graz, 1962.
Rott, Jean. "Bucer et les débuts de la querelle sacramentaire." *Revue d'histoire et de philosophie religieuses,* XXXIV (1954), 234-254.
——. "Forschungen und Arbeiten zur Geschichte des Protestantismus im Elsass. Bericht über die Periode 1918-1940." *Archiv für Reformationsgeschichte,* XXXVIII (1941), 331-349.
——. "Le Humaniste strasbourgeois Nicolas Gerbel et son diairie. (1522-1529)." *Bulletin philologique et historique.* Paris, 1950.
Scheffler, [Heinrich]. *Dr. Wolfgang Capito, der erste evangelische Prediger am Jungen St. Peter in Strassburg.* Strassburg, 1866.
Schmidt, Charles. *Histoire littéraire de l'Alsace à la fin du XVe et au commencement du XVIe siècles.* 2 vols. Paris, 1879.
Schreiber, Heinrich. *Geschichte der Albert-Ludwigs Universität zu Freiburg im Breisgau.* 3 vols. Freiburg, 1857-1860.
Spitz, Lewis W. *The Religious Renaissance of the German Humanists.* Cambridge, Mass., 1963.
——. "The Third Generation of German Renaissance Humanists." *Aspects of the Renaissance* (ed. by Archibald Lewis) Austin, Tex., 1967.
Strasser, O. E. *Capitos Beziehungen zu Bern.* IV, *Quellen und Abhandlungen zur Schweizerischen Reformationsgeschichte.* Leipzig, 1928.
——. *La Pensée theologique de Wolfgang Capiton dans les dernières années de sa vie.* XI, *Mémoires de l'Université de Neuchâtel.* Neuchâtel, 1938.
——. "Un chrétien humaniste: Wolfgang Capiton." *Revue d'histoire et de philosophie religieuses,* XX (1940), 1-14.
Strauss, Gerald. "Protestant Dogma and City Government: The Case of Nuremberg." *Past and Present,* XXXVI (1967), 38-58.

Tracy, James D. *Erasmus. The Growth of a Mind.* CXXVI, *Travaux d'humanisme et renaissance.* Genève, 1972.

——. "Erasmus Becomes a German." *Renaissance Quarterly*, XXI (1968), 221-228.

Usteri, Johann Martin. "Die Stellung der Strassburger Reformatoren Bucer und Capito zur Tauffrage." *Theologische Studien und Kritiken*, LVII (1884), 456-525.

Von Libenau, Theodore. *Der Franziskaner Dr. Thomas Murner.* IX, *Erläuterungen und Ergänzungen zur Janssens Geschichte des deutschen Volks.* Freiburg, 1913.

Von Muralt, Leonhard. *Die Badener Disputation 1526.* III, *Quellen und Abhandlungen zur Schweizerischen Reformationsgeschichte.* Leipzig, 1926.

Wackernagel, Rudolf. *Geschichte der Stadt Basel.* 3 vols. Basel, 1907-1924.

Walton, Robert C. *Zwingli's Theocracy.* Toronto, 1967.

Wendel, François. *L'Église de Strasbourg, sa constitution et son organization, 1532-1535.* XXXVIII, *Études d'histoire et de philosophie religieuses.* Paris, 1942.

Winckelmann, Otto. *Das Fürsorgewesen der Stadt Strassburg vor und nach der Reformation bis zum Ausgang des sechszehnten Jahrhunderts.* V, *Quellen und Forschungen zur Reformationsgeschichte.* Leipzig, 1922.

Williams, George H. *The Radical Reformation.* Philadelphia, 1962.

Wolters, Albrecht. *Der Abgott zu Halle, 1521-1542.* Bonn, 1877.

INDEX